UNFINISHED BUSINESS

UNFINISHED BUSINESS

The Unexplored Causes of the Financial Crisis and the Lessons Yet to be Learned

TAMIM BAYOUMI

YALE UNIVERSITY PRESS
NEW HAVEN AND LONDON

For information about this and other Yale University Press publications, please contact:
U.S. Office: sales.press@yale.edu   yalebooks.com
Europe Office: sales@yaleup.co.uk   yalebooks.co.uk

Set in Minion Pro by IDSUK (DataConnection) Ltd
Printed in Great Britain by TJ International Ltd, Padstow, Cornwall

Library of Congress Control Number: 2017942755

ISBN 978-0-300-22563-1

A catalogue record for this book is available from the British Library.

10 9 8 7 6 5 4 3 2 1

MIX
Paper from
responsible sources
FSC   FSC® C013056
www.fsc.org

To Susan, Elisa, and Stefan
For giving me joy and purpose

CONTENTS

FIGURES

ACKNOWLEDGEMENTS

Many people have helped me with this book. In addition to the IMF, which granted me a sabbatical, pride of place goes to Adam Posen, the director of the Peterson Institute for International Economics, the institution that gave me an office and made me a senior fellow, which allowed me to interact with their fantastic fellows and staff. In particular, during my stay, in addition to Adam, I benefited enormously from conversations with Fred Bergsten, Bill Cline, Nicolas Véron, Simon Johnson, Morris Goldstein, Joe Gagnon, Ana Gelpern, Steve Weisman, Jacob Kierkegaard, Patrick Honohan, Olivier Blanchard, Chad Brown, Monica De Bolle, Marcus Noland, Jérémie Cohen-Setton, Caroline Freud, Olivier Jean, Rory MacFarquhar, Jeff Schott, Ted Truman, Dave Stockton, and Jeromin Zettelmeyer. Their intellectual generosity is an example for us all. Additional important inputs came from Ashok Bhatia of the IMF, who explained the US financial system in terms even I could understand, David Marsh from OMFIF, who constantly encouraged me, and Barry Eichengreen of Berkeley and Harold James of Princeton, who both commented on earlier versions of the text. Many thanks also go to Taiba Batool, my editor, who helped knock the book into shape, and Anish Tailor of the Peterson and Jelle Barkema of the IMF for their invaluable research assistance. Thanks also to Lauren Pettifer, Melissa Bond, and Jennie Doyle at Yale University Press for helping with the finishing touches. Finally, it is important to acknowledge that this book represents my own views, and does not necessarily represent those of the IMF, IMF policy or the Peterson Institute for International Economics.

INTRODUCTION
The Needle (and the Damage Done)

It is often said that it takes a decade to turn current events into history, a reckoning that probably makes this the first true history of the North Atlantic financial crisis.* The moniker is apt, as this narrative chronicles how after 1980 a succession of missteps by financial regulators, aided and abetted by policy makers' intellectual blind spots, made the North Atlantic banking system so brittle that the failure of a medium-sized US investment bank toppled the world into the worst recession since the 1930s and the Euro area into a depression. It highlights the crucial and under-appreciated role played by increasingly shaky northern European mega-banks in financing remarkably similar financial bubbles in the US and southern Europe, which parasitically intertwined with the better known but equally misunderstood expansion of shaky US shadow banks. The common origin of the US and Euro area crises has been missed because it was overlaid by the longer and deeper Euro area recession coming from a flawed currency union that left often cash-strapped national governments responsible for expensive bank rescues. While some of the mistakes in the North Atlantic economy have been rectified, there remains an awful lot of unfinished business before we can be confident that the world will not continue to face serial financial instability and lackluster growth.

* * *

* A central argument of this book is that the 2008–09 US financial crisis and the 2008–12 Euro area crisis were joined at the hip, hence the descriptor the North Atlantic crisis.

The Needle

The North Atlantic crisis is generally dated from the early afternoon of August 9, 2007, Paris time, when this press release flashed on dealers' screens:

BNP Paribas Investment Partners temporally suspends the calculation of the Net Asset Value of the following funds: Parvest Dynamic ABS, BNP Paribas ABS EURIBOR and BNP Paribas ABS EONIA

The complete evaporation of liquidity in certain market segments of the US securitization market has made it impossible to value certain assets fairly regardless of their quality or credit rating. The situation is such that it is no longer possible to value fairly the underlying US ABS assets in the three above-mentioned funds. We are therefore unable to calculate a reliable net asset value ("NAV") for the funds.

In order to protect the interests and ensure the equal treatment of our investors, during these exceptional times, BNP Paribas Investment Partners has decided to temporarily suspend the calculation of the net asset value as well as subscriptions/redemptions, in strict compliance with regulations, for the following funds:

- Parvest Dynamic ABS effective 7 August 2007, 3pm (Luxembourg time)
- BNP Paribas ABS Euribor and BNP Paribas ABS Eonia effective 7 August 2007, 1pm (Paris time)

The valuation of these funds and the issue/redemption process will resume as soon as liquidity returns to the market allowing NAV to be calculated.

In the continued absence of liquidity, additional information on the envisaged measures will be communicated to investors in these funds within one month of today.

Thursday, August 9 was an unappealingly cold and windy day in Paris even before this chilly financial message. Indeed, it turned out to be the coldest day of the month, with an overnight low of 11 degrees Celsius (51 degrees Fahrenheit) rising to a modest 18 degrees Celsius (64 degrees Fahrenheit) in the afternoon. On top of that it was blowy, with average winds of 16 kilometers per hour (10 miles per hour). At least it did not rain, in contrast to the otherwise similar days before and after. In short, it was not a pleasant few days to be a banker in Paris. Not that there were many bankers left in the city. The French predilection for taking August as vacation left Paris largely bereft of workers, replaced by the usual throngs of (in this case often shivering) tourists.

The head of BNP Paribas asset management, Gilles Glicenstein, authorized the press release from the semi-deserted BNP Paribas offices just a
block from the Arc de Triomphe. Gilles was a well-respected up-and-
coming banker who was known for being decent and careful, as well as for
running marathons. He had joined BNP after four years at the French
Ministry of Finance. He never regretted his decision to send out the press
release, which he firmly believed had been the right thing to do. Tragically,
he died of cancer in the spring 2009 at age 44.

The press release underlined how problems initially seen as a minor blip
in US mortgages were affecting the European as well as US banks. The
"certain segments" of the mortgage market that were in distress were securities that bundled subprime mortgages or securities that put these assets
together into more complex collateralized debt obligations (CDOs) or even
into CDOs-squared (CDOs of CDOs). The roaring market in these products
rapidly collapsed as it became apparent that US house prices were falling,
something that the proponents of these products had assured investors had
not happened on a national basis in the United States in the sixty years since
World War II. This unexpected development undid a market in which
subprime mortgages had increasingly been issued with minimal assessment
of the creditworthiness of the borrowers on the happy assumption that
continued house price increases would validate the loans. The mortgage-
backed securitization market collapsed along with its central dogma.

The BNP announcement was the second major blow to the European
banking system from US subprime mortgages, coming less than a fortnight
after the rescue of IKB Deutsche Industriebank AG. IKB was a small
German bank specializing in loans to medium-size enterprises that was
brought down by unwise investments in assets backed by subprime loans.
In many ways, IKB was the more important financial shock. Jochen Sanio,
the lead German bank regulator, is reported to have said that the hurried
weekend rescue involving a wide swathe of the German banking industry
(an arrangement designed to circumvent EU rules on state subsidies) was
needed to avoid the worst banking crisis since 1931.[1] However, the
symbolism of having part of the business of the largest French bank felled
by turmoil in US markets has remained the more potent talisman of the
wider impact of the North Atlantic crisis, a somewhat ironic outcome as
BNP Paribas actually weathered the crisis relatively successfully.

The financial chill that settled over Europe in the summer of 2007 has
yet to be fully lifted. After reaching a peak in mid-July 2007, the rescue of
IKB lowered Euro area equity prices by 5 percent and the subsequent BNP
announcement wiped out another 5 percent.[2] After a brief rally later in the

year, the stock market started a long descent, falling to a nadir of under half its peak value in early 2009. A decade later, it is still below its July 2007 value.

The BNP announcement was also the moment when the two most powerful central banks in the world started finding their traditional policy responses were largely ineffective. The press release prompted an injection of liquidity into the markets by the European Central Bank that was a precursor to many such moves on both sides of the Atlantic as well as policy rate cuts by the US Federal Reserve. Such palliatives had only limited effects, given market jitters coming from uncertainty about the viability of major banks. This financial equivalent of a phony war ended with the market panic that followed the collapse of Lehman Brothers, a mid-sized US investment bank, on September 15, 2008. The subsequent freezing of North Atlantic financial markets, global recession, and painfully slow recovery have forced both central banks to dabble with all sorts of "unconventional" policies such as buying assets and lowering interest rates below zero.

* * *

The Damage Done

Before outlining the origins of the North Atlantic crisis it is worth underlining its massive costs. Calculating the economic losses from a crisis is never easy. For example, it is not enough to simply focus on the output losses after the crisis, as these must be set against the booms that economies experience before financial bubbles burst. Indeed, in normal times economists assume that expansions (when output moves above potential) are offset by recessions (when output falls below potential) so that output is on average at its trend. However, financial busts are different as the disruption coming from sudden losses in access to loans can lead to major net losses in output. In the calculations below, the losses over the cycle are calculated using International Monetary Fund estimates of the deviation of output from its potential value from 2003 to 2021.[3]

Another cost of the financial crisis was the waste due to excessive investment in the crisis countries. In the national accounts, investment is measured by the cost of building (say) a house even though the benefits come only after people start living there. In general, it is safe to assume that each dollar put into housing generates somewhat more than a dollar of value in the future (since investors need to be compensated for patience and risk). In a bubble, however, investments can be much less productive. In the 2000s, a good chunk of the money poured into, for example, Spanish housing went into overbuilt neighborhoods in the wrong places. Such funds could have been much more usefully used to buy machinery, such as computers, or simply been given back to shareholders as dividends. Below, it is assumed that for the crisis countries (the United States, Italy, Spain, Greece, Ireland, and Portugal) any construction spending above the ratio to output prevailing in late 1999 was worth only 50 cents rather than a dollar, which implies that about one-tenth of all spending on construction was wasted.

There were also spillovers to other parts of the world, particularly the core of the Euro area (Germany, France, the Netherlands, and Belgium) whose banks provided much of the financing that supported excessive lending in the United States and the Euro area crisis countries. The resulting banking problems boomeranged back on the core economies. It also included many innocent bystanders, such as the emerging markets that were hit by the wholesale pullback from risky assets as well as the collapse in demand for durable goods in the US and Euro area and associated knock-on to their exports.[4] This suggests three levels of analysis: The costs accruing to the crisis countries themselves, those applying to the rest of the Euro area, and those accruing to the rest of the world.

Putting this together, the United States suffered cumulative losses of around 10 percentage points of output while the typical Euro area crisis country experienced losses of more like 25 percent of output, with the composition varying in an intuitive manner (Figure 1). For example, in Ireland and Spain the bulk of the losses come from inefficient housing investment rather than the cycle since the real estate bubbles were large, the boom before the crisis was extensive, and the recovery from the downturn was relatively fast (details of the calculations for the Euro area crisis countries are provided in Figure 3 at the end of this chapter). Elsewhere, including the United States, direct output losses dominate.

The spillovers to the core of the Euro area from the extended downturn total about 10 percent of output, similar to the United States but less than half that of the crisis countries. These losses reflect the financial problems these countries encountered due to imprudent lending to the United States and Euro area periphery, exacerbated by the inefficient design of the Euro area, where a structure that was intended to shield the rest of the region from national fiscal and financial shocks in practice amplified such spill-overs. In the rest of the world, the losses come more from the immediate impact of the downturn on output. Output in emerging and developing countries, which make up the bulk of the remaining countries, fell by 3 percentage points in 2009 but then rebounded robustly in the subsequent two years for an implied loss in output of around 4 percent.

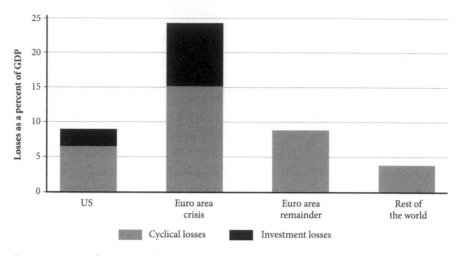

Figure 1: Output losses were the highest in the Euro area periphery.
Source: Haver Analytics.

Overall, the final tally of damages is estimated at some $4½ trillion in 2009 prices or around 8 percent of world output in that year (Figure 2). Put another way, it is as if the world economy shut down completely for a month—no factories, no supermarkets, no electricity, no restaurants, and no new cars. Most of the losses were in the North Atlantic region, with the Euro area crisis countries suffering larger losses than the core, and the Euro area as a whole suffering greater losses than the United States. The crisis cost the rest of the world "only" about $1¼ trillion. Striking as these numbers are, these deliberately conservative calculations are at the low end of estimates of losses from financial crises as they take no account of longer-term costs coming from the erosion in job skills and debilitating impact of lower investment by firms.[5] Less conservative assumptions produce losses of more like 65 percent of output from a typical financial crisis, and can run as high as 140 percent.[6] Using the 65 percent figure for the US and the Euro area crisis countries quadruples the global losses—equivalent to a four-month global shutdown. However you calculate it, the North Atlantic crisis was a massive blow to the global economy.

The stagnation in incomes after the crisis also generated a political backlash against the existing order and associated economic "experts".[7] This is exemplified by the British decision to leave the European Union, the election of President Trump, and the growing support for populist parties in the Euro area. These deep changes in popular sentiment underline the importance of the North Atlantic crisis as a watershed economic, political, and social event. Commensurate with the size of this event, the rest of this

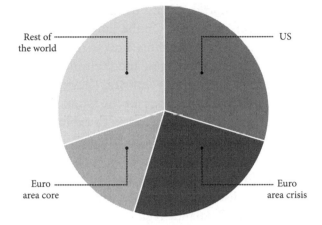

Figure 2: Output losses were mainly in the North Atlantic region.
Source: Haver Analytics.

book explores the historical background that allowed the crisis to occur, and outlines the resulting policy responses and lessons. It focuses on the two regions most affected by the crisis, the Euro area and the United States, and discusses the experiences of other North Atlantic countries such as the United Kingdom and Switzerland only insofar as they pertain to these events. Despite the obvious attractions of including the Swiss and UK experiences (both countries experienced major banking problems) their addition would have involved adding a lot of country-specific detail without a commensurate increase in underlying insights.[8]

* * *

What Went Wrong

There have been many books about the crisis that followed the 2008 collapse of Lehman Brothers in the United States and the 2009 admission of the size of Greek debt in the Euro area. At the risk of oversimplification, the main strand of the US literature involves blow-by-blow accounts of the crisis in which (for example) large and complex banks appear fully formed, while the equivalent narratives on the Euro area are similar except that they provide greater historical background on the creation of the currency union.[9] In both cases, the focus on how policymakers reacted to the new and largely unexpected challenges. In the United States, these include how to provide financial support to institutions that were outside of the Federal Reserve's traditional safety net, how to sort through the long chains of ownership because of banks selling mortgage loans using securitizations, and how to deal with overinflated credit ratings. On the Euro area side, the challenges include regaining access to dollar liquidity, how to respond to market jitters about the solvency of banks, sovereigns, and their interaction, and how to enforce policy conditions on member countries. The experiences from these challenges are then used to distill lessons for the future. Finally, there is also a strand of the literature that uses the crisis to explore the instability of financial systems in capitalist economies and offer policy solutions.[10]

This book takes different and more holistic approach by examining the *origins* of the joint North Atlantic crisis. Rather than using the prism of the immediate crisis to distill lessons, it asks what can be learned from the process by which the North Atlantic region got itself into a position where such a cataclysmic crisis could occur. For example, rather than looking at the problems caused by securitization (the bundling of mortgages and other loans that were then sold to investors), it asks what drove the banks to want to sell mortgages through securitized markets in the United States and not in Europe. Similarly, rather than looking at the problems caused by massive European banks whose governments found difficult to bail out, it asks what led to the creation of so many mega-banks in Europe compared to the United States. Rather than focusing on the different triggers and responses to the US and European crisis, it asks why the major northern European banks were so involved in financing unsustainable financial bubbles in the United States and the Euro area periphery.

A parallel with the literature on World War I may provide a useful analogy. At the end of that bruising conflict there was again a desire to assess the lessons coming from the immediate experience of the war. This focus generated heroes, such as Lawrence of Arabia, and villains, most importantly the leaders of Germany who were seen as bent on aggression. Over time, however, the literature on the *origins* of World War I has come to a much more nuanced view in which the war is seen largely as the inter-action of a range of diplomatic imperatives over a long period.[11] Alliances hardened, military plans were refined, so that when the denouement occurred most of the actors felt like "sleepwalkers".

Similarly, in the wake of the North Atlantic financial crisis there has been a focus on heroes, the policymakers, and villains. In the United States, the villains have generally been reckless financial firms run by greedy and crooked bankers aided and abetted by captured regulators.[12] In Europe, the narrative more often involves malfeasance before the crisis by the central government (Greece), local governments (Spain), bankers (Ireland), and connected firms (Portugal and Italy), followed by an intransigent insistence on maintaining the rules in the face of the crisis by the Germans, due either to the dominance of market-orientated thinking across the elites or to divergences in the historical experience of the French and Germans.[13]

This book incorporates these perspectives, but argues that the structural defects that led to the North Atlantic crisis were more complex and came from a much wider range of actors and motivations. This perspective generates a narrative with fewer heroes or villains. This is not to say that there were not greedy and crooked people in banks in the US and Ireland or malfeasance elsewhere in the Euro area. There undoubtedly were. But then such people always exist. The point is that you can tell a narrative of the origins of the North Atlantic crisis without malfeasance being a central plank. Just as was the case for World War I, most people were playing roles that had been laid out because of earlier decisions—they were sleepwalkers. The system failed, not the individuals. Accordingly, I have almost exclusively used pre-crisis accounts to explain their actions.

Another parallel with World War I comes from the unexpected nature of the North Atlantic crisis, which added immensely to the subsequent costs. In 2008 nobody expected problems in US subprime loans, a seemingly small segment of finance, to fell the entire North Atlantic economy just as, in the run-up to August 1914, misplaced confidence in the ability of the Concert of Europe to finesse earlier crises led to diplomatic complacency over the apparently peripheral assassination of the heir to the Austro-Hungarian Empire by a Serb patriot. The unexpected nature of the North Atlantic crisis matters as it forced policymakers to improvise. Unsurprisingly, some of these decisions were successful while others were not. US policymakers vastly underestimated the impact of allowing Lehman Brothers to go bankrupt. Euro area policymakers were similarly hamstrung by the rules that constrained the Euro area from providing adequate support to crisis countries.

A final parallel with World War I is adequacy of the response. The Versailles Treaty agreed in the aftermath of the war unsuccessfully tried to patch up the pre-war economic order while punishing the Germans with large reparation payments. It led to serial financial and economic instability—and also to World War II. By contrast, the more radical revamp of the global economic order after World War II at the Bretton Woods conference ushered in a long period of growth and prosperity. The crucial question is whether the response to this crisis is a new Versailles or a new Bretton Woods.

The first section of this book, "Anatomy of the North Atlantic Financial Crisis", explains how the North Atlantic financial system became so brittle.

There was indeed a powerful anti-regulatory lobby in the United States comprising the large banks, the Federal Reserve, and (to a lesser extent) the Securities and Exchange Commission (SEC). However, the philosophy was not endorsed by other bank regulators, so that deregulation largely affected the areas where the Federal Reserve and SEC held sway, the (already lightly regulated) investment banks, securitization, and consumer protection of mortgages, even as the core regulated banking system remained relatively sound. Crucially, however, the US anti-regulatory philosophy was exported to the international banking system via the Basel Committee on Banking Supervision, which allowed large international banks to use their own internal models to calculate capital buffers for investment banking operations. This had a particularly large impact on the Euro area, where the European Commission had encouraged universal banking (universal as it combined commercial and investment banking under one roof) and the Maastricht Treaty on Economic Union left financial regulation in the hands of national supervisors. With the scope of banks defined by the Commission and capital buffers by the Basel Committee, national regulators became boosters for their national mega-banks. The resulting boom in loans helped finance bubbles in the US housing market as well as the Euro area periphery. In short, US deregulation did promote the US and Euro area financial crises, but indirectly via Basel and mega-banks in the Euro area.

The following section, "Misdiagnosing the North Atlantic Economy", explains why the financial and macroeconomic warning signs were missed. The answer lies in intellectual overconfidence in the stability of private markets that led to a compartmentalization of policy decisions based on faulty underlying models. Disagreements on the purpose of the single currency between Germany and France led to a flawed Euro area that was designed for good times but not for bad ones. More generally, North Atlantic policymakers underestimated the value of financial regulation and the risks from free international capital flows, while overestimating the ability of central banks to stabilize the economy in the face of shocks. In sum, a free-market intellectual bubble obscured growing domestic, intra-Euro area, and inter-Atlantic macrofinancial bubbles. This explains why the crisis came as such a surprise, and why it was so costly to solve, particularly for the Euro area.

The final section, "Completing the Cure", examines the policy responses to the crisis from this historical perspective. While much has been done to correct the defects that became apparent during the crisis, many deeper weaknesses remain. Examples include the continued focus on bank internal risk models in the Euro area, inadequate oversight of international debt flows, limited buffers to respond to shocks to Euro area members that are not prepared to submit to a program, and a new interest in reducing financial regulations. More generally, the world seems to be drifting back to policy compartmentalization, with monetary policy shouldering the burden of raising growth out of its doldrums while backing away from concerns about financial stability, despite calls for greater coordination with fiscal, financial, and structural policies. There is still an awful lot of unfinished business.

Country	Cycle	Investment	Total
Italy	-19.1	-6.8	-25.9
Spain	-4.9	-15.4	-20.3
Ireland	-5.0	-14.1	-19.1
Portugal	-31.9	0.0	-31.9
Greece	-30.0	0.0	-30.0

Figure 3: Estimated output losses in Euro area crisis countries. Percent of GDP. *Source:* Haver Analytics.

PART I

ANATOMY OF THE NORTH ATLANTIC FINANCIAL CRISIS

Chapter 1

EUROPEAN BANKS UNFETTERED

The massive expansion of the European banking system between 1985 and 2002 is a crucial, and previously underestimated, aspect of the North Atlantic financial crisis. Over this period European bank assets doubled in relation to the economy. The growth was spearheaded by the emergence of a small number of major banks referred to as "national champions" that were mainly located in the northern core of the Euro area—Germany, France, the Netherlands, and Belgium. The assets of these banks ballooned even as their capital buffers—the reserves they held in case their loans went bad—thinned. The upshot was the emergence of a small number of northern mega-banks that were quickly becoming too big to save even as they became less sound in the face of shocks.

In the subsequent boom over the 2000s these trends took on a life of their own. The mega-banks in the Euro area core continued to expand, providing much of the funding for the housing price bubbles in the United States and financial bubbles in the Euro area periphery. When the bubbles burst the losses whipsawed back onto the core of the Euro area, widening the banking crisis across the North Atlantic. Indeed, every banking system in the Euro area experienced a crisis in 2008 except for Finland.[1] The northern European mega-banks were thus major protagonists that helped drive the North Atlantic banking crisis rather than hapless victims, as they are often portrayed.

How the northern European banks were allowed to expand so far, so fast, is a cautionary tale of unanticipated spillovers from financial regulations. Three decisions, directed at differing goals and taken by distinct groups, created the environment for the mega-banks to thrive. In chronological order they were: The 1986 Single European Act, driven by the European Commission; the 1992 Maastricht Treaty, primarily planned by central bankers; and the 1996 market risk amendment to the Basel Accords, under the purview of bank regulators. Together, these three decisions drove an unsustainable expansion of the major European banks that exploited lax regulation and supervision. This business strategy was so successful that by the early 2000s just twelve banks in the Euro area owned one-quarter of all bank assets. Most of these mega-banks were located in northern Europe since this is where the investment banking operations that were central to this strategy were most established. Examples include Deutsche Bank in Germany, BNP Paribas in France, and ING in the Netherlands. Understanding the transformative nature of these changes it is useful to first survey the state of the banking system in the early 1980s.

European Banking in the 1980s

In the early 1980s there was no real concept of an integrated European banking system. Rather, the European Community's banks operated in a series of fragmented national markets.[2] German banks took deposits from Germans in Deutsche marks and lent to Germans, a pattern that was repeated throughout the Community—just 4 percent of bank assets in Germany, Europe's largest economy, came from foreign institutions. Bond and equity markets were also split along national lines, and, in any case, were much less important than in the United States. Banks were the dominant financial intermediaries in Europe, shuffling money from savers to borrowers.[3]

The national focus of European banking is vividly illustrated by the nationalization of the French banking system. In 1981, a socialist government was elected under François Mitterrand on a platform to nationalize major industrial groups and private banks. Accordingly, in February 1982 two conglomerates with major banking interests (Paribas and Suez) and thirty-six individual banks were nationalized, bringing over 90 percent of deposits under state control.[4] Strikingly, this takeover of virtually the entire banking system of Europe's second largest economy was accomplished using legislation crafted for domestic companies. It did not require the complex procedures and negotiations involved in nationalizing foreign-owned firms, such as the French subsidiaries of ITT and Hoechst.[5] European banks were nationally run and nationally owned. As a result, a government takeover, as in France, was easily accomplished.

This was not how the European banking system was supposed to be evolving. The Treaty of Rome that founded the (then) European

Economic Community in 1957 had pledged an "ever closer union" across its members that encompassed an ambitious program of economic integration, including a unified banking system. The Treaty had envisaged a gradual process as barriers to trade were removed and firms were given the right to establish themselves in other members of the Community. This plan was reinforced in the early 1970s, when the European Council directed that banks from across the members of the Community should face the same regulation and supervision.

On the ground, however, it was clear that these provisions were not creating a European-wide banking system. This reflected the existence of separate currencies as well as national policies. The costs involved in swapping one currency for another discouraged cross-border banking. While the charges for a single transfer between (say) the Deutsche mark and the French franc were only a few percentage points, they added up quickly if the same funds had to be transferred back and forth several times as would typically occur in a truly integrated cross-border bank. Capital controls added further headaches by disallowing some transactions and adding time, cost, and paperwork to others. Such controls were particularly prevalent in countries suffering from relatively high inflation, including major European Community countries such as France, Italy, and the United Kingdom. These controls reflected the strains these members faced in maintaining international competitiveness given the commitment to limiting exchange rate fluctuations contained in the European Exchange Rate Mechanism. Finally, every Community country except the United Kingdom required foreign-owned banks to raise local capital, adding costs that further fragmented the European banking system.

Irritating as the costs of different currencies, capital controls, and local capital levies were for banks, the most permanent barrier to cross-country banking would turn out to be the informal barriers created by national regulators. Each country had its own set of banking regulations with which any foreign venture had to comply. Since any entry into the domestic market by a foreign bank required the approval of national governments, regulators could easily block foreign ventures. As noted by an independent report to the European Commission in 1988, while "there are no overt barriers to the establishment of foreign banks" the costs of compliance could be considerable and there was "control over the acquisition of domestic banks by foreign entities in all the countries".[6] Regulators ensured that European banks were stopped at the border, but changes were about to happen. Indeed, 1986 marked a pivotal point in European banking history as the first of the transformative decisions was passed.

* * *

The Road to Hell is Paved with Good Intentions

Three major policy decisions, all aimed at integrating the European banking system, culminated in the long banking boom that ended abruptly with the North Atlantic crisis. Each decision made individual sense, but unforeseen interactions turned these individual palliatives into a poisonous mixture. The first of these was the Single European Act that was the brainchild of the European Commission.

The Single European Act

The institution that is responsible for driving European economic integration is the European Commission, set up in 1957 by the Treaty of Rome. Like most institutions, the fortunes of the Commission have waxed and waned with the quality of its leadership. As a general rule, the leaders of the Commission have tended to be relatively ineffective, in part because weak leadership in the European Commission enhanced the relative power of major members such as France and Germany. In 1985, however, the presidency was given to Jacques Delors, an energetic, ambitious, and efficient former French minister. This choice was no accident. Rather, it signaled the importance that President Mitterrand of France had decided to give to accelerating European economic integration after he turned away from his earlier go-it-alone socialist policies.

Jacques Delors immediately set about re-energizing the push towards European economic integration and a single market. The first fruit of this new sense of leadership and purpose was the passage of the Single European Act in 1986, which committed the members of the Community to the creation of "an area without internal barriers in which free movement of goods, persons, services and capital is ensured" by the end of 1992. As a finishing touch, the act renamed the European Community as the European Union to further emphasize the longer-term commitment to greater economic and political integration.

For the banking industry, the crucial element was the free movement of services and capital. Given the existing constraints on integrated banking, the Commission focused on opening capital markets, imposing a single banking model, and breaking down regulatory barriers to Europe-wide banking. The opening of capital markets was achieved smoothly. Details on how to comply with the Single European Act were provided to the members of the Union by directives crafted by the European Commission. One such directive asked member countries to liberalize all capital movements in the Community and between Community countries and third countries by July 1990.[7]

Looking forward in time, the wider objective of eliminating the costs of exchanging currencies was achieved by Jacques Delors in his most striking accomplishment, the Maastricht Treaty on Economic Union. The Treaty, agreed in December 1991 and signed in March 1992, established the path to European Monetary Union (EMU). It specified that by the start of 1999 wholesale financial transactions would be carried out in a common currency and hence would not involve transaction costs (Euro notes and coins were introduced in 2002). Since the membership of the monetary union was not to be determined until 1998, there remained uncertainty as to which countries would be admitted and hence the group across which transaction costs would be eliminated. However, it was clear from the start that the currency union would incorporate a wide swathe of Europe, almost certainly including the northern core of Germany, France, the Netherlands, and Belgium. European bankers could confidently make plans on the assumption that transaction costs would be eliminated across a much of the continent by the end of the 1990s.

The Single European Act was equally successful in synchronizing European banking models. The Second Banking Directive, issued by the Commission in December 1989, defined what services a bank could perform.[8] Crucially, the proposal encompassed both commercial banking (loans to companies and households) and investment banking (supporting financial markets through such services as brokerage, equity issuance, and arranging mergers and acquisitions). This "universal" banking model (universal because banks could engage in both commercial and investment banking instead of having to specialize in one or the other) was typical in much of continental Europe, including Germany. It contrasted with the approach taken in the United States, where commercial and investment banking activities were required to be performed by different firms, as well as the United Kingdom, which also had a tradition of separate commercial and investment banks (the latter called merchant banks because of their origins in financing trade).

Competition across national regulators within the Union ensured that this universal banking model was rapidly adopted. This was because the Commission's Second Directive allowed a bank to offer all services approved by its national supervisor throughout the rest of the Union. As a result, any country that retained a narrow banking model risked putting its banks at a disadvantage by limiting the services its banks could offer compared to foreign competitors. Depositors might switch from a domestic to a foreign-owned universal bank because the latter (say) could provide brokerage services that allowed clients to invest money. This risk provided a powerful incentive for countries to rapidly adopt the wide definition of banking proposed by the Commission. The universal banking model was a crucial development that helped drive the subsequent expansion of core Euro area mega-banks into investment banking. Before turning to that part of the story, however, it is necessary to explain why regulatory competition foiled the most important part of the Commission's plan to create an integrated European banking system.

At the heart of the Single European Act was a plan to overcome national resistance to cross-border ventures through a new and innovative process called "mutual recognition". Mutual recognition replaced the earlier approach that encouraged integration by ensuring that all European Union firms faced the same regulations within a country regardless of their nationality. Countries had found it easy to thwart this approach since, for example, German regulators could and did use their responsibility to approve new firms to discourage entry by foreign entities, including banks. Under mutual recognition, by contrast, if a French firm wanted to set up a new venture in Germany, it would only be subject to French regulations (as long as the French rules complied with EU-wide standards). Since the foreign entrant was not subject to German rules, German regulators had no basis to reject the entry of a French firm. And the same logic applied to a German firm entering the French market—hence the descriptor "mutual" recognition. In a single stroke, the act promised to speed up the process of economic integration by lowering barriers to cross-border firms. Indeed, it promoted rapid integration in many industries, but not in banking.

Explaining why mutual recognition failed to integrate banking requires an understanding how the rule interacted with the incentives of national supervisors. In the Second Banking Directive, the European Commission introduced mutual recognition through a "passport" system and the principle of source country control. European Union banks were issued a single passport that allowed them to do business anywhere in the Union. Source country control meant that foreign bank branches—parts of the domestic bank set up in a foreign country—operated under the rules and supervision of the source country rather than the host country. Hence, for example, if Deutsche Bank set up a branch in Paris, the branch was allowed to follow German banking law and was supervised by the German bank regulators rather than French ones. By contrast, if Deutsche Bank set up a subsidiary—a bank incorporated in France—it was under French supervision.

This approach was completely different from the traditional role played by foreign bank branches and subsidiaries that still operates in the rest of the world. Typically, in (say) the United States, a branch of a German bank is subject to US regulations. However, since the branch is only allowed to offer limited services such as support for traveling clients, it operates under less stringent rules than a full US bank. If a German bank wanted to offer a wider range of services in the United States then it has to set up a subsidiary bank, fully incorporated in the United States and thus subject to full US regulation. By contrast, mutual recognition meant (and still means) that within the European Union there is no difference between the services that are offered by a branch and a subsidiary. Rather, the difference is who supervises the bank. The Germans supervise all *branches* of German banks elsewhere in the European Union such as France. By contrast, a French *subsidiary* of a German bank is supervised by the French.

In practice, however, this elaborate scheme to create an integrated EU banking system via bank branches was stymied by informal barriers set up by national supervisors. Since banking rests on relationships with clients, expansion almost always occurs through acquisition rather than starting a new bank from scratch, since buying an existing bank automatically transfers its clients. Any attempt by a foreign bank to acquire an existing domestic bank, however, involves negotiations with the existing owners and, importantly, with the current national bank supervisor. So, for example, if a German bank wanted to buy a French bank, the deal would need to get the blessing of the French supervisor. National supervisors used this leeway to resist foreign entry. As one commentator put it in the early 2000s:

> Despite legislation on freedom of entry, rumors abounded of public intervention to deter entry of foreign banks in the case of the sale of CIC in France and of Generale Banque in Belgium, an (unsuccessful) attempt to prevent the sale of a bank of the Champalimaud group to Banco Santander in Portugal, and of a desire by the Central Bank of Italy to keep large banks independent.[9]

As a result, cross-border mergers and acquisitions were lower in the banking industry than in other sectors. In Germany, for example, despite the Single European Act, foreign banks owned just 7 percent of all banking assets by the end of 2002. And Germany was not an outlier. Foreign bank assets represented under one-tenth of all assets in every major Euro area country except France, where they squeaked in just above that threshold.

Another telling sign of the failure of "passporting" and the importance of national bank supervisors in resisting foreign entry was that the vast majority of the cross-border bank mergers involved the creation of locally owned and supervised subsidiaries rather than foreign-supervised branches.[10] For example, between 1985 and 2002 assets of foreign subsidiaries in the German banking system quintupled to 5 percent of output while assets in foreign bank branches remained stuck at around 2 percent, a pattern that was repeated across the Union. There were clear reasons for regulators to encourage cross-border entry through subsidiaries rather than branches. National supervisors had a strong interest in overseeing as much of the domestic banking system as possible, as problems in foreign ventures could spill over onto local banks and markets. Given the risk that problems in one bank could rapidly spread and undermine confidence in the rest of the system, it was eminently logical to discourage foreign branches. The underlying weakness of the bank passport system was that, for instance, a French branch of a German bank was supervised by Germans but the main costs of any problems were likely to be incurred in France.

Equally telling is the exception to this pattern of limited foreign entry occurring largely through subsidiaries, namely the United Kingdom. The UK banking system had a very different structure from the rest of the Union as it hosted a large foreign banking presence focused on the highly internationalized UK capital markets. These investment banks were incorporated as branches rather than subsidiaries so as to integrate market support across the major international financial centers, especially London and New York, while the interaction with UK clients was limited. Such international links were much more easily achieved using a branch that was run out of headquarters than by an independent subsidiary. The importance of investment banking in London led to a relaxed attitude to foreign entry. Almost half of all UK bank assets were in branches of foreign banks—London was the melting pot of the international banking system. The gulf with the rest of the EU is equally striking. By the end of 2002, the assets of EU branches in the United Kingdom were twice the size of such branches in the much larger Euro area. Put another way, while more than 20 percent of UK bank assets came from cross-border EU branches, for the Euro area this ratio was only 3 percent. In addition, the UK harbored numerous bank branches from the rest of the world, a type of foreign entry that barely registered in the neighboring Euro area. This example of the impact of a relaxed attitude to foreign entry underlines the central role played by other EU supervisors in blocking integration of the banking system.

Why Was National Bank Supervision Retained in the Maastricht Treaty?

The second crucial policy decision for European banking actually involved no decision—rather retaining the status quo. In the 1992 Maastricht Treaty that determined the structuring of the future currency union, European leaders decided to keep responsibility for supervising and rescuing banks at the level of individual member countries rather that centralizing at the union level, the arrangement typical in other monetary unions such as the United States. The decision to retain national supervision was crucial as it undermined the European banking system in two ways. Competition across national supervisors meant that they increasingly became supporters for their own major banks. This led to the creation of large "national champions" and promoted a supervisory "race to the bottom" as regulators looked to boost the competitive position of their own champions by not being too intrusive. In addition, the fact that in the end almost all entry into other European countries was through subsidiaries meant that the costs of the eventual crisis were bottled up in individual countries. The quip from former Bank of England governor Mervyn King, that banks live internationally but die nationally, was especially true within the Euro area. This had far-reaching consequences. Regulators and governments in the crisis countries were overwhelmingly responsible for the losses, helping to meld their banking and fiscal problems. On the other hand, because a significant part of the financing for the bubbles came from elsewhere in the Euro area, often through loans to local banks, the potential knock-on costs of bank failures to the rest of the Union produced strong incentives across the Euro area to fudge the assessment of the resulting bad loans.

Given the important role played in destabilizing the Euro area banking system by the decision in the Maastricht Treaty to keep bank supervision with member states, it is worth probing its background more thoroughly. The decision fits with the treaty's broad philosophy of subsidiarity, which means leaving issues that did not need to be centralized at the national level. As a result of this objective, the Maastricht Treaty left most major responsibilities outside of monetary policy with individual members, such as fiscal policy and structural reforms.[11] The general philosophy was to focus on creating a monetary union within the existing institutional structure of the Union rather than adding further federal bells and whistles. In the case of banking, the broad regulatory structure was already defined centrally by the European Commission through Union-wide directives, including on capital controls, the services a bank could perform, and the size of capital buffers. The issue, therefore, was whether day-to-day supervision of these rules should remain a national responsibility.[12]

This question provoked a lengthy discussion in the Delors Committee, the group largely comprised of central bankers that provided the blueprint for the eventual Maastricht Treaty. Intriguingly, in the discussion of bank supervision, the traditional roles of the German and the British officials in discussions about European integration were reversed. The Germans, who were generally sympathetic to a more federated structure for the Union, took a strong view that bank supervision should remain at the national level. This reflected the Bundesbank's concern that the newly formed central bank should be truly independent and not subject to outside pressure. The fear of the German negotiators was that if banking supervision was elevated to the level of the Union then problems in the banking system would also be dealt with by the center. Given the small size of the Commission's budget, this would likely imply a need for the European Central Bank (ECB) to provide support for troubled banks. Such responsibilities would be a distraction from the bank's central objective of maintaining price stability and would encourage political lobbying about its decisions. To avoid this risk, Karl Otto Pöhl, President of the Bundesbank, pushed strongly for national supervision in the Delors Committee. By contrast, the British, who were generally the most skeptical of any move toward federation and obtained an opt-out from the single currency, were sympathetic to a Union-wide regulator. This reflected the size of the UK banking system, which was large even by European standards and therefore potentially costly to rescue. In addition, the British were keenly aware that their supervisors held no effective oversight over the massive assets in foreign branches, especially those from other European Union banks where the Second Banking Directive explicitly cut them out of the process. Accordingly, Robert Leigh-Pemberton, the Governor of the Bank of England, argued for centralized supervision.

In common with most issues in the Maastricht Treaty, the German approach prevailed, albeit with a nod to the British view.[13] The text of the Delors Report stated that the European System of Central Banks (ESCB) would "participate in the coordination of banking supervision policies". Over the Maastricht negotiations, the ESCB's role in financial supervision was further downgraded to "contributing" to the policies pursued by "competent authorities".[14] This clearly left the supervision of banks to national regulators. However, the Treaty also included a get-out-of-jail-free card that allowed supervision to be centralized. More specifically, Article 105.6 authorized the European Council to let the ECB take on bank supervision if the Council acted "unanimously on a proposal from the Commission and after consulting the ECB and after receiving the assent of the European Parliament". Unsurprisingly, given the requirement for unanimity across all member states, this option was not invoked until 2012, four years after the financial crisis first broke.

By hard-wiring regulatory competition into the European financial system, the Maastricht Treaty reduced the incentives of European supervisors to look carefully at the behavior of major domestic banks. That was because their banks competed with banks from other countries whose supervisors might be cutting them more slack.[15] It also meant that there was no institution examining the evolution of the European banking system as a whole. With nobody minding the shop, the mega-banks were able to use changes in the rules on capital buffers to become larger and less safe. This opening came through the Basel Committee rules on international bank capital.

The Rise of Bank Internal Risk Models

The third policy decision that drove the expansion in Euro area banking involved international regulations promulgated through the Basel Committee on Banking Supervision. The Basel Committee, whose decisions played a crucial role in the evolution of the European banking system and the North Atlantic crisis, was formed by the Group of Ten (unintuitively comprising eleven major advanced economies) in 1974 to improve supervisory quality and understanding worldwide.[16] It is housed in the Bank for International Settlements in Basel and, while it has no formal legal standing or permanent staff, it remains the main driver behind regulation for internationally active banks. One of its major roles is to craft internationally consistent rules on capital buffers.

The push for consistent capital standards originated from concerns that differing national rules were providing some banks with a competitive advantage compared to their international competitors by allowing them to hold thinner capital buffers. Bank capital is intrinsically risky as owners are the first to lose their money in the case of financial distress. Accordingly, investors demand a higher rate of return on capital compared to safer forms of borrowing such as bonds or deposits. The concern was that competition across supervisors was creating a regulatory "race to the bottom" in which each country tried to make their banks more competitive by diluting the requirements on their expensive capital buffers, leading to inappropriately thin buffers across the board.[17] The risk had been underlined by the international repercussions of major bank failures, such as that of Continental Illinois Bank in 1984. Even so, while national regulators were putting increasing emphasis on rules on bank capital, in 1985 there was "considerable variation in the mode and details of the capital regulation . . . and little apparent interest in most supervisors in harmonizing their capital regulations".[18]

A crucial breakthrough came in 1986 when, rather to their surprise, negotiators from the US and UK rapidly settled on a common set of capital standards.[19] The two countries were particularly influential members of the Basel Committee, reflecting both the size of their economies and the importance of the New York and London financial markets for international banking. In addition, they obtained an agreement in principle to adopt their new standards from Japan, another important member of the Committee. The core of the US/UK proposal comprised a consistent definition of what types of assets could be included in bank capital, the relative riskiness of different types of commercial loans, and the amount of capital that had to be held against such "risk-weighted" assets. The proposal focused on commercial loans since in both countries investment banking was mainly performed outside of the main banking sector.

The US/UK proposal became the basis for negotiations throughout 1987 on a uniform definition of bank assets and capital across the members of the Basel Committee. The discussions were most contentious around which assets should be classified as capital, with different countries supporting definitions that included less effective buffers that their own banks already held so as to minimize additional capital demands. So, for example, Japanese negotiators supported the inclusion of unrealized capital gains on bank equities and those from the United States advocated the inclusion of certain types of preferred stock. The final outcome was the first set of uniform international capital adequacy standards, known as the Basel 1 Accord. The rules were agreed in 1988 and were to be enforced in all member states by the end of 1992 so as to allow national supervisors the time to amend their existing frameworks.

The preamble to the agreement explained that the objective was "to secure international convergence of supervisory regulations governing the capital adequacy of international banks".[20] The new standards were aimed at strengthening the "soundness and stability of the international banking system" and at "diminishing an existing source of competitive inequality among international banks".[21] Basically, each bank loan was to be placed in one of five possible buckets with risk weights varying from 0 to 100 percent.[22] So, for example, loans to governments of advanced countries were considered extremely safe and were given a risk weight of zero. At the other end of the scale, corporate loans were seen as highly risky, and were given a weight of 100 percent, while mortgages attracted a middling value of 50 percent. These buckets were then summed to get total "risk-weighted" assets. Required capital buffers were then calculated as a percentage of these risk-weighted assets. Reflecting the lack of agreement on what should be included in bank capital, Basel 1 included two levels of minimum capital buffers. "Core" (Tier 1) capital, that was largely equity and retained profits, had to be at least 4 percent of risk-weighted assets, while the sum of core and "supplementary" (Tier 2) capital that included less effective buffers such as subordinated debt (subordinated because in the event of a bankruptcy it would be written down before more senior debt) had to be at least 8 percent of risk-weighted assets.

Since the Basel Committee included seven of the ten members of the European Union, the Basel 1 Accord rapidly unified European bank capital rules. The non-participants were Ireland, Denmark and Greece, who had little alternative but to adopt the rules agreed by the larger members. The accord also covered the major international competitors to European Union as the other members of the Committee were Canada, Japan, Sweden, Switzerland, and the United States. However, as will be discussed in the next chapter, the US commercial banks were also under additional US-specific capital standards. This overlay, which effectively meant that the US banks were under a more stringent capital regime, was to have far-reaching consequences since it provided US banks with incentives to sell loans to the European banks over the boom of the 2000s.

The 1996 Market Risk Amendment

The rapid adoption of the universal banking model in Europe as a result of the European Commission's Second Banking Directive created issues for the Basel 1 Accord. The focus of the existing Basel rules was commercial loans to firms or individuals. The large European banks, however, were increasingly expanding into investment banking and hence held increasing amounts of market assets such as equities and bonds. This involved a different type of "market" risk—losses coming from a fall in the price of these assets. This contrasted with the United States where the Depression Era Glass–Steagall Act continued to separate commercial banking from investment banking (other members of the Basel Committee fell between the wide universal banking model in Europe and the narrower commercial banking one in the United States).

In response to the increase in investment banking activities in its banks, the European Union decided that it needed rules on capital buffers for market risk. The Basel Committee became concerned that this move could lead to disjointed international capital rules, with different countries adopting different rules on market risk. Accordingly, in 1993 the Committee proposed an amendment to the Basel 1 risk weights to cover market risks, closely modeled on the European Commission's European Capital Adequacy Directive issued the previous month.[23] The essence of the proposal was to divide bank activities into traditional commercial loans, held in the "banking" book, and holdings of securities, held in the "trading" book. Assets in the banking book would be subject to the standard Basel 1 credit risk weights. By contrast, securities held in the trading book would be subject to new weights based on market risk. Securities would be classified on standardized measures of the risk of large changes in prices—basically the same "bucket" approach that already applied to credit risk.

To the surprise of the Committee, this proposal ran into strong criticism. This came mainly from the large banks, who argued that the proposed buckets were much less sophisticated than their own rapidly evolving "value-at-risk" models that calculated the risk to the value of an entire portfolio by taking into account not simply the volatility of individual asset prices but also the correlations across such prices. They noted that adopting the Committee's proposal would lessen incentives to continue to develop their own internal risk models. Instead, the large banks asked to be allowed to use their own models to calculate the capital buffers needed for the trading book. The assumption of the large banks, which turned out to be correct, was that internal risk models would allow them to save on capital buffers and provide them with a competitive edge over their smaller competitors.

Disconcerted that banks found the proposed methodology "old-fashioned", the Committee set up a Models Task Force to examine the banks internal models. The task force, led by Christine Cummings from the Federal Reserve Bank of New York, reported back to the Committee that they were impressed with the "obvious sincerity and expertise" of the banks.[24] The report concluded that there were compelling arguments to adopt internal risk models, including "greater precision, avoidance of duplication and incentives to develop adequate systems". Accordingly, the revised proposal on market risk, published in 1995, allowed large banks to use their internal risk models as the basis for calculating capital buffers for market risk.[25]

The decision to allow market risk to be calculated using internal risk models was made despite evidence that results differed widely across banks.

The Models Task Force had earlier asked fifteen banks to calculate risks on several dummy portfolios. It reported that half of all banks had estimates of underlying risk that differed from other banks by over 50 percent.[26] In response, the task force proposed "carefully structured safeguards to minimize the risk of abuse". The report went on to the optimistic observation that "a moderate amount of supervisory guidance as to acceptable risk measurement practices could substantially reduce the dispersion of these results". In response to these concerns the Basel Committee proposed a series of safeguards to reign in the internal models by setting a range of quantitative parameters as well as qualitative standards. In addition, the Committee proposed to top up the results from the risk models with a "multiplication factor", whereby the final capital buffer would be three times that calculated by the internal risk model to compensate for the limitations of even the best models to predict shocks.

In a taste of things to come, these safeguards faced a barrage of criticism from the large banks and the Committee started down the path of negotiating the detail of the rules with them. As a result of these discussions, the final version of the amendment provided some additional flexibility for the banks (although the controversial multiplicative factor was retained).[27] Crucially, however, there was no follow-up to check whether these changes made the results from the internal risk models more similar. Whatever the intentions of the Committee, the answer appears to have been no. Major differences in results were again found in the early 2000s, when the properties of internal risk models were next examined in detail in the run-up to the switch to the Basel 2 capital rules. Indeed, the Basel Committee has still not solved this problem.

The market risk amendment was a watershed moment that involved three crucial changes to the philosophy of the Basel Committee. At a very basic level, the Committee accepted the need for rules on international capital buffers to move beyond the traditional concern of bank regulators, namely the risk of *commercial* loans to individuals or firms going sour, and to provide a benchmark for *market* risks to bank balance sheets coming from buying and selling securities, in other words investment banking. In tandem, the Committee also accepted the principle of using internal bank risk models in the calculation of capital buffers. The Committee tacitly accepted that the large banks understood the risks from market trading better than the supervisors. Finally, as a corollary to that change, the Committee engaged in detailed discussions on bank capital regulations with the banking industry, in particular the major international banks.

The important question is why the Basel Committee decided to farm
out the calculation of capital buffers to large banks. Here, a crucial role was
played by the growing belief that market discipline would constrain risk-
taking. This was largely driven by views coming from the United States. The
major US banks had been at the forefront of developing value-at-risk
models. In addition, Alan Greenspan, Chair of the Federal Reserve, and the
Fed staff in charge of bank regulation were strong believers in the power of
market discipline in controlling the risks taken by investment banks. This
is made clear in Greenspan's memoirs, sent to the printers just before
the North Atlantic crisis and titled (with unintended irony) *The Age of
Turbulence*, where he wrote about his experience at the Fed that:

> Since I was an outlier in my libertarian opposition to most [financial]
> regulation, I planned to be largely passive in such matters and allow the
> Federal Reserve governors to take the lead. . . .Taking office, I was in
> for a pleasant surprise. . . .What I had not known about was the staff's
> free market orientation, which I now discovered characterized even the
> Division of Bank Supervision and Regulation. . . .So while the staff
> recommendations at the Federal Reserve Board were directed to imple-
> menting congressional mandates, they were always formulated with a
> view toward fostering competition and letting markets work. . . .The
> staff also fully recognized the power of counterparty surveillance [i.e.,
> market discipline] as the first line of protection against overextended
> or inappropriate credit.[28]

The Federal Reserve made a clear distinction between the appropriate regulation of commercial banking and investment banking. Depositors in
commercial banks that lent to individuals and firms were protected by
deposit insurance. They had few incentives to monitor the risks the bank
was taking as they were protected from losses should the bank fail and were
in any case relatively unsophisticated investors. Government regulation was
needed to ensure that banks did not exploit this lack of attention by taking
excessive risks. By contrast, investment banks were funded by sophisticated
investors through large, uninsured "wholesale" deposits. Such investors
could monitor the behavior of the investment banks and stop them from
taking excess risks by threatening to withdraw their money. In the Fed's
view, government regulation was not needed and could, indeed, be counter-
productive since it could lessen the incentives for investors to monitor the
investment banks. Far from reinforcing the discipline that markets exerted
on banks, government regulation could undermine it.

These views explain the why the Federal Reserve put its very considerable weight behind the disastrous decision to use internal risk models for market risk that left the banks in charge of calculating the buffers needed for their investment banking operations. While regulators were supposed to monitor the adequacy of these models, in practice such checks were always going to be difficult given large differences in results from models across banks. However, in the view of the Fed such checks were largely irrelevant given "the power of counterparty surveillance as the first line of protection against overextended or inappropriate credit". Internal risk models were not really an instrument for bank regulation, but rather were a rejection of the need for such regulation. This also explains why a Basel task force headed by a Federal Reserve official concluded that there were "compelling arguments" in favor of internal risk models based on information provided by bankers with "obvious sincerity".

The naïve decision to allow major international banks to use internal risk models to calculate their capital buffers for investment banking generated a cascade of destructive incentives in the Euro area banking system. It gave large banks a competitive edge over smaller ones as they could expand into investment banking on the cheap using thin cushions of expensive capital. For similar reasons, it also advantaged banks with more aggressive risk models, as they could operate with thinner capital buffers than their competitors. This incentivised large banks to tweak their internal risk models to be more aggressive, so as to save on capital and become more competitive compared to their peers. All of this helped drive the emergence of the small number of mega-banks that dominated European banking on the eve of the North Atlantic financial crisis. By using internal risk models to calculate the amount of (expensive) capital a bank needed, the market risk amendment changed the nature of the internal models from useful tools for risk management to a constraint on the size of the firm's balance sheet. They became a way of lowering costs rather than assessing the level of risk. As in quantum physics, observation changed the nature of the experiment. Once risk models switched from an internal tool to assess risks to an external measure that determined the needed level of capital, banks altered the way in which these models were used.

Internal risk models also made the banking system inherently more cyclical. The reason for this is that internal risk models use market prices as a signal of the riskiness of an asset. If the economy is booming and asset prices are rising, the models interpret this as meaning that the asset is safer and hence that the buffers can be reduced. The capital thus saved could be redeployed to expand the bank's lending, an increase in loanable funds that reinforced the boom. Of course, the same process works in reverse as became painfully obvious after the North Atlantic crisis. If an unsustainable boom in asset prices turns into a bust, banks' internal models force them to shrink lending which exacerbates the resulting downturn. This contrasted with the standardized approach, where risk weights do not vary with cyclical fluctuations in asset prices. The cyclical nature of internal risk models was a major driver of the boom-bust that started in the late 1990s and reversed course after the crisis.

The irony here is that even though the market risk amendment was largely driven by the US Federal Reserve, it had a much larger impact on the European banks than the US ones. This was because the EU's Second Banking Directive ensured that the European banks were at the forefront of the move toward universal banking involving mega-banks with large investment banking operations. The competitive advantages provided by internal models resulted in an industry increasingly driven by a small number of large and largely national banks that, particularly in the Euro area core, exploited the market risk amendment by expanding into investment banking. By contrast, in the United States investment banking was largely performed by the already lightly regulated independent investment banks.

The Poisonous Mixture

The confluence of the Single Market initiative, the single currency, and the Basel capital rules aimed to create an integrated and competitive European Union banking system. In practice, however, unanticipated spillovers meant that it generated a rapidly expanding and over-banked system that remained overwhelmingly national and was increasingly dominated by ever-larger mega-banks with thin capital buffers that were increasingly involved in investment banking. Key roles were played by the universal banking model coming from the Single European Act, by continuing competition across national supervisors as a result of the Maastricht Treaty, and by the Basel Committee's 1996 market risk amendment. In particular, the market risk amendment allowed major banks to economize on capital buffers in their expanding investment banking operations. The banks used the newly freed capital for further expansion, often plowing it back into investment banking since the associated capital charges were so low. European regulators did little to prevent this process as competition between national regulators provided few incentives to reign in the activities of national banks. A vivid illustration of the influence of regulatory competition in eroding bank supervision was the move to "light touch" regulation in the United

Kingdom and Ireland in the early 2000s, which left their banks relatively free from supervision.[29] In the end, the decision by the Basel Committee to allow banks to use internal models to calculate capital buffers for market risk generated exactly the kind of diminution in capital standards on investment banking in Europe that the Committee had originally been formed to avoid.

* * *

Charting the Transformation of European Banking 1985–2002

The transformation of the European banking system from the 1980s through to 2002 can be clearly seen in the numbers. This narrative opens with a broad-brush summary of developments through the late 1990s, followed by a more detailed snapshot of the system in the early 2000s when more information on European banking becomes available with the advent of the Euro.

Expansion after 1985

The European banking system expanded enormously between 1985 and 1999 as restrictions on bank activities were lifted and universal banking took hold. Assets almost doubled as a ratio to output for the future members of the Euro area for which data are readily available (Figure 4). (Assets are reported as a ratio to output so as to abstract from the natural increase in the size of the banking sector as the economy gets larger.) Almost all of the increase came from the northern core of the future Euro area— Germany, France, the Netherlands, and Belgium. Indeed, the size of the core banking system caught up with that of the United Kingdom, traditionally the largest system in Europe because of its international orientation. By contrast, the size of banks in the periphery of the Euro area (measured as a ratio to output) hardly changed. By the turn of the century the core banking system was twice as large as that of the remaining "periphery" when compared to the size of the economies, having been almost equal in 1985.

The 1996 Basel market risk amendment was a major driver of the increase in the core banking system. Figure 5 reports quarterly data on the banking systems of Germany and the Netherlands, the two countries for which such data are readily available. Assets expanded rapidly as a ratio to output in both banking systems, particularly after 1996. The fact that most of the expansion went into investment banking can be seen by the much faster increase in the darker lines that show the path of total loans compared

	1985	1990	1995	1999
Euro area	116	165	193	216
Core	115	187	217	254
Periphery	118	118	141	132
United Kingdom	167	217	237	239
Belgium	252	273	304	313
Finland	86	135	117	86
France	98	216	240	265
Geremany	117	133	169	235
Italy	116	117	135	127
Netherlands	115	175	216	232
Spain	130	116	159	151

Figure 4: Euro area banking boomed after 1985. Assets as a percentage of GDP.
Source: Dermin (2002) B49 country table except Netherlands in 1999 which comes from the ECB.
Notes: For Belgium the 1999 column is for 1999/2000. Euro area data are weighted using 1999 GDP in euros.

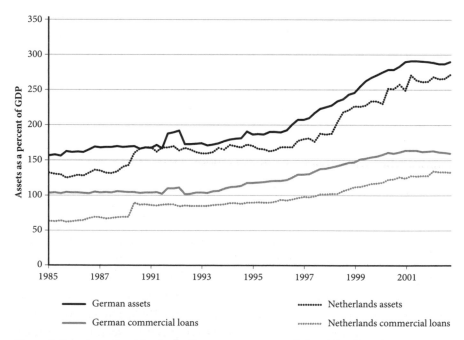

Figure 5: Investment banking in the Euro area core expanded rapidly after 1996.
Source: National Banking Statistics.

with the lighter lines which show the amount of commercial loans (i.e., loans to firms, households, and governments). The expansion into investment banking involved buying overseas ventures. In particular, Germany's largest bank, Deutsche Bank, acquired investment banks in London (where they bought Morgan Grenfell in 1989) and New York (where they bought Bankers Trust in 1999). In the Netherlands, the ING Group bought Bank Brussels Lambert in 1997.

The pattern of mergers and acquisitions in European banking clearly shows how the resistance of Euro area supervisors to cross-border takeovers created large national banks with overseas investment banking operations. In Figure 6 every European bank takeover in the 1990s is defined along two dimensions. Do the banks have the same business model within the industry (e.g., is a commercial bank acquiring another commercial bank) or different business models across the industry (e.g., is a commercial bank acquiring an investment bank)? And is the merger domestic or cross-border? The results show a stark contrast in takeovers between banks with similar business models and those involving banks with different models. Over three-quarters of takeovers of similar banks were domestic (the light grey segments). Basically, commercial banks bought local commercial banks in a process that helped to create nationally orientated banks. On the other hand, the overwhelming number of transactions involving banks with different business models were cross-border (the black areas). This is the dynamic that created universal banks with investment banking operations in market centers such as London. The overseas expansion into investment banking reflected the adoption of a universal banking model in Europe combined with the permissive attitude of the UK regulators to foreign entry, especially after the "big bang" deregulation of the City of London in the late 1980s. Indeed, a significant part of cross-border activity involved the dismemberment of the UK merchant banks (the local name for independent investment banks). By 2002, thirteen major UK merchant banks had been acquired by overseas institutions; seven by European Union banks (including Deutsche Bank's purchase of Morgan Grenfell), two by Swiss ones, and four by US banks.[30] As will be discussed in the next chapter, the independent US investment banks proved much more resilient.

The Banking System 1999–2002

By the early 2000s, the expansion of the Euro area banking system was switching from the core to the periphery of Europe. The rate of increase

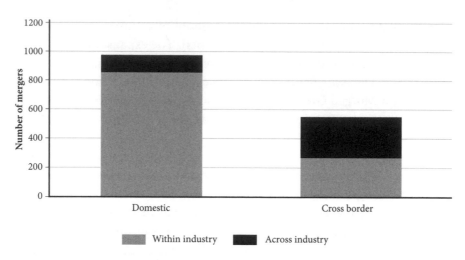

Figure 6: Most European bank mergers involved domestic agglomeration.
Source: Demine (2002) Table 12.

in the banking systems in the core countries (Germany, France, the Netherlands, and Belgium) were slowing as a proportion of output, while those in the periphery were starting to accelerate, albeit from a much lower base. This buoyancy in the periphery reflected the fall in interest rates as a result of European Monetary Union, which was accompanied by accelerating inflation in housing and other asset prices, a trend that would continue through the 2000s.

There were also major differences in the underlying business models between these two halves of the Euro area. The banks in the core were much more focused on investment banking. For example, commercial loans represented only some 30 percent of bank assets in France and Belgium. By contrast, such loans comprised more than half of the assets in the Italian, Spanish, and Portuguese banks. As a result, the assets of the core banks were more diversified internationally. By 2002, around 10 percent of all bank assets in the core Euro area were held in the United States and United Kingdom, the countries that housed the international investment banking hubs of New York and London. For the periphery this ratio was less than 5 percent.

In another trend that was destined to continue in the 2000s, the banking systems started to take off in Ireland and the United Kingdom, the two EU countries that adopted "light touch" supervision. In Ireland, this represented an attempt to repeat the earlier successful strategy of using government policy to attract foreign manufacturing multinationals (in that case through lower tax rates), an approach that had turned Ireland from a poor country into the "Celtic tiger". In the case of banking, the attractions of low taxes were reinforced by a permissive "light touch" approach to supervision. As a result, Ireland's banking system ballooned from two-and-a-half times the economy in 1997 to an enormous five times the economy by 2002 as foreign banks entered the market. The new business was largely in investment banking, and Ireland's ratio of commercial loans to assets fell rapidly to 25 percent, the lowest in the Euro area. A similar transformation occurred in the UK banking system, but it was less dramatic because the United Kingdom started with a much larger foreign investment banking presence.

Despite the push to create an integrated banking system, banking in the Euro area remained mainly domestic (Figure 7). For the region as a whole, less than 10 percent of all assets came from banks based in other members of the Union. This was only modestly higher than the ratio seen in 1999, with an intuitive pattern in which cross-border assets were lower in large economics than smaller ones. Furthermore, despite passporting, the vast majority of such cross-border assets resided in subsidiaries rather than branches as a result of pressure from national regulators.[31] Underlining the importance of such pressure, the much more open UK banking system was the most internationalized in the European Union, with fully half of bank assets owned by foreign banks (equally split between EU and non-EU banks). Boosted by light touch regulation, Ireland was the second most internationalized.

The Creation of the Euro Area Mega-Banks

A wave of bank mergers and acquisitions in the 1990s increased the role of a small number of large banks in the Euro area. While this can be measured in the aggregate—the share of assets in the largest five banks rose in every Euro area country between 1998 and 2002 with the exception of Finland— the more important part of the story involved the rapid rise of a small number of national mega-banks, tellingly called "national champions". By 2002 just twelve Euro area banks already held one-quarter of regional assets and their role continued to expand through to the eve of the crisis in 2007.[32] The increasing dominance of a small number of rapidly expanding mega-banks reflected the competitive advantage conferred on large banks by the ability to use internal risk models to calculate capital buffers on investment banking operations. In some cases, national regulators also supported the creation of mega-banks as a defensive reaction to larger banks elsewhere. This was particularly the case in the south of Europe, which had a tradition of smaller and more local banks.

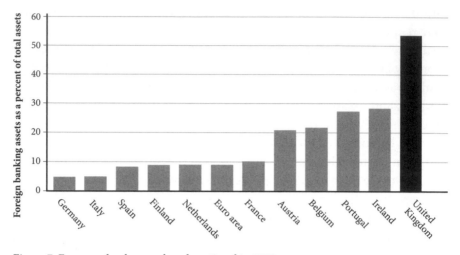

Figure 7: Euro area banks were largely national in 2002.
Source: ECB Structural Banking Statistics.

Strikingly, all of the twelve mega-banks already existed in 2002, with six having been formed in the late 1990s. Given the distinct differences in business models, it is useful to treat the core Euro area banks separately from those in the southern periphery. The largest Euro area mega-banks were universal banks from the core Euro area comprising Germany, France, the Netherlands, and Belgium (Figure 8). They were generally older and more established banks, several of which were expanding into investment banking through acquisitions in the United Kingdom or the United States (Figure 9 provides a potted history of the main mergers and acquisitions that brought these banks into being and expanded them). For example, Deutsche Bank bought Morgan Grenfell in the UK and Bankers Trust in the US, ING bought Barings in the UK, and Société Générale of France bought TCW in the US. The other three core Euro area mega-banks, which also had major investment banking operations, were BNP Paribas and Credit Agricole of France and Commerzbank of Germany. The smallest two mega-banks in the core were more specialized. Natixis was a pure investment bank, while Dexia focused on financing local governments, a business model that was heavily dependent on the Basel Committee's decision to give advanced country government debt a zero risk-weight.

The four mega-banks in the southern Euro area periphery, UniCredit and Intesa in Italy and Santander and BBVA in Spain, had a very different profile. They were all relatively late arrivals, being created by mergers of

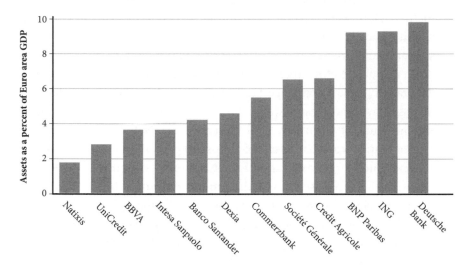

Figure 8: Euro area mega-banks were already becoming too big to fail.
Source: Scientific Committee of the European Systemic Risk Board (2014).

Bank	Rank in 2007	Major takeovers and mergers
Deutsche Bank AG	1	Morgan Grenfell (UK) 1989, Bankers Trust (US) 1999
BNP Paribas SA	2	Merger in 2000 of Societe BNP and Paribas
Credit Agricole SA	3	Crédit Lyonnais 2003
ING Groep NV	4	Barings 1995; Banque Bruxelles Lambert 1996
Société Générale SA	5	Credit du Nord 1997, TCW (US) 2001
UniCredit SpA	6	Merger of Unicredito, Credit Italiano, and others 1998
Banco Santander SA	7	Banco Central Hispanico 1999 Abbey National (UK) 2004 ABN AMRO 2007
Commerzbank AG	8	Eurohypo AG, 2005
Dexia SA	9	Merger of Gemeentekrediet/Credit Communal (Belgium) and the Crédit Local (France) 1996
Intesa Sanpaolo SpA	10	Merger of Cariplo and Aub Verto 1998 to form Banca Intesa, merger with Sanpaolo IMI, 2007
Natixis	11	Merger of Natexis Banque Populaire and IXIS 2006
BBVA SA	12	Merger of Banco Bilbao Vizeaye and Banco Argenteria 1999

Figure 9: Mergers in the late 1990s completed the European mega-banks.
Source: Corporate websites.

smaller commercial banks in 1998 and 1999, often with the support of regulators. They were smaller than most of their rivals in the core and were still basically commercial banks. In many ways, the southern Euro area mega-banks are best seen as a defensive agglomeration of commercial banks in response to the rapid expansion of their northern counterparts.

The rapidly expanding mega-banks were already becoming too large to be managed by the corresponding national governments. The largest three (Deutsche Bank of Germany, ING Group of the Netherlands, and BNP Paribas of France) each had assets of almost 10 percent of Euro area output. They were much larger as a ratio of their national economies. Indeed, the assets of ING handily surpassed the annual output of the Netherlands. Problems in such massive banks were obviously going to have major spill-overs to the rest of the economy, underlining that they were too large to fail. Indeed, given that bank support was provided at the national level, they were arguably also becoming potentially too large to save.

At the same time, the northern mega-banks in particular were using internal risk models to save on capital buffers. Figure 10 shows on the vertical axis the capital buffers using equity against *total* assets, which did not involve risk models, and on the horizontal axis using the Basel capital buffers against *risk-weighted* assets, which did use them.[33] In 1996, before the market risk amendment, these two measures of bank soundness were positively related so that a high regulatory capital ratio also signaled a proportionately high

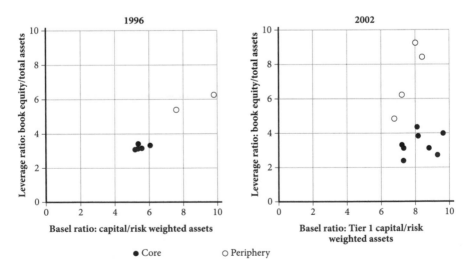

Figure 10: Internal risk models led to thin capital buffers.
Source: Scientific Committee of the European Systemic Risk Board (2014).

ratio of equity to assets. A Basel regulatory capital of 5 percent, for example, corresponded with an equity–asset ratio of about 3 percent, and 10 percent corresponded with about 6 percent. In 2002, this positive relationship still held for the mega-banks in the periphery which focused on commercial banking but had vanished for the mega-banks in the Euro area core with a universal banking model. Indeed, these universal banks showed, if anything, a negative relationship between the size of their equity cushion as a proportion of assets and the regulatory capital ratio based on risk-weighted assets. While the Basel regulatory ratio showed capital buffers to be comfortably above the 4 percent minimum, equity cushions were thinning as a ratio to assets in universal banks such as Deutsche Bank, Commerzbank, Société Générale, and ING. The contrast with the commercial banks as well as with their own behavior in 1996 makes it clear that this change was driven by the corrosive effect of internal risk models.

The loss in correspondence between unweighted and risk-weighted measures of the capital cushion would not have mattered if the internal models were a good measure of balance sheet risk. After all, the main reason for introducing risk weights was to better differentiate the level of risk across types of assets. However, while admittedly crude, the Basel 1 risk weights for commercial banking were consistent across banks and were broadly sensible. Lending to firms, for example, was generally riskier than (say) lending for household mortgages, just as the risk weights implied. By contrast, internal risk models generated bank-specific results that encouraged downward pressure on capital cushions that was to continue into the 2000s. Tellingly, in the North Atlantic crisis, the cruder measure of equity to total assets turned out to be a better predictor of banking stress than more complex risk-weighted ones used by regulators.[34]

In addition, risk weights created opportunities for transatlantic purchases of assets based on differences in regulations rather than economic returns. This was because the regulated US banks were generally (effectively) under a simple leverage ratio that took no account of risk while the European banks were under loose risk-weighted capital rules. Having the two halves of the North Atlantic economy under different capital standards provided incentives for US banks to sell low-risk loans to European banks through securitized assets. The US financial system will be discussed in detail in the next chapter, but the significant holding of US assets by European banks in 2002 with only a limited reciprocal relationship suggests that this factor was already starting to matter.

* * *

The European Banking System in 2002

By 2002, the European banking system was showing evidence of maturing. After a period of rapid expansion of the northern European banks brought about by the single market program and the 1996 Basel market risk amendment, the ratio of assets to output was stabilizing in core banking systems of Germany, France, the Netherlands and Belgium. Growth was continuing in the periphery, partly fed by loans from the core, but banking was generally a smaller part of their economies so some catch-up could be seen as appropriate. At two-and-a-half times the economy, the assets of the banking system were large by international standards, but at least part of this difference was because banks performed more investment banking, services that in many other countries were carried out by specialized non-bank institutions.

At the same time three trends were sources for concern, all of which were linked to the behavior of national supervisors. The first, and most obvious, was the failure to create an integrated European banking system. As discussed earlier, this reflected a strong preference of national supervisors for domestic rather than foreign mergers. This contrasts with the smooth road to national banks in the United States, discussed in the next chapter.

The second trend was the continuing rapid increase in the relatively large banking systems in the United Kingdom and Ireland that specialized in investment banking and where supervisors embraced "light touch"

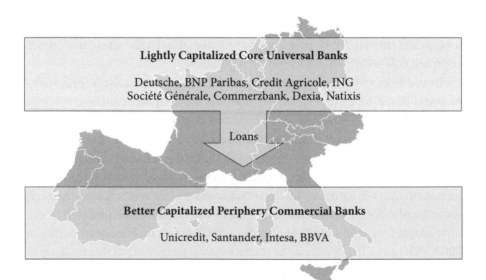

Figure 11: Structure of Euro area banking in 2002.

regulation. This continuing dynamism contrasted with the relative stagnation of the northern Euro area core in the early 2000s. Light touch regulation eroded the authority of other national supervisors, as their banks could argue that they also needed lenient supervision so as to level the playing field. National supervisors who insisted on maintaining a tough approach in the face of such regulatory competition also ran the risk that domestic banks would move major operations to UK and Irish subsidiaries, reducing national supervisors of the ability to observe the full activities of their banks.

The final trend was the increasing importance of a small number of mega-banks from the northern core in the EU banking system (Figure 11). This largely reflected the use and abuse of internal risk models. This is clearly shown by the increasing dissonance between the comfortable Basel regulatory capital ratios—based on risk-weighted assets using internal models being reported to supervisors and markets—and the thinning of unweighted measures of capital buffers in the northern European universal banks. The fact that many of these mega-banks were labeled "national champions" is a telling recognition of the importance of regulatory competition in shaping the European banking landscape. In a truly integrated system, the nationality of the bank would be relatively irrelevant—champions would be defined by competitive advantage rather than by nationality.

None of these trends would have been impossible to solve. However, such a response would have first required an acknowledgement that competition across national regulators was creating unwelcome strains in Euro area banking and that strong central supervision was needed. Such a reassessment was difficult, as it would have required reopening the decentralized structure of financial supervision that had been carefully negotiated in the Maastricht Treaty. In the event, this reassessment did not happen until after the crisis. It would also have required pushback in the Basel Committee on internal risk models, a move which would have met with resistance from the banks themselves and from the US Federal Reserve. Instead, thin capital buffers became central to the business models of the core Euro area mega-banks. Tellingly, after the crisis it was the US and UK regulators that championed tougher bank capital buffers, while French and German regulators supported the continued use of internal risk models that had become intrinsic to the business strategies of their mega-banks.

Chapter 2

US SHADOW BANKS UNLEASHED

The rapid expansion in shadow banks that performed bank-like activities such as taking deposits and holding loans but remained outside of the perimeter of bank regulation transformed US banking between 1980 and 2002. These lightly regulated firms, which held much lower capital buffers against financial shocks than the regulated banks, were the main US institutions that ran into trouble over the crisis.

Reflecting US culture, the transformation of the US banking system was both less structured and more entrepreneurial than in Europe. It involved a series of small steps rather than a few major decisions. It started when the competitiveness of the regulated banks—those with deposit insurance and access to Federal Reserve emergency funding—eroded as the rise in inflation in the 1970s interacted with outdated caps on interest rates on deposits and loans. In response, large depositors managing so-called "wholesale" money drifted away from the insured deposits offered by regulated banks to uninsured but higher paying deposits offered by shadow banks. As their funding base narrowed, the regulated banks increasingly bundled safer and more routine loans such as mortgages into securities and sold them to the shadow banks. The shadow banking system expanded to fill a vacuum created by loss in the competitiveness of regulated banks.

This migration of activity from the regulated to the shadow banking system has often been portrayed as a result of excessively speedy financial deregulation driven by self-interested lobbyists.[1] While such lobbying played a role in the years immediately preceding the 2008 crisis, the origins of the shadow banking system came from the opposite dynamic, namely the slow response of regulators to strains in the banks. The major components of the shadow banking system all emerged between 1980 and 2002, including mortgage-backed securities, investment banks, money market mutual funds (all of which increased by ten-fold compared to the size of the US economy over this period), and repurchase agreements (which quadrupled).

A dual banking system was already in place by 2002. On one side were the relatively stolid, soundly regulated banks such as Bank of America and Wells Fargo. On the other were the much more dynamic, lightly regulated shadow banks such as Goldman Sachs and Morgan Stanley that (confusingly given that they were called investment *banks*) were not subject to bank regulations. The regulated and shadow banks were increasingly linked through mortgage-backed securities issued by the two main housing government-sponsored enterprises (GSEs), Fannie Mae and Freddie Mac, whose assets quadrupled compared to the economy over the 1990s.

These markets and institutions all played major roles in the North Atlantic financial crisis. The prices of mortgage-backed securities plummeted after US house prices started to crumble in 2007. The investment bank groups included Bear Stearns and Lehman Brothers, the two major shadow banks that collapsed in 2008. The market for repurchase agreements froze after Lehman Brothers went bankrupt, depriving the North Atlantic banking system of a major source of cash, while Fannie Mae and Freddie Mac were put into receivership as the crisis unfolded.

The overall outcome was the same as in Europe, with increasing amounts of banking migrating to undercapitalized institutions that could not withstand the shock of the North Atlantic crisis. However, the the process by which this change occurred was completely different. To explain how this happened it is useful to understand quite how constrained the US regulated banks were in 1980.

* * *

Inflation and the Rise of a Dual Banking System

The US banking system in 1980 was even more fractured than in Europe. Banks were only allowed to operate within a single state, so that there were effectively fifty separate banking systems. Indeed, in many states banks were limited to operating out of a single branch. In addition, there were upper limits on interest rates banks could charge—deposits rates were limited by national regulations while charges on loans were constrained by individual state usury laws. Finally, the Glass–Steagall Act of 1933 separated these banks from investment banks that operated outside of the federal safety net. The outcome was a large but highly splintered regulated banking sector as well as a small nationwide investment banking industry which handled other peoples' money but had minimal assets of its own.

This structure reflected the lasting impact of the Great Depression. In popular memory, the national banks of the time had transferred financial instability to the heartland by pulling back from loans to local banks as a result of losses in risky investment banking activities. To avoid a repeat of this experience, regulated banks were kept small, local, and safe, including by being prohibited from engaging in investment banking. The focus was on creating a system that was unlikely to collapse, rather than one that was efficient.

As memories of the Great Depression waned, however, the winds of change started to blow. The rise of inflation in the 1970s initiated a process that undermined the competitiveness of the regulated banks and transformed the banking sector through three interrelated dynamics. Higher inflation and limits on deposit rates reduced the attractiveness of depositing money with regulated banks, and sophisticated investors with large funds increasingly switched their deposits to shadow banks. In addition, limits on lending rates further undermined the profitability of regulated banks, resulting in costly banking crises that led to a hike in capital buffers so as to preserve their financial safety. This further encouraged the expansion of the shadow banks those thinner capital buffers gave them a cost advantage. Finally, these competitive pressures encouraged regulators to dismantle prohibitions on regulated banks engaging in interstate and investment banking, allowing the creation of diversified national banks such as Citi and JP Morgan. Each of these trends had their own dynamics.

The Diversion of Bank Deposits and the Rise in Securitizations

Regulation Q of the Federal Reserve Board, which dated from 1933, limited interest rates that could be offered by banks on deposits. It prohibited paying interest on checking accounts and set upper limits on the rates offered on other types of accounts such as savings and time deposits. The logic of such caps was to discourage banks from exploiting the security provided by federal deposit insurance to offer high rates on deposits and use the resulting cash to make risky investments. The concern was that if these investments did not pan out then the bank would flounder and taxpayers would be saddled with the cost of bailing out the depositors. However, limits on deposit interest rates assumed that inflation remained low and stable. When inflation rose in the 1970s banks were unable to raise their deposit rates to compensate for the faster increase in prices.

The regulators reacted slowly to this loss in competitiveness of bank deposits. It was not until 1980 that Congress amended Regulation Q as part of the Depository Institutions Deregulation and Monetary Control Act, and even this legislation took five years to phase out the caps on deposit rates (checking account rates continued to be frozen at zero). By this time the genie was out of the bottle. Frustrated by the low returns offered on the insured deposits at regulated banks, investors increasingly turned to uninsured deposits offered by the investment banks whose returns were not capped as they were not subject to regulation Q. Ironically, the interest caps that had been introduced with the intention of restricting competition in deposit rates out of fear that that such competition could lead banks to take excessive risks ended up promulgating the growth of the less regulated and riskier shadow banks.

The switch in deposits was particularly focused on large "wholesale" funds that typically deposited sums well above the upper limit on federal deposit insurance. The shadow banks offered two main forms of deposits. Money market mutual funds, where the client bought shares in a mutual fund that invested in safe short-term assets such as government bills and paid interest in a similar manner to traditional deposits. Investors were protected because, if the mutual fund failed to pay interest, they could take possession of the underlying assets. The more complex and popular option for sophisticated investors with wholesale funds was a repurchase agreement, in which assets such as Treasury bonds were sold to the depositor with an agreement to buy back (repurchase) the treasuries at a fixed price at a later time, with the difference between the two prices representing an effective rate of interest. In this case, protection came from the fact that if the shadow bank was unable to repurchase the treasury, then the depositor got to keep it. A discount on the initial selling price of the treasury (called a haircut) provided added security that the depositor would not lose money by making it more likely that the value of the treasury would exceed the value of the cash that had been loaned. The freezing of the repo market after the bankruptcy of Bear Stearns was a crucial driver in the North Atlantic crisis.

The migration of deposits into uninsured deposits led to a massive expansion in the size of investment banks, the institutions at the heart of the shadow banking system, while limiting the size of the regulated banking sector. The regulated banks responded by selling increasing amounts of the loans that they made to their clients to shadow banks rather than keeping them on their books. This was the other half of the dual banking system.

Increasingly, the core functions of banking—attracting deposits and using the money to hold loans—were being farmed out to the shadow banks. The trade worked for both sides because the shadow banks held lower amounts of (expensive) capital against these loans, which had the effect of diluting the capital buffers held by the dual banking system against loans.

The regulated banks used securitized assets to sell loans to the shadow banks. In a securitization, the bank took a bundle of loans such as mortgages and sold them to investors in return for cash. The buyers bought the rights to the loans and hence to the associated repayments. In this "originate to distribute" model, the regulated bank acted as a go-between, using their knowledge of clients to originate loans and collect the associated fees but then bundling the loans and selling them to shadow banks. Securitization was supported by the development of ways of tracking the credit-worthiness of borrowers, in particular standardized credit scores. Credit scores allowed the riskiness of loans to consumers—mortgages, car loans, and credit cards balances—to be independently checked. By contrast, securitization was never used to bundle loans to firms, where much greater knowledge of the client was needed to assess viability.

Securitization occurred in two waves. The first was driven by federal housing policy as promulgated through the main government-sponsored enterprises (GSEs). It was aimed at lowering the cost of mortgages by creating a liquid secondary market where such loans could be bought and sold by investors, just as a stock market lowers the cost of raising money by issuing shares in a company by allowing investors to buy and sell shares easily. Such securitizations were relatively safe as the GSEs provided investors with a guarantee against defaults by home owners. Understanding how this came about requires some knowledge of the GSEs.

Safe Government-Sponsored Securitizations

The GSEs originated during the Great Depression as a way to provide relief to homeowners and banks by buying up troubled mortgages.[2] As the depression gave way to the more stable and prosperous postwar period, their mission switched from providing immediate relief to the housing market to supporting home ownership more generally. By the 1970s, the housing GSEs were dominated by two corporations. The larger, Fannie Mae, took on its pre-crisis form in 1968 when the Housing and Urban Development Act made it into a for-profit shareholding company under the regulation of the Department of Housing and Urban Development. In addition to supporting home ownership in general, Fannie Mae was required as part of its public mission to devote a reasonable proportion of its mortgage purchases to low- and moderate-income housing. It's smaller sister organization, Freddie Mac, was created in 1970 by the Emergency Home Finance Act with the mission of helping specialized mortgage lenders, called Savings and Loans, manage the challenges caused by rising inflation and interest rates. Higher interest rates were particularly problematic for the Savings and Loans as almost all of their loans were thirty-year mortgages with fixed interest rates. As inflation drove short-term interest rates upwards, the costs of attracting deposits rose while the income from the typical thirty-year fixed-rate mortgage remained unchanged.

In the 1970s and 1980s, Fannie Mae and Freddie Mac pursued different business strategies. Fannie Mae kept the mortgages it bought on its balance sheet. As a result, its profits got squeezed by higher deposit rates just like the banks that it served. By contrast, given its mandate to help Savings and Loans avoid interest rate risk, Freddie Mac bundled its mortgages into mortgage-backed securitizations that it then sold to investors with a guarantee that the underlying borrowers would maintain payments. In the jargon of the business, Freddie Mac offered a "wrap"—insurance against defaults by home owners. Because it no longer held the underlying mortgages on its books, Freddie Mac was unaffected by higher interest rates and remained profitable.

In the light of these obvious benefits, in the 1990s Fannie Mae switched to the Freddie Mac model of buying mortgages from banks and then selling them to investors with a guarantee on the quality of the underlying loans. Both of the major GSEs became financial intermediaries, buying loans, bundling them, and selling them to investors with insurance. This business model worked because, even though Fannie and Freddie were theoretically private institutions, their close relationship with the federal government led markets to assume that they had implicit government support (an accurate prediction over the 2008 crisis). A thin capital base and favorable borrowing costs gave Fannie and Freddie the competitive edge needed to support the housing market by creating a successful secondary market in mortgages.

The business model also worked because Fannie and Freddie only accepted relatively safe mortgages that conformed to their rules. For example, they put limits on the size of the loan, the minimum downpayment, and on the credit score of the borrower. This made "conforming" mortgages safer and hence easier for the GSEs to insure. The GSEs also insisted that there were no charges for early repayment of loans, so that consumers were not locked into a loan if a more favorable one became available. Since the typical US mortgage was issued over a thirty-year term at a fixed rate, when long-term interest rates fell some borrowers took out a new mortgage and used it to repay the old one—a one-sided risk as higher rates did not induce the opposite behavior. Investors offset this "duration" risk using derivative markets on interest rates, in which (for example) an investor received a payout if bond yields fell below a certain level. This example illustrates how securitization created demand for other complex derivative markets to offset risks.

GSE securitizations transformed the mortgage market. In 1980, most home mortgages issued by banks were retained on their balance sheets. By 2002, they were typically sold to investors via Fannie and Freddie, a change that led to the creation of a national mortgage market and hence housing market. In the late 1980s, New England experienced a regional housing crash in which house prices fell by one-third in real terms after the local economy was hit by a decline in defense spending and greater competition in the information technology sector, causing major distress to regional banks. As securitization led to an increasingly national mortgage market during the 1990s, however, changes in regional house prices became more coherent, a switch that later created the national housing bubble of the 2000s.

To ensure that the market for mortgage-backed securities stayed liquid, Fannie and Freddie had always kept some of their own securities on the books. Over time, however, they increasingly used their ability to borrow money at favorable rates to buy and hold mortgage-backed securities issued by banks.[3] Since their understanding of the mortgage market allowed them to hedge the resulting interest rate and duration risks, they were able to make money for their private investors. Over the financial crisis, however, it was the losses from defaults on their holdings of higher paying but riskier "private label" securitizations that forced the thinly capitalized Fannie and Freddie into receivership. It is to this market that we now turn.

Risky Private Label Securitizations

After the GSEs successfully developed markets for securitized assets, a second wave of securitization occurred involving regulated banks selling loans directly to investors. Private label securitizations were the second major trend to come from the erosion in competitiveness of regulated banks. In addition to the caps on deposit rates discussed earlier, bank profitability was also hampered by widespread state-specific usury laws. These laws were designed to protect consumers from predatory lending and to ensure that banks did not take excessive risks that could lead to bankruptcy.

As inflation rose, however, these caps eroded profitability of lending and led to a wave of bank failures in the early 1980s.[4]

The largest and most spectacular of these failures was the 1984 bankruptcy of Continental Illinois National Bank and Trust Company, which was the largest US corporate bankruptcy to that date.[5] Despite Chicago's role as a money center, Illinois was a state that limited banks to one branch. Out of its single branch in Chicago, Continental Illinois managed to become the seventh largest bank in the country and the largest US commercial and industrial lender by attracting large deposits (two-thirds of its deposits were above the insurance limit) and lending the proceeds aggressively to risky borrowers such as energy companies and the Mexican government. Controversially, after Continental Illinois filed for bankruptcy regulators decided to fully recompense deposits above the federal insurance cap (including the 179 banks that had deposits worth more than half of their equity capital) and also bondholders, rather than let them absorb the losses. The bailout of these uninsured lenders caused outrage and popularized the phrase "too big to fail".

The outrage was compounded by the even larger and costlier Savings and Loans crisis.[6] Savings and Loans were a specialized sector that lent for home mortgages using savings deposits. Their deposits were popular with investors because under Regulation Q they could offer slightly higher deposit rates than regulated banks. Savings and Loans failures rose rapidly during the 1970s and early 1980s, however, because their business model was particularly susceptible to rising inflation. Their funding came from short-term deposits while almost all of their loans were in thirty-year fixed-rate mortgages. With bankruptcies rapidly depleting the funds available to support failed banks, the dedicated regulator of the Savings and Loans decided to let the industry grow its way out of its problems by expanding into new types of lending beyond their traditional mortgage business. Unfortunately, just as in the case of Continental Illinois, many of the resulting highly speculative loans did not pan out. The result was a prolonged crisis across the industry. Between 1986 and 1995 almost one-third of the Savings and Loans had to be closed, at the cost of some $160 billion (2 percent of 1995 GDP) including $120 billion in taxpayer money.

The political furor over the cost to taxpayers of the failure of Continental Illinois and the Savings and Loans crisis led to a major tightening of US rules on capital buffers for regulated banks that went over and above existing Basel Committee rules.[7] To reduce the potential for costly regulatory forbearance of the type seen in the case of Continental Illinois, a "prompt corrective action" framework was introduced by the Federal

Deposit Insurance Corporation Improvement Act of 1991 that required automatic interventions if a bank's capital fell below certain ratios.[8] To be well capitalized and avoid intervention, a regulated bank needed to have core capital that was at least 6 percent of risk-weighted assets (2 percent above the minimum defined by the Basel Committee in 1988) and total capital that was at least a 10 percent of risk-weighted assets (again 2 percent above the Basel minimum).

In an even more important deviation from the Basel approach, prompt corrective action also required regulated banks to hold core capital that was at least 5 percent of total assets. The unintended side-effect was that it created major incentives for regulated banks to bundle safe loans and sell them to shadow banks using "private label" securitized assets. This was because the regulated banks were under the simple leverage ratio which meant that if they kept a relatively safe loan such as a mortgage on their books, they still had to hold 5 cents of capital. By contrast, the investment banks that funded the shadow banking system were subject to a different capital rule that involved much lower buffers on safe loans such as mortgages. Because it was much cheaper for an investment/shadow bank to hold a mortgage on its books than for a regulated bank to do so, there were clear incentives to transfer such loans through private mortgage-backed securities. Indeed, the same dynamic occurred between US regulated banks and their European counterparts after the 1996 market risk amendment allowed the large European banks to use their internal risk models to calculate capital buffers on investment banking. This divergence in capital standards was the genesis of the massive inflows of northern European banks into the US markets over the financial boom of the 2000s.

The wedge in capital buffers between the regulated and shadow banks explains why the regulated banking sector remained roughly constant as a proportion of the economy even as shadow banks boomed. Regulated banks were creating more loans for customers but, rather than keeping them on the books, they sold them to shadow banks. In this "originate to distribute" business model, regulated banks used their superior knowledge of clients to originate loans, but then distributed them to shadow banks. These transactions had no real social value. Rather, they simply exploited differences in capital buffers between regulated and shadow banks. Ironically, prompt corrective action helped to lower capital buffers against bank loans as the tough capital standards for regulated banks were circumvented as they sold loans to lightly capitalized shadow banks. At the same time, the regulated banking sector was going through its own transformation.

The Emergence of National Banks

The final trend coming from the loss of competitiveness of the regulated banking system after the inflation of the 1970s was the gradual creation of large regulated banks as constraints on theie activities were gradually lifted. This culminated in the emergence of a small number of national US banks, including two that expanded into a universal banking model that was more typical of the European mega-banks.

Small banks had remained a dominant presence in US regulated banking sector through the 1970s partly as a result of laws that restricted banks to operate in only one state. These restrictions were initially driven by the revenues that states obtained from selling bank charters. However, the importance of these revenues had dwindled and by the 1970s state banking rules were effectively simply a protection for small banks. By reducing the cost of communication and transportation, however, information technology reduced the benefits from local banking. For example, the introduction of automatic teller machines in the 1970s allowed larger banks to widen their presence without the need to set up branches.[9] Political support for state banking restrictions eroded along with the competitive position of small banks. Maine was the first state to allow reciprocal inter-state banking in 1978 (out-of-state banks could purchase local banks as long as local banks had the same privilege). The change was initially only symbolic as no other states followed suit, but in 1982 Alaska and (much more importantly given its larger size) New York passed similar laws. A decade later all states except Hawaii allowed interstate banking, and in 1997 the rules were made nationally consistent under the Reigal–Neal Interstate Banking and Branching Efficiency Act. A similar process occurred with intrastate branching. In 1970, only twelve states allowed unrestricted branch banking. By 1994, thirty-eight states had removed such restrictions.

Over the same period, the strongly pro-deregulation Federal Reserve gradually reduced the restrictions on US regulated banks being involved in investment banking. These rules were initially motivated by concerns that banks could have inside information that could undermine the integrity of market transactions. They dated from the 1933 Glass–Steagall Act and had been reinforced in the Bank Holding Company Act of 1956 and its amendment in 1970.[10] The relaxation of these rules started in 1987 when the Federal Reserve determined that "Section 20" subsidiaries of three bank holding companies could underwrite some previously prohibited securities as long as the revenue from such activities did not exceed 5 percent of total revenue. In early 1989 this rule was expanded to a wider range of banks and products. The revenue limit was then gradually raised to 10 percent later in 1989 and 25 percent in 1996. At the same time, the Office of the Comptroller of the Currency loosened restrictions on banks' activities in insurance. By the time Congress formally repealed the Glass–Steagall Act through the Graham–Leach–Bliley Act of 1999 it was largely a symbolic gesture.

The US regulated banking industry thus entered the 2000s unencumbered by limits on interest rates, constraints on location, or prohibitions on engaging in investment banking. The gradual loosening of geographic rules led to steadily larger banks, including three truly national banks, JP Morgan, Bank of America, and Citi.[11] These banks grew through a convoluted burst of acquisitions over the 1990s, as restrictions on bank size crumbled. For example, one strand of the origins of JP Morgan Chase involved the merger of Chemical Bank and Manufactures Hanover in 1991, then with Chase Manhattan Bank in 1996, and then with JP Morgan and Company in 2000. Bank of America went through a similar process, acquiring its California rival Security Pacific Corporation in 1992, Continental Illinois Bank and Trust Company in 1994, and then being taken over by NationsBank, another rapidly expanding "super-regional" bank, in 1999 (the group decided to retain the name Bank of America, which was better known). Finally, Citigroup was formed by the 1998 merger of Citicorp and the Travelers Group, a much more diversified financial institution, to form the first US universal bank and spell the effective end of the Glass–Steagall prohibition on mixing commercial and investment banking.

The Dual Banking System

By the early 2000s bank deregulation had shifted the US regulated banking industry from a mass of small banks to a hodge-podge of large and small ones. However, the expansion of market activities that occurred mainly within the universal mega-banks in Europe took place largely in the shadow banking sector, especially the independent investment banks that were already lightly regulated and remained highly competitive. Only two regulated banks moved to a universal banking model by expanding into investment banking, Citi and JP Morgan, and their operations remained relatively limited by comparison to the major independent investment banks. The remaining regulated banks used the new-found flexibility to expand and make their commercial banking operations more efficient. Rather than diversifying into investment banking, they sold increasing amounts of loans to shadow banks.

The repeal of the Glass–Steagall Act in 1999 has often been seen as a key moment in a deregulatory process that led to banking excesses and the housing crisis.[12] However, by then the important transformation of the US banking system had already taken place, as the relatively heavily capitalized US regulated banks sold standardized loans such as mortgages to the less capitalized investment banks and other parts of the shadow banking system, thereby undermining the capital buffers behind bank loans. The parallel change on the deposit side was that many large depositors switched to investment banks that offered better returns but without federal insurance. Before discussing the expansion of the investment banks, it is useful to first understand why the US financial regulators did not respond more vigorously to the undermining of capital buffers by the shadow banks.

* * *

Bank Regulators Looking Under the Wrong Lamppost

In stark contrast to the dynamic changes occurring within the banking industry, the structure of financial regulation stayed basically unchanged between 1980 and the 2008 crisis. The regulatory system in the United States was much more complex and splintered than in other major countries.[13] This reflected the wider range of institutions involved in the US financial system compared to the bank-centric systems typical in the rest of the world. It also reflected the Roosevelt Administration's predilection for creating complex institutional set-ups with overlapping powers during the "New Deal" of the 1930s that created most of the regulatory structure.[14] Several regulators were responsible for overseeing regulated banks, while the rest (the "nonbanks") were overseen by different agencies that focused on compliance with rules on behavior rather than financial safety. This sharp split between those who regulated the banks and the nonbanks was what allowed the shadow banking system to mushroom.

Bank financial safety was (and still is) primarily overseen by three regulators.[15] The Office of the Comptroller of the Currency is the main supervisor of federally chartered banks while the Federal Reserve primarily oversees the holding companies of the larger and more complex banks that often include nonbank subsidiaries (such as the "Section 20" operations discussed earlier) as well as consumer protection for mortgages. The main job of the Federal Deposit Insurance Corporation (FDIC) is to oversee the deposit insurance system and resolve insolvent banks. The roles of the Fed and the Comptroller are similar—to supervise banks' capital buffers—albeit for different types of banks (small individual banks versus large bank holding companies). The FDIC has a different focus, namely on the risks and costs of bank failures.

The different regulators makes it cumbersome to change the regulation of US banks, a process that had both disadvantages and advantages over the pre-crisis boom. On the negative side, the sluggish response to the challenges to bank competitiveness as a result of higher inflation supported the expansion of the shadow banking sector and the "originate to distribute" model that failed over the 2008 crisis. On the other hand, the slow response to change was the main reason that the US regulated banks remained relatively sound in the face of international rules on internal risk models that eroded capital buffers elsewhere, especially in the Euro area.

The nonbank half of the regulatory system comprised the Securities and Exchange Commission (SEC) and the Commodity Futures Trading Commission. These agencies were primarily tasked with overseeing rules on market behavior, such as ensuring that information in a firm's prospectus is accurately and fairly provided to market participants. Until the crisis, the SEC was also in charge of supervising the investment (non)banks, the institutions at the center of the shadow banking system. This involved enforcing the Net Capital Rule for broker-dealers, the core institutions at the center of the US investment banking groups. The Net Capital Rule required broker-dealers to maintain capital that depended on the perceived riskiness of their assets. Despite the inclusion of the word "capital" and the use of risk-weighted assets, the Net Capital Rule was primarily aimed at ensuring that customers were able to recover their money in the event of a bankruptcy rather than protecting broker-dealers from going broke. Since the rule was not aimed at preserving the broker-dealers from bankruptcy, the SEC did not have the authority that the bank regulators had to conduct examinations or to intervene to ensure that a bankruptcy did not disrupt the payments system. This was a critical difference that became apparent over the North Atlantic crisis after the immediate cessation of trading caused by the bankruptcy of the investment bank Lehman Brothers led to the collapse in many financial market segments.

This splintered regulatory system explains the relatively lax regulation of the investment bank groups. A major weakness of the system was that as the investment banks became increasingly large and influential they continued to be supervised by the SEC when such regulation would have more naturally fallen under the purview of the Federal Reserve, which already oversaw bank holding companies and their associated nonbank subsidiaries. Such a change would have been a major break with the distinction between commercial and investment banking that was hard-wired into the US regulatory system via the Glass–Steagall Act. However, this distinction was already blurring in reality as the Federal Reserve allowed bank holding companies more and more freedom to perform investment banking.

The main reason the investment banks continued to be supervised by the SEC was that the Federal Reserve was not interested in the job. The Fed took the strong view that investors were the most effective monitors of the risks taken by investment banks. They saw private monitoring of risk by investors and government monitoring through regulation as alternatives rather than complements. In particular, they were concerned that stronger government oversight of investment banks could be potentially counter-productive as it might reduce the incentives of investors to monitor risk-taking. As Alan Greenspan stated in a speech in 1996:

> On the other hand, if central banks or governments effectively insulate private institutions from the largest potential losses, however incurred, increased laxity could be costly to society as well. Leverage could esca-late to the outer edge of prudence, if not beyond. Lenders to banks (as well as their owners or managers) would learn to anticipate central bank or government intervention and would become less responsible, perhaps reckless, in their practices.[16]

In the Fed's view, regulation (to the extent it was at all valuable) was a cost imposed on regulated banks in return for access to government support through deposit insurance and access to emergency Federal Reserve funds, both of which reduced the incentives for depositors to monitor the under-lying health of the institution. Since neither applied to the investment banks, they were left outside of bank regulation.

An alternative view argues that Alan Greenspan and the Federal Reserve understood the risks posed by the financial system, but would have been unable to stop the underlying forces behind deregulation.[17] Certainly, Greenspan's 1998 warnings about "irrational exuberance" in markets suggests he was aware of potential financial risks. However, in the end the view that Greenspan understood the risks to the financial system is not convincing. The Federal Reserve promulgated market discipline as an alter-native to government regulation in many fora. Crucially, this included the Basel Committee on Banking Supervision where the Federal Reserve's firm support for internal risk models was crucial to the disastrous decision to adopt the 1996 market risk amendment. As discussed in the last chapter,

European regulators were skeptical about risk models, having agreed to a completely different framework in 1993, building off the existing "bucket" approach to credit risk. It was the Federal Reserve that pushed internal risk models over the finishing line.

The commitment of the highest echelons of the Fed to internal risks models is illustrated by the following passage from a speech to international bank supervisors made by Chair Greenspan in July 1996, soon after the market risk amendment had been released:

> The decision to craft bank's capital requirements for trading activities around accepted and verifiable internal risk measures was an important step in the supervision and regulation of large, internationally active, banks. . . . Within the United States, the Federal Reserve and other bank supervisors are placing growing important on a bank's risk management process . . . We are also working to develop supervisory tools and techniques that help supervisors perform their duties with less disruption to banks.[18]

Another result of the complex and fractured US regulatory arrangements was that before the crisis no institution was charged with overseeing the entire dual banking system. In particular, there was a split between those who oversaw regulated banks and those who oversaw conduct in securities markets, including the rapidly expanding shadow banks. Fundamentally, as a result of the Fed's rejection of regulation of investment banks, the US regulatory system failed to modernize as the investment banks moved from bit players holding other people's money to major cogs in the financial system. Inattention to the risks posed by investment banks helped drive the 2008 crisis. It is to these entities that we now turn.

* * *

Investment Bankers Become Masters of the Universe

Investment banking is a general term used for firms that support financial markets.[19] Typical services include the placement of initial equity and debt issues, including assessing the appropriate price and providing a backstop should the issue flop. They also play an important role in creating secondary markets that allow assets to be traded across investors, including providing advice on investment strategies, executing transactions, and assisting in negotiating the terms of mergers and acquisitions.

The essence of investment banking is summed up by the term "broker-dealer", the legal description of the entities at the center of investment banking groups. The broker side of the equation involves accepting money from investors and placing that money on their behalf in the market. The dealer half of the equation initiates these trades. Together, brokers and dealers take money from individuals and invest it. This is very different from a commercial bank, which accepts deposits at a fixed rate of interest and uses the money to make loans to people or firms.

Broker-dealers are at the center of financial markets as much of their business depended on their smooth functioning. Deep and liquid markets encourage firms to raise money by issuing securities, lower the costs of mergers and acquisitions, and make investment advice more predictable. It also explains why investment banks are interested in creating new products as they would benefit from the resulting transaction fees. No other financial institution has such an incentive to make sure that markets function smoothly. Indeed, choppy and illiquid markets provide opportunities for firms that focus only on making profits from trading, such as hedge funds, as price volatility increases the potential to make money. At the same time, before the crisis the investment banks were largely outside of the rules on safety, soundness, and deposit insurance that had been developed for the regulated banks. This is why they became the center of the largely unregulated shadow banking system.[20]

The information technology revolution gradually transformed the markets investment banks served. Settlement of trade moved from a cumbersome process involving people and paperwork to lightning-fast deals based on electronic matching of offers, and increasing algorithmic trading dictated by computer programs rather than human dealers. Lower costs of information also ushered in a wider variety of assets, including complex derivatives, and gradually changed the nature and size of investment banking. As costs of trades fell and transactions rose, the potential profits from trading increased. The importance (and pay) of dealers rose while the status of brokers fell. Increasingly, the modestly boring business of looking after other people's money was transformed into a highly paid and high-stakes business centered around trading their own money. As the balance sheets of investment banks expanded, they became one of the preferred destinations for graduates from top business schools. In addition, as trading became increasingly complicated, the business attracted mathematicians and statisticians or, as popular imagination put it, "rocket scientists" who used advanced mathematic techniques to maximize returns compared to risk. Investment bankers became the "masters of the universe"

and were increasingly lauded (or derided) in books and movies.[21] This
expansion was also aided by the permissive regulatory environment in
which (for example) financial derivatives were exempted from federal oversight since markets were assumed to be able to police themselves. In many
ways, the markets became a financial wild west.

Lower costs of trading and lax regulations also created the hedge fund
industry.[22] Hedge funds were trading firms that used advanced strategies to
achieve high returns (and charged fees to match). Since they only used
money from high-value individuals who were assumed to understand and
be able to handle the risks involved, hedge funds were largely exempt from
the laws governing entities that were available to less savvy investors, such
as mutual funds. The name, which came from the 1960s, was something of
a misnomer as "hedge" funds did not hedge (i.e. reduce) risks. On the
contrary, hedge funds generally took significant risks and as a result had a
relatively high attrition rate.

Hedge funds were useful to investment banks for two reasons. The first
was that as firms that specialized in market trading, they made markets
more liquid, thereby making investment banking easier. In addition, hedge
funds created much of the demand for new products that investment banks
created. The rocket scientists in the investment banks not only invented
new trading strategies, they also dreamed up new assets to accomplish such
trades. Given this symbiotic relationship, the investment banks increasingly
provided hedge funds with cash to supplement their investor equity and
finance larger trades.

Not all went smoothly. In particular, in 1998 Long-Term Capital
Management (LTCM) had to be rescued.[23] LTCM was a high-profile hedge
fund whose general partners included a former head of bond trading at
Salmon Brothers (John Merriweather), a former vice-chair of the Federal
Reserve (David Mullins), and two Nobel laureates in finance (Myron
Schoales and Robert Merton). It also returned high profits for the first three
years after its formation in 1994. However, by early 1998 LTCM was using
huge amounts of borrowed money to bet that emerging market risk-
spreads, which had spiked over the Asia crisis, would fall. This did not
happen. Rather, they rose after the Russian government declared a moratorium on payments of part of its government debt in August 1998. In early
September, LTCM advised the Federal Reserve Bank of New York of its
financial difficulties, which led to a rescue financed by its creditors. Tellingly,
these were major domestic- or foreign-owned broker-dealers, including
Goldman Sachs, Merrill Lynch, Morgan Stanley, JP Morgan, Barclays, and
Credit Suisse First Boston. In an interesting plot twist, the only major

investment bank to not participate in this rescue was Lehman Brothers, thereby creating a certain amount of animus that may have contributed to the reluctance to rescue it over the 2008 crisis.

Despite this setback, the hedge fund industry continued to prosper. Increasingly, investment banks became go-betweens, borrowing funds from institutions with large pools of cash looking for a safe place to put their money and lending to risky hedge funds and similar institutions. Cash was provided to hedge funds using repurchase agreements (repos) in return for relatively safe assets. These safe assets were then reused to raise cash from wholesale investors through money market mutual funds or new repos. Through most of the period repos were the most important source of investment bank funding. However, this started to change in the late 1990s due to limited collateral for repo deals, which the SEC limited to a small number of safe assets such as treasury assets. As the market expanded the amount of collateral available for repos became a constraint. As discussed in the next chapter, the desire for wider collateral for repos was to be a crucial driver of the crisis.

The business of creating derivative assets that rebundled existing assets in attractive new ways also gradually changed the relationship between the investment banks and the ratings agencies whose job it was to assess the riskiness of bonds. When the vast majority of debt instruments were plain vanilla assets such as corporate bonds, the business of the rating agencies was to look at the characteristics of the underlying firm and the seniority of the debt and provide an assessment of the safety of the bond. As assets became increasingly complex pools of loans, with characteristics determined by their creators, this inevitably generated a closer relationship between the investment banks and the rating agencies because the investment banks needed to understand the ratings models in order to design their products.

This inversion of the relationship between issuers of bonds and the ratings agencies tended to increase market risk for a given rating. As bonds began to be designed with the rating in mind, the investment banks aimed to achieve the maximum possible returns for a given rating by creating products that exploited weaknesses in the links between the rating agency models and the risk as assessed by market prices. In particular, they took advantage of the focus of some rating agencies on the likelihood of default rather than the losses to investors associated with a default. They did this by creating securitized assets as well as more complex derivatives such as collateralized debt obligations (CDOs) in ways that lowered the likelihood of default but increased the losses should default occur (called "waterfall"

structures since if you fell, you fell a long way).[24] The relatively favorable
ratings on such structures allowed investment banks to sell risky loans on
the cheap but had little or no social value as they simply reflected deficiencies in the rating system. That being said, this activity can be seen as a
consequence of the natural to and fro between investment bankers creating
new instruments and the ratings agencies. This contrasts with the typical
narrative portrayed in popular accounts of the crisis that views the generous
ratings of CDOs as part of a plot between the investment banks and rating
agencies to exploit the general public.

* * *

Charting the Transforming US Financial System

The emergence of a dual banking system comprising of both regulated and
shadow banks between 1980 and 2002 can be clearly seen in the data. In the
early 1980s, the banking system was dominated by small, local regulated
banks which kept most of their loans on their books. Securitized bonds and
investment banks were bit-players in this landscape. By 2002, the regulated
banking industry had been transformed in style if not in size by conglom-
eration, including the emergence of national banks, and by the widespread
use of securitized assets to sell relatively standardized consumer loans to
shadow banks while retaining riskier and more complex commercial loans.
Securitization and the increasing diversion of deposits away from the regulated banking system (and the associated federal deposit insurance) had fed
a massive increase in the size of the shadow banking system. This was
epitomized by the growing size of the broker-dealers, the core institutions
in the investment banking groups. And beyond the investment banks was
an increasing penumbra of largely unregulated hedge funds and the like
that focused on trading increasingly complex and largely unregulated
instruments.

The size of the regulated banking industry was an area of relative stability
within this dynamic environment (Figure 12). While changes in regulation
resulted in the emergence of national banks, the balance sheets of private
deposit institutions (a description that includes banks, Savings and Loans,
and credit unions) as a ratio to US output fluctuated within a relatively
narrow band (the size is measured as a ratio to output so as to abstract from
the natural increase in the size of the sector as the economy expands due to
more activity and higher prices). Although the debacle of the rapid expansion and subsequent contraction of the Savings and Loans industry in the

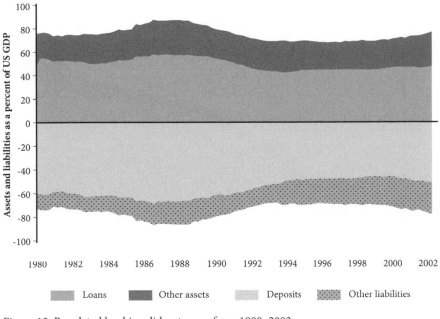

Figure 12: Regulated banking did not grow from 1980–2002.
Source: US Flow of Funds.

late 1980s is visible, by the end of 2002 assets represented 75 percent of output, almost exactly the ratio at the start of 1980. Furthermore, the basic business model of attracting deposits (the light gray segment) and using them to make commercial loans (the medium gray segment) was largely unchanged. Deposits and loans made up around two-thirds of the balance sheet throughout the period.

This apparent stasis, however, masked a profound transformation in the banking system. Regulated banks were making more loans, but the additional loans were sold to shadow banks via mortgage-backed securities (Figure 13). The vast majority of this activity took place through the Fannie Mae and Freddie Mac, the two major GSEs. The amount of mortgage-backed securities that the GSEs issued and insured against defaults rose by almost a factor of ten compared to the size of the economy, from slightly over 3 percent of output in 1980 to almost 30 percent by the end of 2002. Private firms also started to issue mortgage-backed securities. Like the GSEs these private companies took pools of mortgages and sold them to investors, but without an insurance on creditworthiness of the underlying loans that was provided by the GSEs—a crucial difference over the 2008 crisis.

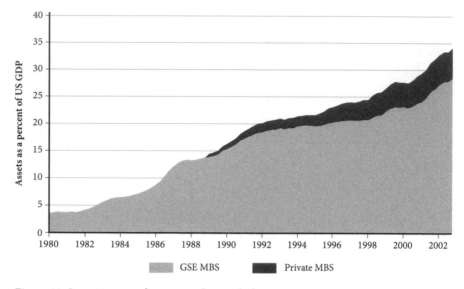

Figure 13: Securitization of mortgages boomed after 1980.
Source: US Flow of Funds.

Securitization transformed the market for residential mortgages
(Figure 14). In 1980, banks retained about three-quarters of residential
mortgages on their books (the dotted segment) and sold only about one-
tenth of them to investors through GSE securitized assets (the black
segment)—the remainder being mainly mortgages issued by the federal
government through Federal Home Loan Banks. By 2002, banks were only
retaining one-quarter of residential mortgages on their books and were
selling well over half through GSE and private securitizations (the black and
light gray segments). The originate-to-distribute model in which banks
originated mortgages and then distributed them to investors that featured
prominently in the financial crisis was already in place by 2002. In addition,
private securitizations extended well beyond residential mortgages. Similar,
if less spectacular, transformations occurred in the multifamily mortgage
market (apartments and condos), where banks went from holding over 90
percent of all mortgages on the books in 1980 to holding under two-thirds
by 2002, and in consumer loans, where securitization rose from nothing in
1980 to 20–30 percent of the market by 2002. In all, over one-third of bank
loans were being securitized by 2002.

The counterpart to securitization was the diversion of deposits away
from the regulated banks to shadow banks. Regulated bank deposits as a
ratio to output peaked during the Savings and Loans boom, and then went

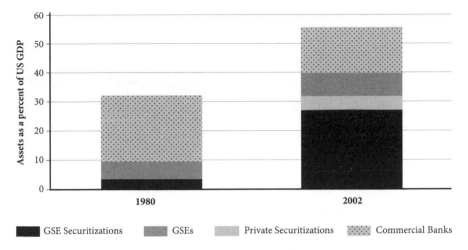

Figure 14: Banks sold most mortgages via securitizations by 2002.
Source: US Flow of Funds.

into gradual decline. This was particularly true of large bank deposits that exceeded the insurance cap. In their place, there was a surge in deposits placed outside of the regulated banking system using money market mutual funds and repos. These uninsured deposits rose from under 10 percent of output in 1980 to over 40 percent by the end of 2002, by which point their size rivaled that of insured bank deposits.[25]

The major beneficiaries of the increase in nontraditional cash deposits were the investment banks (Figure 15). The assets of the core market operations of these groups, the broker-dealers and their holding companies (called funding corporations), exploded more than ten-fold as a ratio to output, from barely 2 percent in 1980 to well over 20 percent by 2002. The broker-dealers were central to markets. They sucked in large deposits of wholesale cash via repos and money market mutual funds (the medium gray and black areas) and used repos to lend this cash out to firms that traded such as hedge funds (the light gray area). This transfer of funds from holders of cash to traders comprised around two-thirds of assets and liabilities of the broker-dealers by 2002. This link was at the heart of the shadow banking system. The lightly regulated broker-dealers borrowed cash from investors and then lent it out to the even less regulated firms such as hedge funds, which bought and sold securitized assets and derivatives. Indeed, the expansion in the assets of broker-dealers closely mirrors the increase in securitized assets.

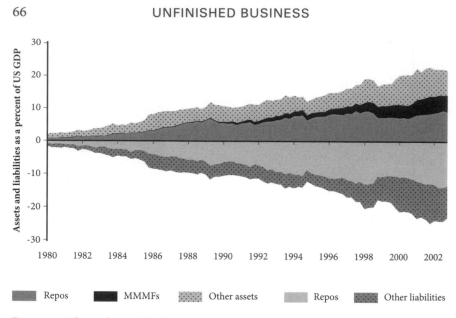

Repos   MMMFs   Other assets   Repos   Other liabilities

Figure 15: Balance sheets of broker-dealers, the core of investment banks, exploded.
Source: US Flow of Funds.

The Rise of National Banks

These shifts took place against a background in which the size of regulated banks expanded rapidly, creating massive institutions with a national reach (Figure 16). As in Europe, the regulated banking industry went through a period of mergers and acquisitions in the 1990s that created a small number of dominant institutions. By 2002, the three regulated banks, Citicorp, JP Morgan, and Bank of America, had aggregate assets of almost one quarter of the economy, well over twice the size they were in 1989 (dark gray segment). The average size of these banks rivaled those of the (more numerous) European mega-banks. By contrast, the ten or so other regulated banks that figured in the largest thirty US financial institutions remained at about the same size as a proportion of output.

The large US regulated banks retained strong capital buffers throughout this period. All of the major regulated banks had equity buffers of over 5 percent of unweighted assets in 2002, in stark contrast to the experience of the Euro area mega-banks. This was because the simple leverage ratio that was part of prompt corrective action limited the ability of large US regulated banks to reduce capital buffers by manipulating risk weights from internal risk models. Within this group, capital buffers tended to be somewhat lower at the two emerging universal banks, Citi and JP Morgan, that

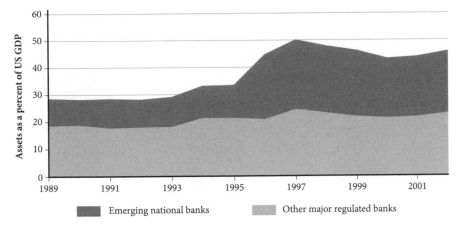

Figure 16: Emerging national banks became increasingly important.
Source: SNL.

followed the European model of combining commercial lending and investment banking under one roof, because prompt corrective action only applied to their commercial banking operations.

While the number of regulated banks was thinning, the booming US investment banking industry was attracting new entrants. The investment banking industry had always been more concentrated than the regulated banks, reflecting fewer regulatory constraints and the greater economies of scale that came with market trading as opposed to making loans to individual customers. The assets of the five main independent investment banks mushroomed five-fold from 1989 to 2002, rising to 20 percent of output. At the same time, however, the sector was becoming more diverse as US and European universal banks entered after the repeal of the Glass–Steagall prohibition on regulated banks owning investment banks.

Competition was putting pressure on the smaller independent investment banks. While Morgan Stanley and (at the time) Merrill Lynch were much larger than their rivals, the smaller independent investment banks (Goldman Sachs, Bear Stearns, and Lehman Brothers) were competing with the investment banking arms of the two major US universal banks and similar offshoots of several European universal banks (such as Deutsche Bank from Germany and Barclays from the United Kingdom, as well as Credit Suisse and UBS from Switzerland) that were backed by large commercial banking operations. It was the second tier of independent investment groups, which lacked the deep pockets of the market leaders or the more stable backing of the universal banks, that got into trouble over the financial crisis.

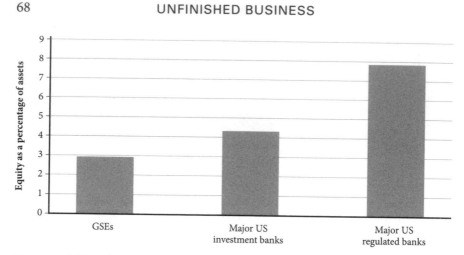

Figure 17: GSEs and investment banks had thin capital buffers in 2002.
Source: SNL.

The two main GSEs, Fannie Mae and Freddie Mac, had also become major financial players by 2002. As they increasingly used their low capital buffers and favorable cost of borrowing to issue bonds and use the proceeds to buy securitized loans, their combined assets had risen to 15 percent of the economy in 2002, quintupling since 1989. This expansion was a distraction from their fundamental role in the financial system, which was to accept conforming mortgages, securitize them, and charge banks for providing insurance on the creditworthiness of the loans to investors.

The rapidly expanding investment banks and GSEs had much thinner capital buffers than the regulated banks (Figure 17). At 2 to 5 percent of assets, their equity cushion was similar to those exhibited by the major European universal banks (although different accounting rules muddy the comparison).

* * *

The US Financial System in 2002

In 2002, the US financial industry had taken on most of the characteristics that were to be seen over the crisis but remained relatively sound (Figure 18). Securitization and uninsured deposits had led to a massive expansion in the shadow banking system centered around the investment banks. Increasing amounts of mortgages created by regulated banks were being securitized and sold to shadow banks, reflecting the incentives coming from differences in regulation. However, the market for home mortgages securitization (by far the largest part of the market) were dominated by the two main housing government-sponsored enterprises, Fannie Mae and Freddie Mac, who were limited to securitizing relatively safe "conforming" mortgages and who provided guarantees on the credit-worthiness of the underlying loans. While these two entities were increasingly exploiting their low funding costs by issuing debt and buying their own securitized assets, these products had many other willing buyers. The riskier private label part of the mortgage-backed securitization market, which lacked insurance on the creditworthiness of the underlying loans, was still only one-sixth of the size of the GSE pools, a proportion that had only crept up slowly since the early 1990s.

Within the regulated banking sector, changes in rules had allowed the creation of three major national banks even as the aggregate size of the industry had remained relatively constant. While two of these mammoths had moved toward being universal banks, with part of their business in investment banking, the trend was not being followed by others and the industry as a whole remained focused on deposits and commercial loans. The market for deposits was also changing, with an increasing proportion bypassing federal insurance. New deposit instruments were generally most attractive to managers of wholesale funds whose deposits were typically above the limits to qualify for deposit insurance. However, since these had not been insured in the first place, there was limited reason to be concerned about the diversion to shadow banks.

Figure 18: Structure of US banking in 2002.

Within this relatively benign picture, however, were three areas for concern. The first was the rapid expansion of the lightly regulated investment banks. While it was true that investment banks had never been regulated for safety and soundness, the explosion in the size of the sector boosted the potential risks to the financial system from a failure. Assets of the broker-dealers at the core of the investment banking groups had increased steadily from just 2 percent the economy in 1980 to 10 percent in 1990 and over 20 percent by the early 2000s. The risks to the investment banking industry posed through financing reckless market behavior were well illustrated by the rescue of Long-Term Capital Management, which had managed to amass over a trillion dollars in assets on a narrow capital base. When it collapsed, the investment banks had to band together for a rescue.

The second area for concern was the increasing participation of rapidly growing European universal banks in US markets. These firms further supported the expansion of investment banking and derivative markets and also provided a conduit to European banks to buy securitized assets with which they were less familiar. Between 1980 and 2002, foreign ownership of corporate bonds (which included securitized assets) doubled to one-tenth of the size of the US economy.

The final area of concern was the acceleration in house prices. After a long period of stable house prices in the early 1990s momentum in the housing market was gradually accelerating. By the end of 2002, house prices (as measured by the yet-to-be-invented Case Shiller index) were rising by almost 10 percent a year even as inflation remained quiescent and real house prices had already risen by one-third compared to their nadir in early 1993.

None of these trends made a crisis inevitable. Indeed, it is relatively easy to think of policies that could have prevented these trends from magnifying over the coming years. The failure to reign in these financial excesses reflected misguided regulatory decisions on both sides of the Atlantic, largely driven by a misplaced belief in the power of market discipline of investors to limit risk-taking by major banks. This dynamic is the topic of the next chapter.

Chapter 3

BOOM AND BUST

The trends observed from 1980 through to 2002 were gradually making the North Atlantic financial system more brittle. The rapid expansion of the balance sheets of the Euro area mega-banks and erosion in their capital buffers were creating risks for that region, especially against a backdrop of a monetary union that was badly designed for negative shocks. In the United States, the boom in shadow banking involving the nexus of securitization, non-insured deposits, and investment banks was well under way and house price inflation was starting to gain steam. However, these strains were limited and essentially isolated from each other.

The boom of the 2000s saw these risks grow and intermingle (Figure 19). The core Euro area banks were central protagonists in the unsustainable financial boom and bust, in stark contrast to the popular portrayal of them as hapless victims of US financial deregulation. To be sure, US deregulation played a role. In particular, reforms designed to provide greater liquidity in US repurchase (repo) markets supported the explosion of substandard mortgage-backed assets and gave foreign banks easy access to dollars. However, this coincided with a massive boom in lending by the core Euro area banks as a result of inadequate regulation and supervision. As domestic lending opportunities dried up, the core Euro area mega-banks expanded into foreign markets, financing housing booms in the United States and the Euro area periphery. Indeed, this lending was a major catalyst in making these housing and financial bubbles larger and more destructive—the road to the housing crashes went through Basel and Berlin, not Baltimore and Barcelona. The subsequent collapses in house prices created banking and economic crises in the United States and the Euro area periphery that blew back onto the Euro area core, broadening the crisis to the entire North Atlantic region.[1] The jaws of the North Atlantic crisis clamped shut.

This is not to say that the banks in the Euro area core all behaved alike, or that the booms in the Euro area periphery did not have their own national flavors. The broad-brush split of the Euro area into a core and a periphery masks significant differences across countries. Within the core, the German banking system included large numbers of small banks whereas larger institutions dominated the French banking system. Less sophisticated German banks bought significant amounts of questionable US assets, including the cash-rich Landesbanken (owned by the German states, or Länder) whose spending spree in the mid-2000s was further boosted by a hump in borrowing before the option to use government-guaranteed bonds expired. Turning to the periphery, the Spanish housing boom was much larger than the one in Italy. This largely reflected the activities of unsophisticated local-government-owned "caja" savings banks that drove much of the Spanish housing boom. Indeed, the cajas followed a similar trajectory to the Landesbanken in terms of investing heavily in real estate, except that the bad investments were national instead of international. By contrast, in Italy banks loans were much more closely linked to local firms. For that matter, there were also major differences across US regions, where house price increases were much larger in the west and east coasts (especially Arizona and Florida) than in the middle of the country. In the end, the similarities between the behavior in the Euro area core (Germany, France,

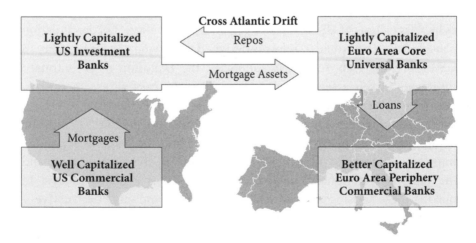

Figure 19: The North Atlantic financial boom.

the Netherlands, and Belgium) and in the periphery (the remainder) justify a narrative that splits the Euro area into these two regions, just as the United States is treated as a single entity. These simplifications allow a coherent story to be told without multiple digressions.

* * *

Regulators and the Cross-Atlantic Financial Drift

Pro-market changes in regulation helped propel a cross-Atlantic financial drift in which Euro area banks financed the US housing bubble by buying increasing amounts of securitized US mortgage loans. Regulators focused on updating rules that supported markets and hence investment banking. This motivation was different from the earlier wave of regulatory changes in the 1980s and 1990s, which had aimed at integrating the European financial system and freeing regulated US banks from outdated depression-era rules. These objectives had essentially been completed by 2000 with the introduction of the Euro (helping to create a single European financial market), the repeal of the US Glass–Steagall Act separating commercial and investment banking (integrating the US banking system), and the Basel 1 Capital Accord on international capital buffers (harmonizing rules on capital charges across international banks). The new push was in response to lobbying by banks to make markets more efficient and, by extension, increase their profits. This accession to bank self-interest was to have tragic consequences.

How US Repo Markets Funded the Housing Bubble

The expansion of collateral that US broker-dealers could use in repurchase agreements with clients was the first and most important of the regulatory decisions aimed at enhancing markets. In April 2003, Release 47683 of the US Securities and Exchange Commission (SEC) widened the collateral that US broker-dealers could use with clients from "cash, U.S. Treasury bills or notes, or irrevocable bank letters of credit" to include two major additional types of assets.[2] These were, firstly, foreign paper such as sovereign bonds, highly rated non-government securities, certificates of deposit, and bankers' acceptances, and, secondly, securities associated with the US housing market. Crucially, the second category included mortgage-backed securities.

The SEC release was responding to complaints from the US investment banking industry that the size of the repurchase market was being

constrained by limited amounts of eligible collateral. Repurchase agreements were a flexible and convenient instrument to borrow and lend cash
on a short-term basis. For example, an investment bank could sell a financial asset to a client in return for cash and an agreement to buy the asset
back (repurchase it) the next day at a fixed price, with the difference between
the current and future prices representing the return for the depositor. The
investment bank then either used the cash to invest in the market or, more
typically, lend it to a market trader such as a hedge fund using another repo.
Clearly, collateral was central to these arrangements as it provided the client
with an assurance that they would get their money back in case anything
went wrong.

In a political and intellectual environment that was sympathetic to
loosening financial regulation, the SEC assessed that the benefits from
deeper repo markets to investors and US investment banks outweighed
any risks to clients. The release explained that benefits included "lowered
borrowing costs and increased liquidity in the securities lending markets,
and greater opportunities for US firms to compete abroad".[3] It observed
that broker-dealers (the legal description for the firms at the core of the US
investment banking groups) often found it more economical to borrow
and lend with each other than with clients. This was because there were no
restrictions on the collateral that could be used in repos with fellow broker-
dealers, in contrast to the restrictions on the collateral employed for such
transactions with clients. Allowing a wider range of assets to be used as
collateral would allow clients to lend more to broker-dealers and "earn the
fees associated with such transactions and thereby realize greater returns
on their securities portfolios". These benefits, which not incidentally also
included solidifying the pre-eminent place of US broker-dealers in global
markets, were deemed to outweigh the risks "of customer losses associated
with permitting a new category of collateral".

Two years later, similar motives led the US Congress to give repo
markets a further boost with the passage of the Bankruptcy Abuse and
Consumer Protection Act in April 2005. This act extended "safe haven"
protection to most of the expanded repo collateral granted by the SEC two
years earlier.[4] Safe haven status meant that if the broker-dealer went bankrupt the lender was able to automatically keep the collateral behind the
repo. By contrast, if the broker-dealer borrowed money by (say) issuing
money market mutual funds or commercial paper, lenders could only get
their money back through a lengthy bankruptcy procedure. Safe haven
thus increased the attractiveness of repos over other ways of lending
money.

The justification for extending safe haven status to the expanded collateral was to limit the systemic risks of repo transactions. There was a concern that if clients started to worry about the financial stability of a broker-dealer, this could create risks to the wider financial system, given the size of the repo market. But there was a strong element of circularity in this line of reasoning. First, the SEC widened the repo collateral after investment banks complained that a lack of safe collateral was constraining the market. Then the resulting expanded repo market based on less secure collateral was supported through changes to the bankruptcy code. The Congress was trying to minimize a concern about riskier collateral that had been created just two years earlier by the SEC. The ultimate irony is that the collapse of the investment bank Lehman Brothers created exactly the run on the repo market that the safe haven provision was supposed to avoid. This was because over the crisis lenders to the investment banks simultaneously questioned the viability of banks *and* the value of the underlying collateral. The safe haven provision protected them from the first of these concerns but not the second.

The third and final regulatory lift to the repo market, particularly as regards the participation of foreign banks, came when the Basel Committee loosened its capital requirements for repos in July 2005.[5] These changes had been anticipated in the previous year's agreement on the overall Basel 2 framework (discussed later). At that time, the Committee promised to "maintain its active dialogue with the industry to ensure that the new framework keeps pace with, and can be applied to, ongoing development in the financial sector".[6] One ongoing development where it had indicated that "immediate work should be done" concerned exposures to "certain trading activities" (which was code for repos).

These seemingly technical changes to regulations sparked two trends that drove the US housing bubble and internationalized the spillovers from the eventual bust. The first trend was the increased participation of foreign banks in the US repo market. Before collateral was widened to include foreign paper, overseas banks had almost no presence in this market. By contrast, they were major players by the time of the crisis, using foreign paper to obtain dollars that were then generally invested in US assets. As the SEC predicted, easier access to the repos market further deepened the already substantial role of US assets in international banking, including the booming market for mortgage-backed securities. The deep involvement of European banks in US repos markets explains why the seizing up of these markets after the collapse of Lehman Brothers over the crisis immediately translated into dollar and liquidity shortages at European banks.

The second and even more corrosive trend was to increase the desirability of high-yielding mortgage-backed securities issued by private firms. Before the SEC decision, mortgage-backed securities represented a useful way of pooling risk and selling bundles of loans to investors. With a stroke of the pen, the SEC also made mortgage-backed securities into liquid assets that could be swapped for cash in the repo market. This added a powerful incentive for traders to own, lend, and sell mortgage-backed securities. As these securities increasingly became a vehicle for borrowing and lending cash, purchasers became progressively more focused on the short-term goal of obtaining high returns rather than on the long-term business of providing people housing through sound mortgages.

This search for higher yield boosted the demand for riskier private label securitizations over the safer but lower-yielding assets provided by the GSEs. Private banks were able to offer better yields on mortgage-back securities because they could accept riskier mortgages that by-passed the rules on safety and soundness for "conforming" mortgages that GSEs could accept. In addition, unlike the GSEs, private banks did not provide insurance against the risk that the underlying mortgages would default. This moved the potential losses on defaulting mortgages as a result of a US housing collapse away from the GSEs, with their deep pockets derived from implicit government backing, and toward shadow banks with thin capital cushions.

The nonconforming mortgage loans bundled by private banks in securitized assets included "jumbo" mortgages, whose value exceeded the upper limit on loans that Fannie and Freddie would accept, and where demand was rising along with house prices. In their desire to satisfy the rising demand for high-yielding mortgages, however, private firms increasingly bundled mortgages from borrowers that did not meet the "prime" credit standards required by Fannie and Freddie. Expanding the quantity of "subprime" mortgages was relatively easy as they were being offered to people who wanted to own a home but had been previously locked out of the mortgage market. The expansion met with little opposition from regulators as it coincided with the federal government's desire to widen home ownership.

The subprime mortgage market exploded after the SEC decision to widen repo collateral to mortgage-backed securities. In 2002, only 7 percent of US mortgages were subprime and only half of those were sold to investors. By 2006, subprime loans were almost half of the market and almost all were sold on to investors; research also finds a major fall in the spread of mortgage-backed securities to treasury notes in the summer of 2003, soon after the SEC decision.[7] Because the banks sold the mortgages, they no longer had "skin in the game" and the quality of subprime loans deteriorated to the point where they became known colloquially known as "liar loans" due to the lack of due diligence on the borrowers.[8] Due diligence was skimped as banks and investors increasingly saw house price appreciation as the main guarantee against default rather than the ability and willingness of borrowers to repay. This unconventional lending approach was justified by the observation that that US national house prices had never fallen in the postwar period. Unsurprisingly, after this assumption proved incorrect and house prices did start to fall in 2006, the default rate on these loans rapidly escalated. The market collapsed along with its central dogma.

Obviously, changes in rules on repo collateral was not the only driver of the US housing market bubble. Many other factors were involved, most importantly a massive failure of US consumer protection for subprime mortgage borrowers which allowed mortgage lenders to offer increasingly unsafe loans based on miniscule downpayments, low initial charges on the loan, and minimal documentation. This lax attitude largely reflected the Federal Reserve's overinflated belief that risks taken by banks would be limited by market discipline from investors (the Federal Reserve was the main regulator of mortgage lending standards). However, this deterioration in lending standards only emerged once the subprime market had already been established. The initial takeoff of the subprime market occurred on the heels of the SEC decision to widen repo collateral in 2003. More generally, while the internal dynamics of the US mortgage market boosted the US housing bubble by increasing the *supply* of mortgage-backed assets, much of the *demand* for these assets came from the Euro area as expanding northern banks created a cross-Atlantic financial drift into US markets using repos. It is to this story that we now turn.

* * *

How the Basel Committee Encouraged Euro Area Mega-Banks

The most important change to international banking regulations in the early 2000s was the 2004 Basel 2 Accord. In this landmark decision, the Basel Committee agreed to widen the use of risk models to credit risk on commercial loans to firms and households in addition to market risks from trading securities. Since Basel 2 was not implemented until the end of 2007 for the large Europe banks and never really adopted in the United States, the direct impact of these regulations on the North Atlantic banking system was limited. However, in anticipation of lower future capital requirements, European banks reduced the capital that they held in excess of current minimums. In addition, the Basel 2 negotiations illustrate the increasingly cozy relationship between the European mega-banks and their supervisors. This explains why these banks were able to manipulate their internal risk to thin their capital buffers on investment banking without regulators intervening.

The Long and Winding Road to Basel 2

The road to Basel 2 started almost immediately after the January 1996 passage of the market risk amendment, as the Basel Committee refocused on rules for commercial lending to consumers and firms. Most members of the Basel Committee agreed that the existing Basel 1 system that put each loan into a broad risk bucket was relatively crude, with the risk weights often deviating significantly from actual risk, but that it reflected a practical compromise between simplicity and complexity. US Federal Reserve Board officials, however, became increasingly strident advocates of altering this system. As early as May 1996, Chair Greenspan noted that the weaknesses in Basel 1 were becoming ever more evident. By 1998 "calls for change in Basel 1 became a regular theme in public statements by Federal Reserve Officials concerning bank regulation".[9]

In addition to a general bias against financial regulation, Fed concerns with Basel 1 stemmed from two trends that were particularly advanced in the US banking system. The first was the expansion in securitizations of mortgages. Fed officials noted that the Basel 1 risk weights encouraged such securitizations since the weight assigned to a mortgage-backed security was lower than the weight assigned to the underlying mortgages.[10] Fed officials were correct that securitization was being encouraged by differences in capital charges. However, standardized Basel risk rates were a minor issue. The main driver were differences in required capital coming from the high capital buffers embodied in the US prompt corrective action framework for US regulated banks versus the much lower capital buffers for securitized bundles of such loans required of US investment and major European banks that used internal models to calculate market risks. Fed officials were in the right neighborhood, but looking under the wrong lamppost.

Second, just as they had done for market risks, the Federal Reserve argued that risks from commercial loans were better calculated using internal "value-at-risk" models. The Fed had by now widened its view that market discipline was a better constraint on bank risk-taking than crude government regulations to include commercial banking as well as investment banking. The Fed argued that extending the use of internal models to credit risk would improve the calculation of capital buffers while also providing incentives for the major banks to further refine their risk models. It was therefore little surprise that a month after Federal Reserve Bank of New York President William McDonough became chair of the Basel Committee in June 1998 that its members agreed to review Basel 1.[11] While the Basel 1 regime came from a need to unify and beef up international capital rules, Basel 2 was born from a vaguer dissatisfaction with the existing regime. The lack of a clear final objective complicated and confused the process. For example, it was never clear whether the plan was to maintain bank capital buffers at existing levels or to allow some erosion in light of the banks' use of more sophisticated risk management tools.

Against this background, it is little surprise that the Committee's conservative initial 1999 proposal to change the capital standards by using credit ratings to assign loans to risk weight buckets was badly received.[12] Even the rating agencies opposed the plan, saying that it risked "ratings shopping" by clients, while the large banks (correctly) pointed out that many borrowers did not have external ratings and that the track record of such ratings as predictors of future risk was not encouraging. Instead, the large banks lined up behind the Fed and asked to extend internal models to credit risk. For example, the Institute for International Finance (a trade group for large banks that had already advocated the use of internal risk models) and the International Swaps and Derivatives Association each organized groups of senior bankers to lobby the Basel Committee in favor of using internal models.

The Committee's second consultative paper, published in January 2001, caved into this pressure and agreed to let large banks use internal bank models to calculate credit risk. This was despite misgivings about the internal ratings approach by some European members of the Committee, most notably the German supervisors. Under the Committee's proposal, small banks would continue to use the existing "standardized" approach to calculate credit risks while somewhat larger banks would be allowed to use the "foundation" approach, which combined bank estimates of the likelihood of default with supervisors' estimates of the associated losses. Crucially, the largest and most important banks would be allowed to use the "advanced" approach in which internal risk models were used to calculate the probability of default and the associated losses on commercial loans—i.e., their capital buffers—just as they were already doing for market risks. Depending on their size and sophistication, banks could therefore be under three different capital adequacy regimes—the standardized regime, the foundation internal ratings regime, or the advanced internal ratings regime.

Reactions to this proposal were not tepid. The Committee receiving over a thousand pages of largely negative comments. Many academic and quasi-academic commentators (correctly) questioned the advisability of using internal ratings models given the potential for manipulation. By contrast, the large banks supported the framework but suggested numerous modifications arguing that, based on their initial calculations, internal risk models could lead to a rise in regulatory capital requirements.[13] As observed by a knowledgeable commentator at the time (who subsequently helped clean up after the US financial bust) these detailed comments obscured the fact that:

> In another sense, though, the banks' objections to capital levels required by the CP–2 [the second consultative paper] was their *only* complaint . . . any feature of CP–2 that boosted capital requirements was unwelcome. On the other hand, the banks were quite rationally prepared to accept regulatory features that they found arbitrary, costly, or even ill-conceived, so long as their capital requirements declined enough to make the changes on net profitable [emphasis in the original].[14]

After the acceptance of internal risk models had demonstrated the ability of large banks to sway decisions, the Basel Committee engaged in more or less constant negotiations with the banking industry and frequent revisions of its proposals. The Committee was on the defensive, responding to a nearly constant barrage of criticism mainly from large banks, whose focus was on lowering capital charges and hence improving their competitiveness relative to banks that were not able to use the advanced approach.[15] As a result:

> In many instances, it is not easy to determine if the Committee's modifications in response to the many objections from banks reflected an enhanced technical understanding of matters not fully grasped in CP–2, on the one hand, or tactical accommodations in the face of broad-based opposition, on the other hand (or some of both).[16]

The final Basel 2 proposals (released in June 2004) added further layers of complexity and hence more discretion on implementation of rules and standards.[17] Reflecting these characteristics, it was agreed that the advanced system should come into force at the end of 2007, a year after the rest of Basel 2. Lobbying by the large banks produced a complex and opaque system using internal models that were easy to manipulate.

Internal Risk Models as the Golden Goose

Astonishingly, the Basel Committee agreed to extend internal models to cover credit risks without detailed information on the consequences for bank capital, just as had occurred earlier with the 1996 market risk amendment. As one commentator put it at the time, this "calls into question the degree to which the Basel Committee understood the implications of its proposal".[18] Eventually, the consequences of the switch from Basel 1 to Basel 2 for banks' capital buffers were assessed by regulators through a series of Quantitative Impact Studies (QISs). While such studies started early in the negotiating process, because the proposals changed so much over time the only studies using assumptions fairly close to the final rules were the last two (QIS–4 and QIS–5). US regulators and the Basel Committee both published analyses of the results of QIS–4 and QIS–5 in 2006, well after the Basel framework had been agreed (in 2004) and adopted by the European Union in (2005).

The carefully written and highly factual report by four US regulators, which masked considerable differences in opinion across the institutions, found that Basel 2 facilitated a major reduction in bank capital.[19] This quietly devastating study focused exclusively on the potential impact of the "advanced" internal ratings approach using the "best-efforts" of twenty-six US institutions. It found that capital requirements for a typical bank would fall by 26 percent, implying that on average banks would be able to add one-third more loans for the same capital base (confusingly, as a result of a dubious weighting procedure, the aggregate reduction was calculated as only 15 percent, but the 26 percent figure is a better estimate).[20] Even more strikingly, the US regulators found wide variations in estimated capital charges across institutions. They reported that "much of the observed dispersion [in results] was caused by the underlying source data and methodologies used by institutions to quantify their risks".[21] While this partly reflected the fact that the institutions were at various stages of implementing the framework, the report noted that it also reflected the *"flexibility allowed within the framework governing the selection of risk inputs"* (emphasis added). They concluded that "portfolio composition was not as important a contributor to dispersion as differences in data and methodologies used". The models were wildly inconsistent with each other when tested on identical portfolios, just as been found with the 1996 market risk amendment.

The Basel Committee study of the impact of Basel 2 found similar results for a wider range of countries that encompassed all three methods for calculating capital requirements.[22] Using the same dubious weighting strategy, the study estimated that capital buffers would fall by 7 percent for banks using the advanced approach, broadly in line with the US results once changes in rules between QIS–4 and QIS–5 are taken into account.[23] Like the US report, the Basel study also reported major differences in results across institutions, from a +60 percent to a –60 percent change in capital requirements.

The wide variation in estimates of needed capital buffers coming from different internal risk models is crucial to understanding why the European banks were able to manipulate these models. In the face of such diverse outcomes, it was extremely difficult for supervisors to assess the accuracy of any given model or whether changes to models reflected genuine improvements or a desire to lower costs by minimizing capital buffers. The Basel 2 negotiations had made clear that banks were more than happy to minimize their capital charges. Complex and widely varying internal risk models gave them an easy means to do so.

Another characteristic that became evident is that internal risk models amplify the business cycle. They encourage more lending during booms and less lending during slumps. This is because internal risk models assume that the rise in asset prices during a boom signaled a reduction in risk, which allow banks to reduce the capital support on existing loans and redeploy it to back new lending. As the Euro area was to find out over the crisis, the same mechanism applied during a bust, only with the opposite effect. The US regulators were the most explicit about the pro-cyclical nature of Basel 2, stating that "the relatively benign economic environment prevalent when QIS–4 was conducted resulted in lower minimum risk-based capital requirements than would had been observed had QIS–4 been conducted during a more stressful economic period, *since the Basel 2 framework is designed to be more sensitive to expected macroeconomic conditions than current U.S. rules*" (emphasis added). The Basel Committee paper broadly agreed, stating "some supervisors noted this [better economic conditions for QIS–4 and QIS–5] likely affected estimates of probabilities of default (PD) through strong credit quality conditions". By lowering capital charges at the height of the bubble and raising them in the subsequent bust, internal risk models amplified both halves of the 2000s financial cycle.

Implementation of Basel 2 in Europe and Not in the United States

There was never any doubt about the implementation of Basel 2 rules in the European Union. Indeed, one of the reasons that European negotiators wanted to make the final Basel Committee rules so specific was to minimize the need for additional work on implementation via an EU Capital Adequacy Directive. The directive was duly passed in October 2005 without any significant changes compared to the Basel proposals. The "flexibility within the framework" (in the words of the US regulators) provided room for large European banks to take an aggressive approach toward the calculation of capital buffers. The European banking industry was increasingly driven by a small number of bloated national mega-banks who were already using the flexibility provided by internal risk models for investment banking to lower capital buffers and thereby gain a competitive advantage over smaller rivals who were operating under standardized weights. The Basel 2 plan to extend the use of internal risks models from investment banking to the entire operations of a bank provided further incentives to manipulate internal models, particularly as the mega-banks were increasingly competing against each other.

Competition across national supervisors within the European Union undermined incentives to closely examine bank behavior. The lack of engagement in the difficult task of supervising large universal banks with internal risk models was exemplified by the adoption of "light touch" regulation in the United Kingdom in early 2001 (a similar approach was taken in Ireland). The principles-based approach to regulation (the formal title for "light touch") adopted by the UK Financial Services Agency involved close collaboration between supervisors and regulated banks. In the words of the 2005 *Better Regulation Action Plan*, the agency committed to "continue to work with the industry where possible, so that they own solutions to market failure problems".[24] Or, in the words of Chancellor Gordon Brown's accompanying press release "Not just a light touch but a limited touch". Looking back after the crisis, the Former Chief Executive of the Agency, Hector Sants, commented: "The prevailing climate at the time and indeed right up till the crisis commenced was the market really does know best".[25] UK regulators accepted the US Federal Reserve's view of the power of market discipline in limiting risks taken by banks.[26]

There were several reasons why the United Kingdom in particular was happy to publicly embrace light touch regulation. First, UK supervisors had less incentives to be tough on domestic banks as almost half of its banking system was foreign-owned branches and hence supervised by other countries. Second, UK supervisors had a much more active relationship with its banks than was typical on the continent, where the greater reliance on auditors in the supervision process already implied a more hands-off process. Finally, UK regulators were much closer to the Federal Reserve, which espoused the advantages of market discipline, than other European regulators due to similarities in culture, legal systems, and financial market structure.

More generally, the 2000s saw a gradual erosion in capital cushions across the major European Union banks. The process had its own dynamic, as lax supervision in some countries (such as the United Kingdom and Ireland) put pressure on others European supervisors to lighten their own approach as their banks requested a level playing field on the enforcement of regulations. There was also the risk that if supervisors continued to take a tough approach then national banks would divert some of their business to subsidiaries in countries with lighter supervision such as Ireland, thereby reducing the control that national supervisors could exert over their national banks.

The outcome was a massive and unsustainable expansion of European mega-banks. As their domestic markets became saturated, the additional lending went into overseas ventures. The core Euro area banks lent increasing amount to the United States and the Euro area periphery. They also became the dominant players in various other types of loans, such as trade finance or funding projects in developing countries.

It is ironic that the Basel 2 framework that the Federal Reserve supported so strongly was in effect never implemented in the United States.[27] The main reason for this was splintered financial regulation that required Basel 2 to be agreed across different banking regulators. While the Comptroller of the Currency was modestly positive about the Basel 2 Accord, the Federal Deposit Insurance Corporation (FDIC) viewed the drop in required bank capital as a result of adopting Basel 2 with concern. Lower capital implied a higher chance of banks insolvencies, and the FDIC was primarily responsible for avoiding such insolvencies and for organizing and paying for any rescues. As a result, the FDIC was not prepared to scrap the leverage ratio that had been incorporated into the US prompt corrective action framework. This was important as the leverage ratio used total assets to calculate capital needs, and hence was not affected by any reduction in risk weights coming from internal risk models. It set a floor below which the capital buffers of the US regulated banks could not fall.

A compromise between the pro-Basel 2 Fed and the more cautious FDIC was eventually reached in July 2007 after long and difficult negotiations. This instituted some relatively aggressive transition floors that limited the short-term erosion of capital under Basel 2. Crucially, it also retained the leverage ratio and prompt corrective action for US regulated banks (the compromise was effectively overtaken by the financial crisis and the decision to revamp bank regulation through Basel 2.5 and Basel 3, discussed in a later chapter).

The experience of the US investment banks vividly illustrates the problems associated with internal risk models. After the European Union decided that investment banking groups operating in Europe had to be subject to safety and soundness supervision, the five major US investment banking groups (called the Consolidated Supervision Entities or CSE) agreed to switch from the Net Capital Rule to the Basel system in 2004. Although this switch has often been portrayed as a weakening of supervision given the problems that the investment banks experienced over the crisis, in actual fact the Basel system was, if anything, more stringent since the Net Capital Rule was only focused on ensuring clients were repaid rather than avoiding bankruptcy. It also had the advantage of unifying the capital rules faced by the US investment banks and the European universal banks. Despite this, however, the outcome of the Consolidated Supervision Entities program was not pretty. As the Congressional Research Service put it:

> Whatever the intent of the CSE program, it did not succeed in preventing excessive risk-taking by the participants. By the end of September 2008 all five CSE investment banks had either failed (Lehman Brothers), merged to prevent failure (Merrill Lynch and Bear Stearns), or applied for bank holding company status (Morgan Stanley and Goldman Sachs) [in order to gain access to emergency Federal Reserve funds]. On September 26, 2008, SEC Chairman Cox announced the end of the CSE program, declaring that "[t]he last six months have made it abundantly clear that voluntary regulation does not work".[28]

While voluntary regulation may have been part of the problem, this assessment is much too generous to the Basel Committee. The European experience indicates that the internal risk model approach did not provide adequate capital buffers to cover risks from investment banking. The entire Basel system was faulty, not simply its US implementation.

The core US banking system was protected from the excesses of internal risk models by the FDIC's insistence that the simple leverage ratio be retained. This explains why the crisis had its worst effects on the US investment banks and the European universal banks, while the major US regulated banks were generally financially strong enough to help rescue the system, including by buying troubled investment banks. This is not to say that the Fed-led drive to financial deregulation had no impact on the United States. It did. Lax consumer protection allowed a flood of subprime mortgages without adequate regulatory oversight. The biggest impact of the Federal Reserve, however, came through their championing of internal risk models that allowed a massive expansion in core Euro area bank lending that was ferried back to the United States via the cross-Atlantic financial drift. The ability of the US regulatory process to reject the major reduction in bank capital requirements implied by Basel 2 underlines the advantage of a slow process in which multiple institutions with different viewpoints need to agree on changes. So how did the North Atlantic boom unfold? It is instructive to start with the Euro area banks.

* * *

Charting the Unsustainable North Atlantic Financial Boom

The Unwise Overseas Expansion of Core Euro Area Banks

The Euro area banking system expanded massively over the 2000s boom on the back of thinning capital buffers (Figure 20). Strikingly, the rate of increase tripled after 2004, the year that the passage of Basel 2 ensured that internal risk models would be extended to credit risk by the end of 2008.[29] Nor was the process limited to the Euro area. Similar percentage increases in assets were experienced elsewhere in Europe, including the already large UK banking system.

In particular, the core Euro area banks expanded their investment banking operations (Figure 21). Noticeably, very little of the increase in the size of the banks in Germany, France, the Netherlands, and Belgium came from commercial loans (dotted segments).[30] By contrast, in the Euro area periphery (Italy, Spain, Portugal, Ireland, Greece, Austria and Finland) the expansion in assets was much more balanced, as the dramatic reduction in interest rates in southern Europe as a result of Euro area membership provided opportunities for more loans to customers.[31]

Facing limited lending opportunities at home, the core banking system expanded rapidly into foreign ventures, most notably in the United States, United Kingdom and Euro area periphery (Figure 22). The expansion into US and UK investment banking (the black segment) was spearheaded by mega-banks such as Deutsche Bank and BNP Paribas. The expansion to the

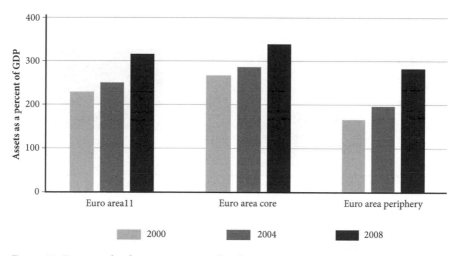

Figure 20: Euro area bank assets grew rapidly after 2004.
Source: ECB Banking Statistics.

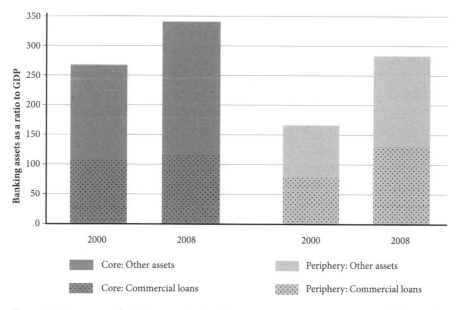

Figure 21: Investment banking grew in the Euro area core, expansion was more balanced in the periphery.
Source: ECB Banking Statistics.

Euro area periphery (dark gray segment) came through a mix of subsidiaries, branches, loans to local banks, and purchases of government and private paper. By 2007, the assets of core Euro area banks in the US, UK, and periphery were almost equal to core Euro area output. Furthermore, this

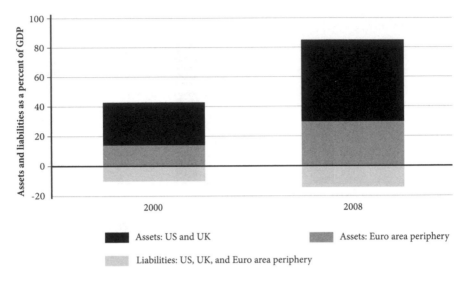

Figure 22: Core Euro area banks expanded overseas.
Source: Bank for International Settlements.

was a one-way expansion as the corresponding liabilities remained small (light gray segment). Similarly, the core Euro area banks dove into other regions, such as eastern Europe (where areas such as the Baltics also suffered banking crashes) and business lines (such as trade credit, which also suffered over the crisis).

This rapid overseas expansion provided significant parts of the funding for the US and periphery financial bubbles, and ensured that the subsequent busts fed back to the core Euro area banking systems despite limited housing excesses at home. In 2007, on the eve of the US subprime problems, the northern European banks (Euro area core plus UK) owned US assets worth over one-quarter of US output, three times the ratio of 2000. By this time, they also owned assets in the Euro area periphery of around half of the periphery output, double the 2000 value. The result was that when the bubble burst the Euro area suffered a generalized banking crisis.

The twelve mega-banks identified in Chapter 1 (see Figure 3) drove these shifts in the Euro area banking system.[32] Indeed, they accounted for the entire increase in bank assets over the 2000s as they expanded from one-third to one-half of the assets of the overall system through a combination of internal expansion, and mergers and acquisitions (Figure 23). By 2008, Deutsche Bank had assets of over 20 percentage points of Euro area output and six other mega-banks had balance sheets greater than 10 percentage

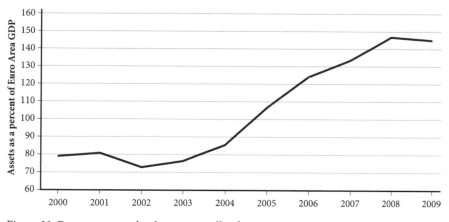

Figure 23: Euro area mega-banks grew rapidly after 2004.
Source: ECB Banking Statistics.

points, a threshold than no bank had surpassed in 2000. Their mergers with smaller banks in other EU countries also drove the limited integration of the European banking system. Examples included UniCredit's 2005 takeover of the German group HBV in 2005, BNP Paribas's acquisition of Banca Nazionale di Lavoro in 2006, and the massive purchase of the Dutch group ABN AMRO by Royal Bank of Scotland, Fortis, and Santander in 2007. These mega-banks were often not just too big to fail but too big to save. By 2007, many had assets that were over half of national output, while those of ING Group were over double the output of the Netherlands. The delays in acknowledging the true size of the banking problems after the North Atlantic crisis, which slowed the repair of the financial system and lengthened the recession, was more of a necessity than a choice.

Even as the assets of the mega-banks expanded, their capital buffers eroded (Figure 24). Capital buffers were lower and fell more steadily for the universal mega-banks in the Euro area core. By contrast, the larger capital buffers of the commercial mega-banks in the Euro area periphery were more volatile, but fell notably in 2004, when Basel 2 was agreed, and in 2008, when it was adopted.

The Basel measures of capital buffers used by regulators obscured this fall in bank soundness because of the manipulation of risk-weighted assets. Figure 25 plots the ratio of equity to total assets just discussed for individual mega-banks on the vertical axis and the Basel regulatory ratio of core capital to risk-weighted assets on the horizontal axis. Already by 2002 the relationship between these different ways of measuring capital buffers had broken

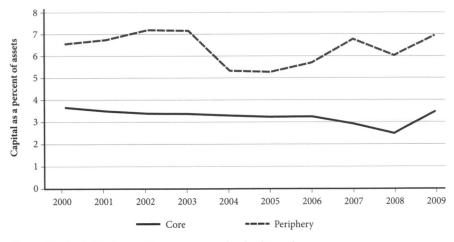

Figure 24: Capital buffers of Euro area mega-banks thinned.
Source: SNL.

down. In 2008, after the introduction of Basel 2, the relationship had turned *negative* across the mega-banks. In this topsy-turvy world, Dexia and Deutsche Bank exhibited exemplary Basel regulatory capital ratios despite having capital below 2 percent of total assets while Intesa Sanpaolo, which boasted the highest ratio of capital to assets (8 percent), registered the second *lowest* Basel regulatory buffer. Put another way, at "well-capitalized" Deutsche Bank a Euro of capital was backing about 60 Euros in assets while at the apparently less well capitalized Intesa the same Euro backed only 12 Euros in assets. In short, over the European banking boom of the 2000s the system became larger, more dominated by mega-banks, less well capitalized, and more exposed to the emerging bubbles in the United States and the Euro area periphery. So what was happening in the United States?

The Changing Face of US Securitization

Investment banking was also booming in the United States. The US banking system retained its dual structure, with regulated banks originating loans and then selling many of them to the less regulated shadow banking system centered around the independent investment banks. Indeed, even in the case of the two US banks that developed a universal banking model involving both commercial and investment banking (Citigroup and JP Morgan Chase), the US Flow of Funds data continued to separate the activities of their "deposit taking institutions" (the regulated banking side) from their "broker-dealers" (the core of the investment

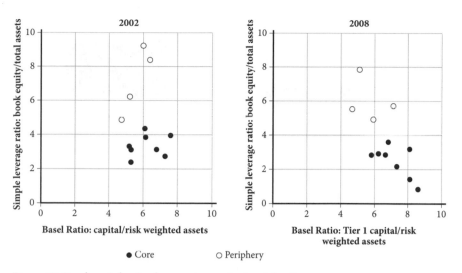

Figure 25: Basel capital ratios became increasingly misleading.
Source: Scientific Committee of the European Systemic Risk Board (2014).

banking side)—a residual statistical tic from the Glass–Steagall law separating the two activities. Accordingly, the assets of regulated banks and of
broker-dealers should be combined to get a sense of a US "universal"
banking system equivalent to that in Europe. While regulated banking
remained the dominant segment, it was becoming a smaller part of
the system up to the crisis as broker-dealer assets doubled as a ratio of the
economy between 2000 and 2008.

The rise in importance of the shadow banking system can be clearly
seen in the surge in riskier private-label mortgage-backed securities after
the Securities and Exchange Commission (SEC) widened rules on repo
collateral in 2003 (Figure 26). With house prices rising faster than inflation, mortgage-backed securities increased rapidly as a proportion of the
economy, while the nature of the issuers changed dramatically. Through
2002, the securitization market was dominated by Fannie Mae and Freddie
Mac, the two major housing government-sponsored enterprises (GSEs),
but after the 2003 SEC decision issuance was dominated by riskier private
mortgage-backed asset companies. By the time the housing market soured
in 2007, one-third of all mortgaged-backed securities had been issued
through private firms that had no credit guarantee. These were the assets
whose values collapsed over the crisis.

Foreign banks use of the repo market to borrow dollars also surged
after the SEC decision (Figure 27). In 2002, foreign banks were bit players
in the repo market (black segment). By 2007, they comprised a quarter of

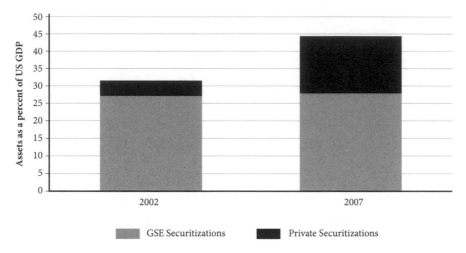

Figure 26: Private mortgage securitizations surged after repo collateral was widened in 2003. *Source:* US Flow of Funds.

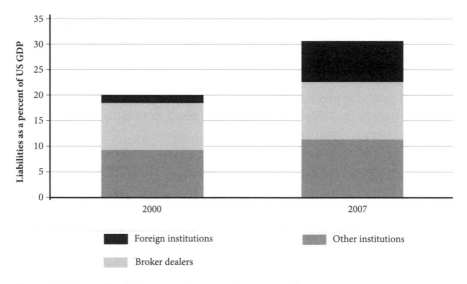

Figure 27: Foreign banks borrowed more cash via repos after 2003. *Source:* US Flow of Funds.

a much larger market (by the eve of the crisis, the repo market was twice the size of that for money market mutual funds, compared to near equality in 2002). Consequently, when the repo market froze over the crisis, Euro area banks had to scramble to replace the loss in dollar wholesale cash that they needed for their market operations.[33]

Euro area banks provided much of the funding for the US housing bubble. Strikingly, between 2002 and 2007, the increase in US assets owned by northern European banks (the Euro area core plus the United Kingdom, which housed many Euro area investment banking operations) was almost exactly equal to the increase in US private-label mortgage securitizations. While the creation of so many subprime mortgages was a product of faulty consumer protection and US-specific changes in regulation, including for repo collateral, much of the financing came directly or indirectly from European banks using internal risk models (that the Fed had championed) to save on capital buffers. The road to the collapse of the US housing market went from the Fed through the Basel Committee and then core Euro area banks before flowing back to the United States via the cross-Atlantic financial drift.

These changes were aided and abetted by a major increase in the size of the US national regulated and investment banks. Figure 28 shows the assets of the major investment banks (Morgan Stanley, Goldman Sachs, Merrill Lynch, Lehman Brothers, and Bear Stearns) and the three regulated national banks (Citi, JP Morgan Chase, and Bank of America, of which the first two were becoming universal banks that included investment banking operations). At the peak in 2007 the assets of these institutions were almost as large as US output.

Despite rapid expansion, the smaller US investment banks were coming under increasing competitive pressure.[34] The five major independent US investment firms remained the most important presence in the sector but

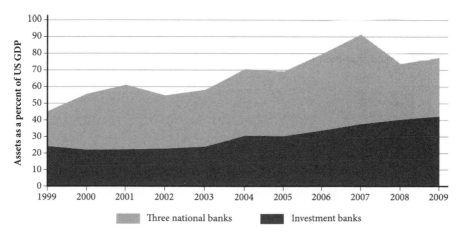

Figure 28: Investment and national banks grew rapidly through 2007.
Source: SNL.

their clout was shrinking as they faced increased competition from subsidiaries of universal banks, including JP Morgan, Citi and the northern European mega-banks—Deutsche Bank, Barclays, BNP Paribas, and, from 2006, HSBC. While the leading independent US investment banks, Morgan Stanley and Goldman Sachs, continued to be much larger than these newcomers, the same was not true of Bear Stearns, Lehman Brothers, and Merrill Lynch, all of which floundered in the crisis.

In contrast to Europe, the three regulated national banks never became too big to save because support was centralized at the federal level. While the assets of Citigroup, the largest of the three national banks in 2007 and the one that experienced severe problems over the crisis, were similar in size to the Euro area mega-banks, they represented only about 15 percent of US output a much smaller ratio than in European countries. Consequently, the US government was able to provide adequate support to Citigroup over the crisis, which meant that the US banking system did not suffer the same obfuscation that prolonged banking problems in the Euro area.

The capital buffers of the shadow banks were much thinner. The investment banking groups as well as the two major GSEs (Fannie Mae and Freddie Mac)—the segments that included most of the failures over the crisis—had buffers that were only about half of those of the regulated banks.

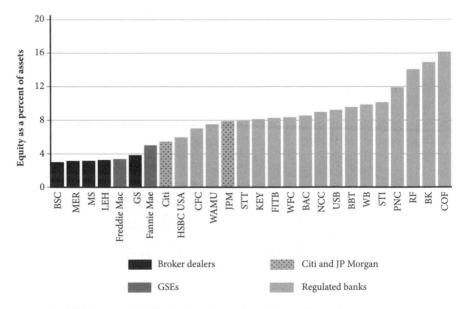

Figure 29: Thinly capitalized banks faced more trouble over the crisis.
Source: SNL.

This dichotomy between well–capitalized regulated banks and thinly capitalized shadow banks in the United States was similar to that between the core universal banks and the periphery commercial banks in the Euro area. However, in the United States the thinly capitalized institutions were a smaller part of the overall system.

Examining the capital buffers of individual institutions in 2007 illuminates the vulnerability of the shadow banking system and Citigroup (Figure 29). Across the twenty-six largest US-owned financial institutions, three of the four lowest capital ratios were associated with investment banks that subsequently failed or had to be rescued, Bear Stearns, Merrill Lynch, and Lehman Brothers. In addition, Freddie Mac and Fannie Mae—the seventh and eighth largest financial institutions in the country that had to be put into receivership after their holdings of private mortgage-backed securities went sour—also had thin capital cushions. Finally, within the regulated banking sector, Citigroup had the lowest capital buffer.

Was the Behavior of the US and European Banking Systems Typical?

An important question is the degree to which the expansion in the Euro area and US banking systems were unique, or part of a more general global trend. This international perspective is useful for explaining the origins of the North Atlantic financial boom and its consequences, as larger banking systems are costlier and more difficult to resolve. Comparing the size of the US and other banking systems is complicated by differences in accounting practices. Assets of financial firms under the US accounting standard (GAAP) do not include holdings of derivative assets such as options and futures contracts that are included in the international accounting standard (IFRB) used by the rest of the world. A second complication is that the broker-dealers whose assets are tracked in the US Flow of Funds data are only one part of the investment banks. Examining pre-crisis balance sheets of investment banks suggests that broker-dealer assets should be doubled to get a sense of the size of the overall US investment banking system on an equivalent basis to the international accounting system (the difference for regulated banks is trivial).

Making this adjustment generates a US banking sector that was larger, expanding faster, and had a larger role for shadow banking than is generally recognized. The US "universal" banking system peaked at 160 percent of output in 2009 with the investment banks making up some 40 percent of the system. The magnified role of investment banks makes it easier to understand how the shadow banking system was able to absorb so many securitized assets and why problems in the US investment banks generated a global financial crisis. Even so, the US banking system remained only about half the size of the European system relative to output. The massive size of the European banks, as well as their presence in the US investment banking sector, explains why the European banking crisis was so generalized and so difficult to fix.

Most other major banking systems did not expand as fast as those in Europe or the United States, suggesting that the Basel rules alone were not the main driver of the North Atlantic debacle. Figure 30 compares bank assets as a ratio to output for European banks (Euro area plus the UK, which includes a lot of Euro area investment banking) and the (adjusted) US banking system since 1999 with the banking systems of Australia, Canada, and Japan, all of which were also members of the Basel Committee. The assets of the Canadian and Japanese banking systems, which were dominated by commercial banks, remained relatively stable as a ratio to output just like the regulated part of the US banks, albeit at vastly different sizes. The Canadian system was the smallest throughout the period while the Japanese banking system started as the largest. The Australian banking system, which

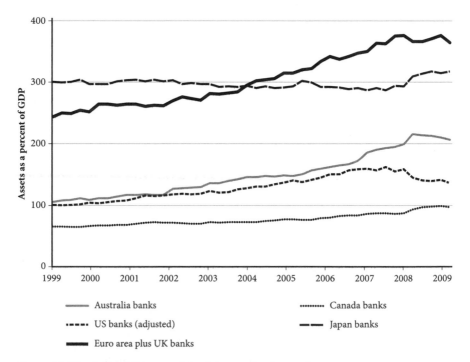

Figure 30: The size and increase of the European banks stands out.
Source: National Data Sources from Haver Analytics.

unlike the other two countries had a universal bank model, did expand over the boom of the 2000s but remained much smaller than the European system. The Australian banks also suffered a wholesale funding run over the crisis, but this was quickly solved through government guarantees. This suggests that the major drivers of the expansion of the European banks were the universal banking model and overexpansion from lax oversight due to regulatory competition. But what created the demand for loans that the rapidly expanding North Atlantic banking system produced?

* * *

Charting the North Atlantic Macroeconomic Boom and Bust

The booms in the Euro area periphery and the United States that started in the late 1990s were propelled by a potent cycle of rising lending, spending, output, and asset prices. In addition to the "yin" of lax financial regulation, the North Atlantic crisis reflected the "yang" of macroeconomic booms. The US boom that started in the late 1990s exhibited a larger and more persistent imbalance between spending and output than had been seen previously. Figure 31 measures US aggregate spending as a percentage of output. From 1970 through to the mid-1990s there is a clear cycle with spending rising above output in expansions and then falling back over recessions. From the late 1990s on, however, spending rose consistently compared to output. By the eve of the crisis, Americans were spending a record dollar and 6 cents for every dollar that they produced. The flip side to this spending boom was a growing trade gap. As Americans spent more they sucked in more imports and borrowed increasing amounts of money from abroad to pay for them.

The same pattern holds for the Euro area periphery. Figure 32 reports the same ratio of spending to output for Italy, the only country in the group for which data from 1970 is readily available, as well as a shorter series for the periphery as a whole. Through to the mid-1990s, there is again a clear cycle as spending rises and falls compared to output, followed by an extended boom in spending from the late 1990s until the crisis. Indeed, the increase in spending over the pre-crisis boom is similar to that in the United States, albeit from a somewhat lower base. Again, the flip side was a growing trade deficit.[35]

The macroeconomic "yang" of lower interest rates explains why the Euro area financial boom occurred in the periphery even though much of the additional lending capacity was concentrated in the core. The spending

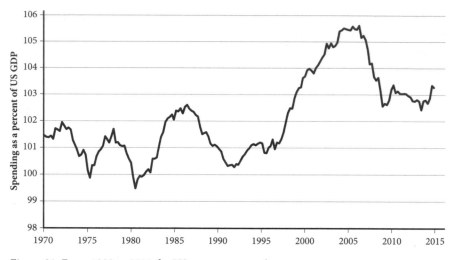

Figure 31: From 1998 to 2008 the US went on a spending spree.
Source: US National Accounts.

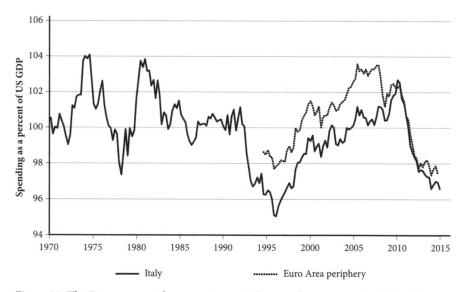

Figure 32: The Euro area periphery went on a similar spending spree to the United States.
Source: Italian and EU National Accounts.

boom in the periphery was sparked by the rapid fall in long-term interest rates as entry into European Monetary Union reduced risk premiums (Figure 33). Yields on ten-year bonds in Italy, Spain, and Portugal were in double digits as late as 1995. By the time the Euro was introduced in 1999, they were below 4 percent and essentially identical to German rates (a pattern that was repeated when Greece joined the Euro area in 2003). While some of this compression in nominal yields reflected the reduction in inflation as a result of joining the Euro area, "real" rates adjusted by inflation also fell markedly. This reduction in real interest rates also partly reflected the pressure on core Euro area banks to find places to lend their rapidly expanding loan portfolio.

Low funding costs boosted by overconfidence in the benefits from European Monetary Union and the need to find new places to make loans led to a boom in investment spending in the Euro area periphery (Figure 34). The left chart below traces how the rise in spending as a proportion of output discussed earlier was apportioned between investment and consumption (with each series measuring changes compared to the situation in early 1995). The entire pre-crisis spending boom in the Euro area periphery came from higher investment, which then collapsed well below its 1995 level after the crisis. Figure 35 shows the same decomposition for the components of investment—machinery, residential housing, and commercial buildings. Over time, the boom in spending became increasingly dominated by residential housing, financed by mortgages to households and loans to property developers.

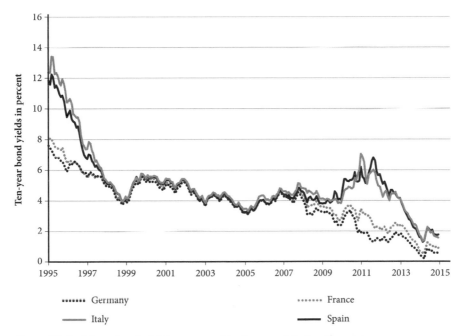

Figure 33: Periphery bond yields converged to Germany's before the crisis.
Source: ECB.

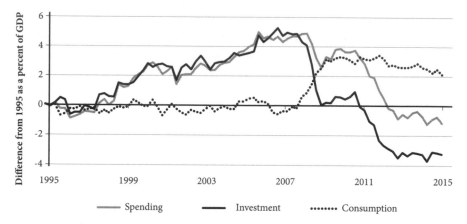

Figure 34: Investment spending surged in the Euro area periphery before the crisis.
Source: EU National Accounts.

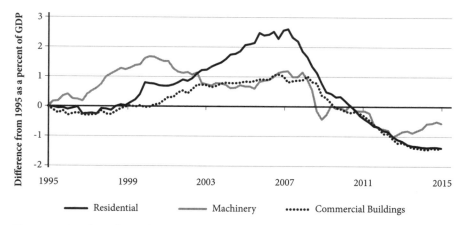

Figure 35: Residential spending drove higher investment.
Source: EU National Accounts.

A similar pattern was seen in the United States (Figures 36 and 37). While consumption played a more important role in the early stages of the US boom than it did in the Euro area periphery, plausibly reflecting the wider use of credit scores that allowed US banks to automate consumer loans, the latter stages of the US boom were increasingly driven by rapid increases in spending on residential housing.

Higher spending on residential housing was both a cause and a consequence of booming housing prices (Figure 38). Here, again, there are striking similarities between the Euro area periphery and the United States. In both regions house prices rose by about two-thirds compared to the

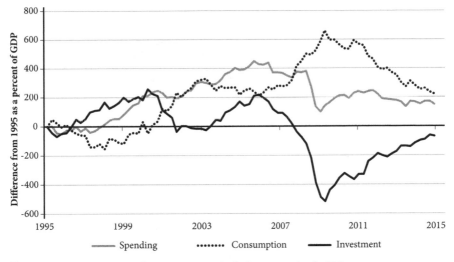

Figure 36: Investment spending was increasingly important in the US.
Source: US National Accounts.

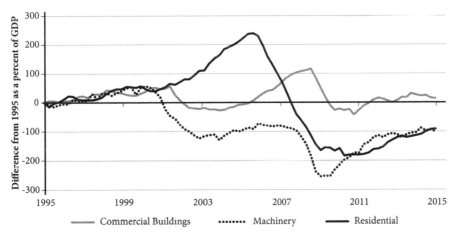

Figure 37: US residential investment surged in the 2000s.
Source: US National Accounts.

overall price level between the late 1990s and the peak of the boom. The
subsequent fall in house prices, however, was much faster in the United
States. As will be discussed further below, this largely reflected the fact that
the US housing boom was financed by traded assets whose prices fell
rapidly while in the Euro area periphery the real estate loans were generally
kept on bank balance sheets which made it easier to delay recognition of
losses.

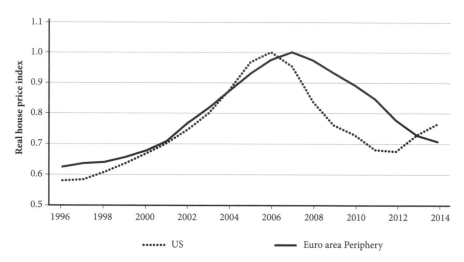

Figure 38: US and Euro area periphery experienced similar house price booms.
Source: Europe: National data on All Dwellings from Haver Analytics. US: FHFA Purchase Only Index.

What Lowered US Bond Yields in the 2000s?

The US boom was accompanied by a gradual fall in long-term interest rates whose cause is less clear than the European Monetary Union-induced reduction in the Euro area periphery. Three main hypotheses have been put forward to explain the fall in US yields. The first is that it reflected the inflows into US Treasury and Agency assets coming from the build-up in reserves in emerging markets, including China—often referred to as the "global saving glut".[36] The second is that financial inflows from European banks lowered rates.[37] The final explanation is that the rise in repos led to a reduction in yields as mortgage-backed assets became more liquid.[38] Each explanation highlights a different potential driver, self-insurance by emerging markets, financial deregulation in Europe, and the widening of repo collateral in the United States.

The evidence suggests that all three drivers mattered. Figure 39 provides a sense of the relative importance of these three explanations by comparing the amount of money that was pumped into US markets from each source. For the global saving glut, the chart shows the increase in reserve holdings as a proportion of US output.[39] Holdings rose by some 8 percent of US output between 1999 and 2007 (unlike the other explanations, this flow accelerated after the crisis). For European bank inflows, the chart shows the increase in net ownership of US assets by core Euro area and UK banks, which start at a very similar level to reserves but rise twice as fast through 2006.[40] Even accepting that capital gains may have played a part in the increase in European bank assets and that not all of these inflows went into the US housing market, it is clear that such inflows played an important role in easing US financial conditions, as it also did in the Euro area periphery. Finally, the expansion in US repos was similar to the increase in European bank assets, partly because the two were interlinked, since Euro area banks used repos to access dollars.

The counterpart to these asset purchases was a rise in the US trade deficit. This was important as the Federal Reserve focused on stabilizing domestic inflation rather than domestic demand. As the rise in the trade deficit limited the amount to which the rise in domestic demand translated into higher output and inflation, the Federal Reserve kept monetary policy relatively expansionary.[41] This maintained output close to capacity, but at the cost of supporting the housing bubble.

All in all, it seems reasonable to conclude that the fall in US bond yields reflected a combination of all three drivers—higher reserve asset holdings by emerging markets, European expansion into investment banking, and greater liquidity of safe assets. This suggests that in the United States a significant portion of the fall in yields reflected the internal dynamics of the US financial system, and hence a melding of macroeconomic and financial drivers. This is similar to the Euro area periphery where, in addition to the fall in bond yields linked to entry into monetary union, inflows from core Euro area banks also played a significant role.

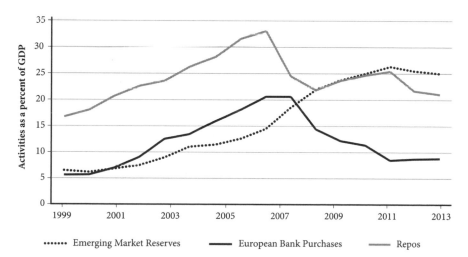

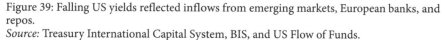

Figure 39: Falling US yields reflected inflows from emerging markets, European banks, and repos.
Source: Treasury International Capital System, BIS, and US Flow of Funds.

* * *

Similar Macroeconomic Booms, Dissimilar Busts

The US and Euro area crises were driven by the same underlying dynamics. A steady loosening of financial regulation led to an expansion in bank assets on both sides of the Atlantic, complemented by higher spending coming as a result of lower borrowing costs. Easy borrowing, higher assets prices, and pro-cyclical financial regulation fed on each other to create spending booms that sucked in money, particularly from the core Euro area banks, that artificially supported spending and output.

If the components of the unsustainable asset bubbles were so similar, why then was the timing so different between the financial crises in the United States and Europe? After all, the US crisis started in 2007 with problems in subprime loans and reached a peak in September 2008 when Lehman Brothers went bankrupt. By contrast, the Euro area debt crisis is generally dated from the Greek government's announcement of much larger government deficits and debt in late 2009, and peaked in mid–2012. The answer to this questions matters because the association of the European crisis with the problems of Greece and unsustainable debt elsewhere in the periphery diverted attention from the more important fact that the real problem in the Euro area was that the European banking system had become dangerously undercapitalized, particularly in the Euro area core.

The answer to why the Euro area crisis lagged that in the United States lies in the type of lending used to finance the bubbles. In the United States, most of the bad loans were sold to investors through mortgage-backed securities. The prices of these securities reacted immediately when problems in subprime mortgages first started to appear in mid-2007 and took a larger dive in the aftermath of the collapse of the investment bank Lehman Brothers, when a loss of confidence in counterparties led to a freeze in repo markets. This fall in market prices led to rapid write-downs of US mortgage-backed securities that affected US and core Euro area banks immediately. By contrast, in the Euro area periphery most of the bad loans were retained on bank balance sheets, which gave banks much more leeway as to when to acknowledge that the borrowers were unable to pay.

In addition to the delayed recognition of bad loans, the much more destructive impact of the crisis on Euro area than on the United States largely reflected the region's deeper structural weaknesses. In the Euro area, the bloated universal banks went into the crisis with thin capital buffers, which meant that the financial shocks in the US and Euro area periphery whipsawed back and created a banking crises in the core of the banking system. In addition, the design of the Euro area made it difficult to provide the periphery with fiscal or banking support. Weak bank supervision and a deeply flawed monetary union were at the root of why a collapse in housing prices in the United States and European periphery led to a prolonged Euro area economic crisis.

While the crisis in the United States was dramatic, the regulated banks were significantly better capitalized than in Europe. Hence, while large parts of the shadow banking system had to be rescued—especially the smaller investment banks, government-sponsored enterprises, as well as Citigroup—most of the regulated banks were able to support this effort and absorb many of the failed institutions. In addition, US policymakers were not constrained by an incomplete monetary union. The Federal Reserve responded to the crisis by almost immediately funneling money into illiquid markets and institutions (including many Euro area ones). Similarly, the US federal government was able to provide banking support without creating serious doubts about the viability of its finances.

This is not to say that individual decisions taken during the crisis were unimportant. In the United States, the bankruptcy of Lehman Brothers— while possibly understandable given the constraints being faced—was clearly a policy blunder. Similarly, even given its legal mandate, the European Central Bank could have been more proactive as problems in the periphery mounted—after all, the Federal Reserve showed considerable ingenuity in its crisis response, including finding ways to channel funds to distressed investment banks. In the end, however, it was always much more likely that the bursting of housing and financial bubbles in the United States and the Euro area periphery would create bigger shockwaves in the Euro area for the simple reason that the Euro area started with a weaker banking system and a more limited set of policy responses. The next chapter explains why the Euro area was so badly designed.

PART II

MISDIAGNOSING THE NORTH ATLANTIC ECONOMY

Chapter 4

A FLAWED MONETARY UNION

The costs of the Euro area banking crisis were enormously amplified by the flawed design of European Monetary Union (EMU). By joining EMU, Euro area members gave up the ability to print money in the face of a crisis. For regions within a typical currency union, such as California within the United States of America, the inability to print money is of limited concern as the federal government provides an emergency backstop. By contrast, European Monetary Union was designed in a highly decentralized manner, with little or no ability for countries in crisis to access centralized support. Rather, the risk of a crisis was supposed to be constrained by rules that limited unwise behavior, in particular too much government borrowing. Lax enforcement of these rules allowed the Greek government to borrow excessively in the 2000s using the financial credibility of the union as a whole. The discovery of this subterfuge in 2009 led to a rapid increase in borrowing costs for governments in the Euro area periphery, which rapidly turned the unsustainable economic booms in the periphery into crises as governments floundered in the face of the mounting fiscal costs associated with banking crises and recessions.

The flaws in European Monetary Union reflected longstanding differences between France and Germany on the role of monetary union in the wider project of European economic integration.[1] The French saw a single currency as a crucial step to bringing about European economic integration, while the Germans saw a currency union as a validation after economic integration had been achieved. The interaction between these different views explains why the Euro area was so badly designed. It is also crucial to thinking about the future of EMU since exactly the same tensions manifested themselves in Franco-German disagreements about the response to the crisis, with the French wanted to provide emergency support to the crisis countries while the Germans focused on maintaining the discipline implicit in existing rules.

The Maastricht Treaty that laid out the road to monetary union was a finely honed compromise that papered over these tensions rather than resolving them. This reflected several dynamics. First, the Treaty was a rushed job that reflected the political imperatives coming from the unexpected fall of the Berlin Wall and the 1989 reunification of Germany. The single currency was created as a defensive reaction to German reunification rather than as a positive affirmation of European integration. Reflecting this speed, the final treaty closely followed the plan created by the earlier Delors Committee that had been dominated by European central bankers. These bankers produced a plan for EMU that focused on ensuring that the new European Central Bank remained independent of political pressures while leaving existing national fiscal and financial arrangements in place. The Delors Committee planned a fine central bank but a substandard monetary union.

Another crucial dynamic was the close relationship between President Mitterrand of France and Chancellor Kohl of Germany. To a large extent, the overall direction of the final Treaty signed by ten heads of state at Maastricht was the product of bilateral agreements between these two leaders, neither of whom was very interested in economics. The resulting Treaty succeeded in its *political* objective of ensuring that the newly unified Germany remained anchored in western Europe but unfortunately retained the *economic* deficiencies of the Delors Committee plan. More generally, while in any major policy decision there is inevitably some separation between the "visionaries" who initiate the project and the "planners" who implement it, the degree of separation between the two processes was exceptionally large for the Maastricht Treaty. While the vision agreed between President Mitterrand and Chancellor Kohl was driven by the need for a political compromise between European Union governments with a focus on Paris, Berlin, and Brussels, the implementation was based on earlier work by central bankers. The technical bent of the Delors Committee that planned the monetary union is illustrated by the fact that the Committee met at the Bank for International Settlements in the Swiss city of Basel, an international organization located outside of the European Union and equally far removed from its politics.

* * *

Differing Visions of Monetary Union

The signing of the Treaty of Economic Union on February 7, 1992 in the picturesque town of Maastricht in the south of the Netherlands remains an historic moment. After centuries of nationalism and conflict, the leaders of the future Euro area came together to agree on an "irrevocable" path to monetary union that was to start at the latest on January 1, 1999. Despite a ratification process that proved more challenging than expected, this is indeed what transpired.

Maastricht was an appropriate venue for the Treaty on Economic Union even if the location was largely determined by the vagaries of the revolving Community leadership. It nestles conveniently between France or Germany without being part of either. It is some 100 kilometers from Bonn (the seat of the German Bundestag until June 1991), 250 kilometers from Frankfurt (the location of the Bundesbank, the independent German central bank whose views were a vital ingredient in the negotiations), and 350 kilometers from Paris, which housed both the French government and the Banque de France. Equally symbolically, it is only 250 kilometers from Brussels, the home of the European Commission that led the drive for a single currency. By contrast, it is a much longer and more difficult trip from London or Rome, the capitals of the other two major European Union members.

Postwar European economic integration embodied the Franco-German desire to cement their peace and create an economic counterweight to the United States. The first step was the European Coal and Steel Community of 1951, which integrated these two vital industrial sectors that straddled their common border. The Community had six members—West Germany, France, the Netherlands, Belgium, Luxembourg, and Italy. The inclusion of Italy in the initial agreement was an important step. It could easily have been left out as its citizens were much poorer than those of the other five members and also more distant—all of the other countries had contiguous borders with at least two other members while Italy touched only France. It was included because of a strong political wish to widen the Community beyond the narrow confines of France, West Germany, and the nations in between, particularly to a country that was also a protagonist in World War II. This desire for a wide membership was to be a recurring feature of the drive to European integration, including the decision to include the subsequent crisis countries—Italy, Spain, Portugal, Greece, and Ireland—in the Euro area.

The Treaty of Rome, signed in March 1957, was a milestone that set out an ambitious vision of future European economic integration. It created the

European Economic Community comprising the same six countries that had entered into the coal and steel pact. It accelerated the process of economic integration by promising the elimination of taxes on trade across the six by 1970, thereby creating a customs union within which trade could thrive. It also committed the six governments to move toward the more ambitious goals of a common market of goods, workers, services, and capital and a monetary union. In addition, the Treaty of Rome also created the European Commission, whose job was to oversee the achievement of the objectives of the treaty. The Commission was an important addition to the landscape as it created an official body whose job was to make progress on European economic integration, thereby ensuring that the project was kept alive even when members' short-term political considerations were unfavorable.

Since this ambitious future vision was embodied in an international treaty, it was and remains extremely difficult to change its provisions. Hence, the members of the European Economic Community (subsequently renamed the European Union) were officially committed to "ever closer" economic integration. By contrast, two other proposed communities that would have moved towards a broader vision of a federal Europe, one on defense and the other on political integration, never came to fruition.[2] Agreeing to economic convergence was one thing; meshing political and defense systems was seen as quite another. This unwillingness to surrender sovereignty to the center was to be a key feature of the Maastricht Treaty.

Within this relatively unified Franco-German vision of an integrated European economy, however, were two very different views about the role of monetary union in the process.[3] On the one hand were the so-called "Economists" who saw a single currency as the *culmination* of a broader process of creating a truly common market and at least some form of federated budget able to react to shocks. In this view, closely integrated markets for goods, workers, services, and capital were necessary precursors for an effective monetary union. It reflected the opinions of the German government, the Bundesbank (the fiercely independent German central bank), and like-minded "hard money" governments such as the Netherlands. In the parlance of the theory of optimum currency areas, the union should only be formed once the preconditions for such a union were already in place. It was the cherry on top.

An extremely different view was held by the "Monetarists", who saw monetary union as an important step to *creating* economic integration in Europe. The Monetarists (not to be confused with the followers of Milton Friedman who also went under this name) felt it would be impossible to create a truly integrated European economy across countries that still had their own currencies. The risk of disruption to international commerce would always discourage deep economic integration. Only in the case of an irrevocable commitment to a single currency would the private sector be prepared to see political borders as irrelevant. In optimum currency area terms, they saw monetary union as a vital ingredient toward creating an integrated European economy. This was the view held by successive French governments as well as by other "soft money" countries such as Italy.

This bifurcation in views about the value of a single currency reflected the different historical experiences of France and Germany.[4] In France, the franc was made legal tender in 1795 before the centralization of the political system under Napoleon. This sequence led to a belief that a strong central government could and should respond flexibly to events. By contrast, the German mark was only made legal tender in 1873, after Bismarck's wily diplomacy had created the highly decentralized German empire in 1871 and well after the creation of a customs union that aimed, but largely failed, to promote German political integration. The decentralized German federation emphasized the importance of binding rules across its constituent parts, as opposed to the French focus on flexibility at the center.

The differences over the relationship between monetary union and economic integration resulted in different views on the role of the central bank. For the Germans, the central bank should be independent of governments and precluded from providing financial support. After all, if the region was already prepared for a single currency because of its high level of fiscal and economic integration, no further support would be needed for governments. Indeed, such support would muddy incentives as a government could game the system by running reckless policies with the prospect of being bailed out. By contrast, for the French, it was essential for the central bank to be under some form of political control and be allowed to provide significant support to national governments, for example by buying national debt. Similarly, fiscal policy across the union should provide a means of support for ailing members. Such support would be particularly necessary in the transition phase as the monetary union evolved from a region with limited economic integration into a smoothly functioning currency area. These differences stymied earlier attempts at a single currency, most notably the 1970 Werner Report.

Irreconcilable Differences: The Werner Report

Plans for European monetary union can be traced back to around 800 AD, although the early concepts were linked with imperial ambitions (of

Charlemagne or Napoleon, for example) or utopian visions of a United States of Europe (Victor Hugo).[5] Somewhat more relevant are the multi-country currency unions created during the late nineteenth century. The 1865 Latin League, comprising France, Italy, Belgium, Switzerland and (later) Greece, created francs and liras of a standard weight and purity of silver that circulated freely across the members.[6] Indeed, in 1869 there was talk of joining this system with the gold-based monetary standards of Britain and the United States, but the British parliament baulked at the implied devaluation in the gold value of the British sovereign (the coin, not the monarch). Similarly, the 1873 Scandinavian monetary union unified the currencies of Denmark, Sweden, and Norway. This came about in response to the shift by Germany, their dominant trading partner, from a silver standard to gold. While both monetary unions survived on paper into the 1920s, they were effectively ended by the financial and inflationary strains created by World War I.

In the light of the Franco-German debate about the role of a single currency in economic integration, it is of interest that neither the Latin nor the Scandinavian monetary unions seem to have created a significant move to closer economic and political union. The collapse of these multi-country currency unions stands in contrast to the successful German and Italian monetary unions that were created at around the same time following the unification of both countries, strongly suggesting that political cohesion is a vital element for a successful monetary union.

With all of that said, the main precursor to the Maastricht Treaty was the Werner Report of 1970 which, like the Delors Report almost 20 years later, set out a plan and a timetable for a currency union. The Werner Report was part of an effort to deepen as well as widen the European Community to create a counterweight to the US dollar. Unlike the earlier gold standard, the Bretton Woods system set up at the end of World War II involved a two-tiered global system, with the dollar pegged to gold and other currencies pegged to the dollar. Since the dollar was the major international reserve asset (with sterling playing a smaller and diminishing role as the British Empire faded) the United States was guaranteed a steady increase in demand for its assets as the need for reserves expanded along with the global economy. In the view of the Europeans, the low cost of borrowing coming from this "exorbitant privilege" (in the words of then Finance Minister Giscard d'Estaing of France) was being used to finance excessive fiscal deficits such as those used to pay for the Vietnam War in the late 1960s.

This US financial recklessness in the 1960s was seen as creating international financial instability, including pressures to appreciate the currencies of the competitive and fast-growing West German and Japanese economies. It is worth noting that tensions were not limited to the United States, and that similar strains were occurring within the European Community, where low West German inflation was creating pressures for Deutsche mark appreciation against higher-inflation currencies such as the French franc. Indeed, it was only following a significant (and overdue) devaluation of the French franc and a revaluation of the Deutsche mark in 1969 that leaders of the six countries in the Community agreed to set up the Werner Commission to produce a detailed plan for European economic and monetary union. At the same time, they decided to increase the potential heft of the Community by opening negotiations for entry of four additional countries—the United Kingdom, Ireland, Denmark, and Norway.

While the desire to create a viable alternative to the dollar created some unity across the Werner Committee, different views on the role of a monetary union in economic integration generated divisions.[7] In line with the Economist/Monetarist split, Germany with support from the Netherlands argued that greater economic coherence was a prerequisite for monetary union while France, Luxembourg, Belgium, Italy, and the Commission backed an early union. The final report was a compromise between these two positions with a focus on "parallelism"—in which progress would be made in all areas. The text opened by arguing that because policy cohesion across the Community had not kept up with the increase in trade and interconnectedness coming from the customs union there was a risk that instability in one country could be transmitted to others. To solve this problem, the report envisaged a gradual transformation in stages from the existing situation to union where "goods, and services, people and capital will circulate freely and without competitive distortions, without thereby giving rise to structural or regional disequilibrium".[8] This would be overseen by a federal state in which the "principal decisions of economic policy will be taken at the Community level and therefore the necessary powers will be transferred from the national plane to the Community plane". This would lay "a leaven for the development of political union, which in the long-run it [monetary union] *cannot do without*" (emphasis added).

The report only contained a detailed discussion of the first stage in this process, in which "the [European] Council will be the central organ of decisions of general economic policy". Coordination of short-term policies would gradually improve through three regular annual surveys of member policies. The first survey would mainly gather facts, the second would provide some guidance to members on policies, while the third would give more detailed instruction and would also be formally sent to the European Parliament. Such guidance to members would become "more binding and ensure a sufficient degree of harmonization in monetary and budget polices". The text was vague on timing, suggesting that the first stage get underway at the start of 1971 and might last three years, after which an intergovernmental conference would have to agree to the needed changes to the Treaty of Rome required to move to stages 2 and 3.

The report opened up the familiar Economist/Monetary fissures. The German government's response was positive, with the cabinet accepting a plan to work on initial steps "in coming weeks". However, the independent Bundesbank was much less enthusiastic, with its Central Bank Council arguing that monetary policy should not be under the ultimate purview of the European Council, but should be determined independently by central bankers via the long-windedly named Committee of Governors of the Central Banks of the member States of the European Economic Community. (I will follow the normal convention of shortening this to the Council of Governors.) Privately, President Emminger of the Bundesbank was much more suspicious, seeing this as a French plan to use "a European currency block as a battering ram against the dollar" to "put shackles as quickly as possible on what they see as our sinister German monetary policy".[9] He considered that "improved access to mutual balance of payments assistance" underlay French thinking. The French were even less happy because of the implied loss in sovereignty. Finance Minister Giscard d'Estaing, the senior official most likely to be sympathetic to the report, commented that it offered "too centralized a conception".

Given this frosty reception, Chancellor Brandt and President Pompidou met in early 1971 to try and sort out Franco-German differences. With Pompidou unwilling to give up any significant degree of sovereignty over fiscal policy, however, Brandt concluded that the French were not serious about the Werner Report and the Germans pushed for a sunset clause on moves to monetary union.[10] Based on these concerns, it is no surprise that when the European governments formally adopted the Werner Plan in March 1971 there was no timetable for implementation. Rather, they agreed that the European currencies would fluctuate in modestly narrower limits against each other than those implied by bands around the dollar in the Bretton Woods system, an extremely modest move to European monetary integration.[11] These new bands were supposed to be put in place in June 1971, but this was upended in the spring when the Germans unilaterally floated their currency against the dollar in the face of mounting inflows from international investors.

Interest in forming a currency union continued. Indeed, in October 1972 a Community summit in Paris agreed to start the transition to the second stage of the Werner Plan in January 1974 as well as the creation of a European Monetary Cooperation Fund to support this move.[12] This distinctly half-hearted agreement, however, did not survive the final collapse of the Bretton Woods fixed exchange rate system in 1973. Ultimately, the unwillingness of the French, in particular, to surrender sovereignty over fiscal policy to the European Council torpedoed the Werner Report. The future Delors Report was to take a much more decentralized approach to sovereignty, in large part because it was driven by French dissatisfaction with the growing dominance of the Deutsche mark in European monetary policy, a dynamic to which we now turn.

The Hard D-Mark

In the period from the early 1970s to the mid-1980s plans for monetary union were overshadowed by monetary instability coming from the collapse of the Bretton Woods system of fixed exchange rates. Globally, the main challenges were managing the switch from fixed to floating exchange rates and taming inflation, which rose in the wake of the 1973 oil price shock. On curbing inflation, Germany and Japan were notably more successful than other major economies including the United States and other members of the European Economic Community such as France, Italy, and the United Kingdom. Within Europe, interest in wider European integration faded as policymakers grappled with the task of achieving exchange rate stability across the expanded Community despite continuing pressure for Deutsche mark (or D-mark as the Germans called it) appreciation.[13] As early as March 1972, the European Community Council of Ministers (ECOFIN) launched a plan to limit intra-European currency fluctuations via the "snake"—a system in which European Community currencies limited their fluctuations to within 2¼ percent of each other's central parities, half the amount allowed under the Smithsonian Agreement that attempted to resuscitate the doomed dollar-based Bretton Woods fixed exchange rate system. The snake was also widened to include prospective new members of the Community, with the United Kingdom, Ireland, Denmark, and Sweden joining the arrangement. However, the United Kingdom and Ireland left after only two months.

On March 11, 1973, European finance ministers reaffirmed the 2¼ percent fluctuation margins between European currencies while ending any efforts to stabilize their currencies against the dollar. This marked the moment when the Bretton Woods exchange rate system was replaced by a global float of the major currencies overlaid by attempts to stabilize intra-European exchange rates via the snake. The strains caused by different inflation rates, however, ensured that the membership of the snake was partial. It excluded two major European countries, Italy and the United Kingdom. Even more importantly, the French franc was forced to leave the snake in early 1974 in the face of speculation and persistently higher infla-tion in France than in West Germany. Although the franc rejoined the snake in July 1975 it was again forced to exit in March 1976. In the absence of these major European currencies, the snake effectively became a Deutsche mark zone in which smaller European currencies fixed against the West German currency with occasional realignments. This was a long way away from the broad region of European financial stability that had been initially envisaged.

The dissatisfaction of the French and German leaders with this state of affairs led to the replacement of the snake by the Exchange Rate Mechanism (ERM) in 1979. The new arrangement was driven from the top, cooked up in bilateral meetings between President Giscard d'Estaing and Chancellor Schmidt and done, in the view of the British Foreign Office, "in spite of their own bureaucracies".[14] The ERM was formally proposed by Schmidt at a "fireside chat" of leaders (without ministers or advisers) in Amalienborg castle during the Copenhagen European leaders summit of April 7–8, 1978. The idea was to relaunch the snake but with a more symmetric system involving the creation of a European Monetary Fund modeled after the International Monetary Fund. The new European Monetary Fund would pool part of the reserves of member countries and would be responsible for a European unit of account which would help to ensure European currency intervention was more symmetric.[15]

The ERM proposal reflected two powerful political forces: German Chancellor Schmidt's desire to bring the French into the European exchange rate system and French President Giscard d'Estaing's desire that more of the burden of staying in such a system be taken on by the countries with stronger currencies (in other words Germany) rather than being borne almost entirely by countries with weaker currencies (such as France). This was a new version of the familiar Economist/Monetarist split. Germany wanted France to follow more conservative "German" policies to make the system work while France wanted Germany to meet the costs of divergent policies halfway.

The central issue of who should bear the burden for maintaining the system was negotiated under the guise of a technical discussion about whether intervention would be defined relative to a basket of European currencies or only take account of the deviation of individual bilateral rates from their central parity. The crucial difference was that the former would tend to isolate the Deutsche mark as the exchange rate furthest away from the basket, thereby triggering German intervention rather than requiring intervention from countries with weaker currencies. Unsurprisingly, this larger role for Germany in maintaining European exchange rate stability was strongly opposed by the Bundesbank and the German Finance Ministry.

In the end, the ERM arrangement agreed in late 1978 and implemented in early 1979 made few concessions to French desires. It was a long way away from the initial vision, with marginal decisions almost always favoring the preferences of the German bureaucrats to maintain the existing system. For example, while the system included a new unit of account—the European Currency Unit (ECU) which was officially stated to be "at the center of the system"—in practice, currency intervention and debt settlement rules remained asymmetric and favored stronger currencies. There was also little progress on reserves. The agreement made some concessions to French desires by allowing more borrowing across central banks within the system, but the creation of the proposed European Monetary Fund was delayed for two years and with it plans to pool reserves, provide loans, and potentially issue ECUs. The fund was eventually abandoned, given irreconcilable differences about its level of independence from political controls and its role in national policies. In practice, the ERM was essentially a reworking of the snake with a wider membership.

Crucially, the need to obtain agreement from the independent Bundesbank led Chancellor Schmidt to make a side deal. On a visit to the Bundesbank, Schmidt told its Council that whatever the theoretical rules in place, the German central bank would not have to intervene in unlimited quantities if this would undermine German economic and financial stability. He also explained, however, that the sensitivity of this arrangement made a formal written agreement impossible and hence this decision was not communicated to Germany's partners. This piece of subterfuge may have been crucial to keeping both the French and the Bundesbank on board with the ERM but stored up resentment when it was revealed in the later ERM crisis in 1992.

Like the snake, the Exchange Rate Mechanism was a semi-fixed exchange rate system that limited bilateral European exchange rates to within 2¼ percent of a central parity. The main exceptions were the lira, which was allowed wider bands of 6 percent, and the pound, as the British chose not to participate (both currencies, however, were part of the ECU, complicating and eventually marginalizing the ECU as the central peg for the exchange rate regime). Parities could be altered, in theory after discussion with other partners, although in practice this was often ignored (as in the earlier Bretton Woods exchange rate system). Initially dismissed by some as "a mere crawling peg", the early years saw relatively frequent changes in parities given major difference in rates of inflation rates across members.[16] Over time, however, the mood shifted. Smaller Community countries increasingly saw ERM parities as a useful way of importing German policy credibility and of constraining domestic inflation.

French policies, however, were creating increasing strains in the ERM. In 1981, President François Mitterrand became the first postwar socialist leader of France.[17] The new government set out a radical and expansionary agenda, including nationalizing the banking system and some major industrial companies, activist employment policies, and increasing social spending. Unsurprisingly, this agenda led to inflation, a drop in investor confidence, and a series of devaluations of the French franc within the ERM. France's Community partners made it increasingly clear to President Mitterrand that he would have to choose between his desire to follow his own political leanings and to continue as a key member of the European project.[18] In 1983, in the aftermath of a series of political setbacks for the government and after a significant period of indecision and consultation, Mitterrand followed the advice of his market-orientated ministers Michel Rochard (Agriculture) and Jacques Delors (Finance) and switched to a "franc fort" policy involving keeping the franc strong (fort) within the European Monetary System.

This was a crucial step. By choosing European economic integration over his initial go-it-alone expansionist socialist policies, Mitterrand accepted the dominance of the Deutsche mark within the European Monetary System and the need to adapt French policies to maintaining the peg by reversing course and imposing fiscal austerity. The franc fort policy led to a steady hardening of the ERM. A series of changes in parities in 1985 and 1986 were topped off in January 1987 by a revaluation of the Deutsche mark and the Netherlands guilder (by 3 percent) and the Belgium franc (by 2 percent). The next realignment did not occur until January 1990 and was in any case a technical one as the lira switched from 6 percent to 2¼ percent intervention bands. It was in this atmosphere of apparently successful exchange rate stability, but French dissatisfaction with the asymmetry of the ERM, that the next plan for monetary union was born.

* * *

Jacques Delors and His Committee

After the franc fort policy unified European views on the virtues of monetary stability, the focus of European policy returned to achieving greater economic integration. The new agenda was significantly boosted by the arrival as the head of the European Commission of the energetic, ambitious, and diplomatically savvy Jacques Delors. Indeed, the two developments were linked. In 1984, when contemplating a needed reshuffle of his government, Mitterrand considered making Delors his prime minister. However, Delors was a known advocate of fiscal austerity, the domestic counterpart to the franc fort policy. As Mitterrand did not want to advertise his switch to austerity, he chose a more traditional socialist for the job. This left Delors, a powerful up-and-coming force in the French Socialist Party, without a position but with strong market-orientated bona fides. As Mitterrand had decided to make European economic integration into a major plank of his future agenda, he proposed Delors as the head of the European Commission. Delors was chosen as his market orientation made him acceptable to more right-wing leaders, in particular Prime Minister Thatcher and Chancellor Kohl.[19]

The first major initiative from the Delors Commission was the 1986 Single European Act. The act, the first amendment to the Treaty of Rome, set a deadline of the end of 1992 for completion of the single market by freeing the movement of goods, services, labor, and capital within the European Union. Its passage reflected the new pro-market political alignment across the three major European powers as Mitterrand's conversion to market economics moved France into step with the long-standing desire of Germany for a larger market for their goods and with the Thatcher government's pro-market philosophy.

The importance Mitterrand placed on the Single European Act is illustrated by his use of carrots and sticks to overcome Prime Minister Margaret Thatcher's concerns about the centralization of power implied by the extension of the use of majority voting in the European Commission, which was also contained in the act. The carrot was an agreement on a permanent British rebate from the Community budget, which had been a major issue for Thatcher and on which Mitterrand made concessions against the interests of the powerful French agricultural lobby. Regarding the stick, Mitterrand and Kohl brought up the possibility of moving to a two-stage Europe in which some countries would be in an inner circle and others part of a fringe, with its implied threat to make the United Kingdom into a second-class member of the Community.

The Single European Act was seen as having a mixed impact on the future of monetary union. The text reinforced this goal by mentioning it in the preamble, and the commitment to allow the free movement of funds across the Community by the end of 1992 reduced the ability of members to pursue divergent monetary policies. On the other hand, the new rules required a unanimous vote for any changes to existing monetary arrangements. This gave Britain, a known skeptic of monetary union, veto power over any proposals for a single currency. It is to how UK skepticism and the Monetarist/Economist split were overcome in the Delors Committee that we now turn.

The Delors Committee

After the passage of the Single European Act, the French government refocused on making European monetary arrangements more symmetric. In particular, in early 1988 Prime Minister Balladur presented a memorandum to European finance ministers on the reform of the Exchange Rate Mechanism. In addition to rehashing old French concerns that weaker currencies were being forced to adjust even when they were not necessarily the source of any strains, the memorandum added a new twist by arguing that the liberalization of capital markets required a zone with a single currency, managed by a common central bank. The Balladur initiative created confusion in the German government. Hans-Dietrich Genscher, the "febrile" West German Foreign Minister, presented his own memorandum which emphasized the need for an independent European Central Bank pledged to price stability but without the traditional German emphasis on political and economic convergence.[20] Finance Minister Stoltenberg responded with a more traditional plan that focused on the need for political union, while the Bundesbank argued that any plans for a future monetary union be channeled through the central banks themselves via the Council of Governors. Faced with this range of advice, Chancellor Kohl bucked his advisors and chose to back French plans to look into the feasibility of a monetary union.

In early June 1988 at Evian on the shore of Lake Geneva, Kohl and Mitterrand agreed that a committee of experts was needed to set down a road map for monetary union.[21] The committee was duly proposed by Kohl at a European leaders meeting in Hanover later that month. The committee was to be composed mainly of central bankers, a necessary step to gain support from Prime Minister Thatcher as well as to avoid problems with the Bundesbank. Relatively late in the discussions, as agreed at Evian, Kohl successfully proposed that the Committee be chaired by Jacques Delors. This was a crucial step. All of a sudden, the new committee of experts would be under the stewardship of a powerful and strongly pro-monetary-union politician. Indeed, when he first heard about the chairman, President Pöhl of the Bundesbank wanted to refuse to join the proposed committee, a move which would have severely undermined its effectiveness. He asked his closest central banking counterpart, Wim Duisenberg of the Nederlandsche Bank, to do the same, but he was eventually persuaded by Duisenberg and others to participate.

The success of the Delors Committee in overcoming the headwinds to monetary union owed much to its design. All members worked in their own capacity, were not accompanied by any staff, and agreed not to quote each other.[22] In addition to its chairman, the Committee comprised the twelve Community central bank governors, four experts, and two staff (Tommaso Padoa-Schioppa, a past director of monetary affairs in the European Commission, and Gunter Baer, an official from the Bank for International Settlements). The staff positions were the most controversial, with Pöhl vetoing Delors' proposal that the second staff member be another ex-Commission employee and instead insisting on a German. Pöhl also unsuccessfully proposed adding a third, British, staff member, which would have further increased the number of monetary union skeptics in staff positions.

An important factor forging consensus on the report was that the central bank governors already met on a regular basis and hence were known quantities to each other. In addition, the three most important governors (De Larosière of the Banque de France, Leigh-Pemberton of the Bank of England, and Pöhl of the Bundesbank) took seriously the fact that they were working in their own capacity and deviated from the policies of their governments in crucial ways. Governors Jacques de Larosière and Leigh-Pemberton enlisted technical support from their central banks but kept a distance from their finance ministries. Both were also extremely polite and tactful. In particular, Leigh-Pemberton (who had been told by Thatcher "I have confidence in Karl Otto Pöhl. If he is proposing something, you can accept it.") helped to harness and constrain Pöhl.[23] Karl Otto Pöhl was a more difficult member of the Committee. He chose to work completely on his own, but his boast that he "played things by ear" did not always result in clear or consistent positions. One example of this was that, having got agreement in the Committee that the new central bank should be modeled after the Bundesbank, in a subsequent meeting he confused the discussion by switching his position and suggested that the US Federal Reserve system was a better blueprint. He also showed an element of disdain for the rest of the group, sometimes reading papers during meetings and at times leaving others to debate significant issues. This lack of consistency strengthened the position of the staff. In particular, Padoa-Schioppa, who was close to Delors, was able to drive the agenda.

The mixture of monetary union enthusiasts and skeptics made the Committee complicated to handle. To improve the chances of reaching consensus, it was made clear that the objective was to set out a possible path to economic and monetary union, not to adjudicate its value, so that "even skeptics in the Committee could believe they were achieving their goals by just spelling out precisely what monetary union would involve (and thus precisely showing how difficult it would be)".[24] The agenda was also formulated as questions coming from earlier initiatives—the Single European Act, the Exchange Rate Mechanism, and the European Currency Unit. This led to a less clear final paper, but avoided the radicalism that doomed the Werner Report.

The Committee's arrangements allowed agreement on two major sticking points in the Economist/Monetarist debate, the relationship of the central bank to political authorities and fiscal policy arrangements. On the former, the crucial moment was the decision by Governor de Larosière to support an independent central bank focused on price stability. Given the importance of this deviation from the typical French policy, he discussed this at a one-on-one meeting with President Mitterrand. According to his own account, he explained that

> if France wanted agreement with the Germans, we had to accept that monetary policy would be a single policy and that national central banks would be members of a system of central banks where all would have to be independent of governments. The European Central Bank would work only if its policies were not subject to negotiations between governments. . . . President Mitterrand did not answer specifically. . . . I said to myself 'I'm going to take that as giving me the green light.'[25]

With Governor de Larosière on board, the other central bank governors quickly agreed to an independent central bank. This was relatively easy as the necessary intermediate step of making the national central banks independent of the government gave them more power.

The discussion on the relationship of the central bank to fiscal policy became a debate on the relative merits of market discipline, mechanisms to promote coordination, and fiscal rules. The initial draft of the report proposed greater coordination through non-binding guidelines on fiscal deficits, on access to monetary financing, and on government borrowing in non-Community currencies. Later, these guidelines were to be overseen by a new institution, the Centre for Economic Policy Decisions (CEPD), which would promote convergence and coordination of economic policies in the Community. Following a new Treaty, legislative and executive measures leading to the creation of a European fiscal system of the type envisaged in the Werner Report were to be taken at the Community as well as the national level.[26] Alexandre Lamfalussy, the general manager of the Bank for International Settlements and one of the experts on the Committee, argued that a "Community-wide macroeconomic fiscal policy would be the natural complement to the common monetary policy of the Community".[27] Whatever its technical merits, such a change in the fiscal architecture and reduction in sovereignty would have created political tensions of the kind experienced in response to the Werner Report.

It was Pöhl who switched the plan from policy coordination to binding and relatively inflexible budget rules. He argued that coordination would be less effective than rules, so that a better approach would be if "all member states of the Community would commit themselves to a policy which would lead to inflation rates, let us say below 3% as an example, and to reduce their budget deficits to levels, let us say below 3% of GDP, very concrete steps which wouldn't need any institutional change but would be a very major step in the direction of a monetary and economic union".[28] It was thus the President of the Bundesbank who successfully championed the replacement of Community-wide coordination on fiscal and other economic issues, with its implication of further political integration—a hallmark of the federalist program that the Bundesbank and German government had traditionally championed, including in the Werner Report—with a decentralized fiscal system that maintained national sovereignty of the type supported by the French, albeit in return for accepting rules on fiscal deficits and debt.[29]

The only issue that the Committee could not agree on was whether or not to recommend the creation of a European Reserve Fund to pool reserve assets in Stage 2 of monetary union. In the end, this was left open. Other areas of contention—for example whether to move to a central bank in Stage 2 (de Larosière) or Stage 3 (Pöhl) and pressure to progressively weaken Stage 1 (Pöhl and Leigh-Pemberton) were generally resolved in favor of Pöhl. That said, the report was almost upset at the penultimate meeting of the Committee when (after a visit to the Bundesbank by Margaret

Thatcher) Pöhl came with thirty pages of "quite radical comments".[30] Wim Duisenberg—who was trusted by Pöhl as he saw him as a fellow skeptic of the single currency—produced a winning compromise by suggesting that the relevant Community bodies, the Monetary Committee and the Council of Governors, be invited to make concrete proposals on the basis of the existing report.

While the final report published in April 1989 claimed to be about economic and monetary union, it focused almost entirely on monetary union. Considerable space was given to economic integration, but the text was vague except in stating that no new institutions were needed as existing ones could be adapted. This was consistent with the principle of subsidiarity, namely that tasks should continue to be performed at the national level unless there were compelling reasons to change the architecture, and helped the plan gain political acceptance. On fiscal policies, for example, the text proposed rules to limit government deficits and debt but had only a vague discussion of greater cooperation. Equally crucially, bank supervision and support remained at the national level. Lofty and largely meaningless calls to better coordinate policies across countries were a hallmark of the discussion outside monetary issues, which otherwise largely repeated policies that had been previously agreed.

On monetary union, the text made clear that the final monetary union involved irrevocable parities and a new autonomous Community institution to run policy, but hedged on whether there would be a single currency (probably). The union was to be achieved through three stages. The first stage of the union involved little more than the adoption of narrow ERM bands by all countries and an enhanced role for the Committee of Governors in monetary policy decisions, including the creation of subcommittees on monetary, foreign exchange, and banking supervision (the last only in an advisory role since banking supervision was to remain a national responsibility). After agreeing on the needed revisions to the Treaty of Rome, stage 2 would provide a trial run for stage 3 as the new European System of Central Banks absorbed the European Monetary Cooperation Fund (which oversaw the ERM) and the Council of Governors. Finally, in stage 3 the System of Central Banks would take over control of monetary and exchange rate policy.

Few members of the Committee expected the Delors Report to have much impact. Pöhl described the Report as "a confused piece of work" and said that "when it was formulated, I did not think that monetary union with a European Central Bank could come about in the foreseeable future. I thought it might come in the next hundred years".[31] Leigh-Pemberton was also doubtful, saying in private that "most of us, when we signed the Report in May 1989, thought we would not hear much about it. It would be rather like the Werner Report." Even supporters of the process were cool. Tommaso Padoa-Schioppa, close to Delors and a key author, declined to write a paper on the report because he thought the outcome would not be significant. As one historian of the process has put it, "the outcome looked more like an extension of the principle of international monetary cooperation and coordination—which is exactly what it was".[32]

* * *

The Maastricht Treaty

It was the unanticipated collapse of Soviet control in Eastern Europe later in 1989 that triggered a rapid push for monetary union that embraced the only plan readily available, the one in the Delors Report. On November 28, 1989, just three weeks after the fall of the Berlin Wall, Chancellor Kohl presented a ten-point plan for German unity to the Bundestag without consulting his allies. Two days later, President Mitterrand told German Foreign Minister Hans-Dietrich Genscher that Germany was now a "brake" on European integration and that unless Germany agreed to serious nego- tiations on a single currency by the end of 1990 it risked a revival of the pre-1913 "triple alliance" between France, Britain, and the Soviet Union.[33] Faced with the prospect to diplomatic isolation, Chancellor Kohl agreed to initiate an intergovernmental conference on monetary union at the Strasbourg summit of European leaders on December 8, 1990, just before Mitterrand's deadline expired.

Chancellor Kohl clearly felt pushed into a rapid monetary union. He described the Strasbourg summit as the most "tense and unfriendly" he had ever attended.[34] Concern about the role of a unified Germany abounded. For example, Thatcher declared: "Twice we beat the Germans and now they are here again." In a bilateral meeting with Mitterrand she took out a map of German borders before and after World War II. Strikingly, Kohl confessed to the US Secretary of State James Baker that such a union "was against German interests. For example, the President of the Bundesbank is against this development. But the step is politically important for Germany needs friends." Germany accepted monetary union for political reasons, not economic ones.

Almost exactly a year later, a summit of Community leaders at Maastricht agreed on the Treaty on Economic Union. The Maastricht proceedings were closely choreographed by President Mitterrand and Prime Minister Andreotti of Italy.[35] In particular, the Treaty specified that economic and monetary union would take place by January 1999 for all countries that fulfilled the convergence criteria without any possible renegotiation of the rules. The only exception was the United Kingdom, which obtained a specific opt-out (later, Denmark also pulled out after a referendum rejected EMU). Prime Minister Thatcher had pushed for a more flexible opt-out option but was rebuffed so as to avoid any further delay or new demands from Germany, for example involving greater political integration. While this was an understandable ploy given German doubts about the speed of EMU, the feeling of being pushed into an excessively early monetary union explains German intransigence over reinterpreting the rules when Euro area went into crisis after 2008. In the end, the Maastricht Treaty did not solve Franco-German differences over monetary union, it merely papered over them.

In retrospect, Mitterrand's decision to use the centripetal intra-European political forces from German unification to achieve a binding treaty preserved monetary union from the centrifugal economic effects of German unification. German unification was always going to lead to some overheating of the German economy and pressure to revalue the Deutsche mark, implying inevitable strains across the ERM. These strains were exacerbated by the decision to convert East German Ostmarks to West German Deutsche marks at the inflated rate of one-to-one, as well as by larger-than-necessary pressures on German government spending coming from the decision to subsidize new capital investments rather than new jobs in the former East Germany. This led to an influx of plants with large amounts of machinery that benefited from subsidies but created few jobs for unemployed East Germans.

The Bundesbank responded to German economic overheating by raising interest rates aggressively, which left Germany's partners with the conundrum of how far to raise rates to defend the currency peg at the cost of slowing growth. The final outcome of these strains was a crisis in the Exchange Rate Mechanism that resulted in the ejection of the British pound and the Italian lira in 1992 (the lira rejoined in 1996) followed by a face-saving widening of the intervention bands from 2¼ percent to 15 percent to avoid French ejection in 1993. If the Maastricht Treaty had not been in place before the economic effects of German unification became apparent, it is difficult to imagine that the plan for monetary union would have survived.

Unsurprisingly given the haste involved, the Treaty closely followed the plan laid down in the Delors Report. It involved a highly independent central bank whose statutes were written by the Committee of Governors under the chairmanship of Bundesbank President Pöhl until his resignation in early 1991. In particular, the new central bank's Governing Council was made essentially immune from interference by national governments, in part by defining its objective as maintaining price stability with no responsibility for ensuring adequate growth. In addition, the new central bank was forbidden from providing monetary financing to member governments by directly buying their bonds. The Treaty also included a no-fiscal-bailout clause that specified that the debts of individual national governments were not the responsibility of the Community or of any other members of the currency union. Governments that got into fiscal difficulties were on their own, while remaining responsible for supporting their own banking systems.

The Treaty stipulated four convergence criteria that were needed for a country's entry into EMU: (1) the inflation rate should not be more than 1½ percentage points higher than the average of the three lowest inflation rates in the Community; (2) the long-term interest rate should be no more than 2 percentage points higher than the average of the three lowest members; (3) the members should have been part of the Exchange Rate Mechanism for two years before entering and the central parity should have not been devalued in that time; and (4) the fiscal deficit should be below 3 percent of output and the debt level below 60 percent of annual output, or should be approaching this value at a satisfactory pace.

Details on how to police the fiscal rules that aimed to ensure probity after entry into monetary union, which were delayed to Stage 2, brought further Franco-German disagreements. The German government proposed a system of large automatic fines for transgressors. However, the French proposal of a softer version involving the European Council was adopted at a difficult summit in December 1996. Tellingly, the agreement that had been initially proposed as simply a Stability Pact was renamed the Stability and Growth Pact, signaling the introduction of a wider view on the impact of such rules on economic activity.[36] This erosion of rigorous surveillance of the members of the Euro area was underlined in 2003 when, facing a recession, France and Germany backed by Italy suspended sanctions for fiscal deficits above 3 percent of output.

Gradually, the 3 percent fiscal deficit figure that had been originally seen as an upper limit for governments aiming for budget balance came to be seen as more like a target, as France, Germany, and Italy, under pressure from low growth and (in the case of Germany) the cost of unification, continued to run significant government deficits. The lack of support for rigorous surveillance is what allowed the Greek government in the 2000s to go on exactly the type of lending and spending binge based on the credibility of the Euro area as a whole that the Stability and Growth Pact was supposed to protect against.

A similar "pragmatism" and acceptance of modest rule-bending was evident in 1998 when it came time to choosing which countries could enter the monetary union. Both Germany and France preferred a wide union although for somewhat different reasons—the French in order to dilute the influence of German on the union, the Germans to avoid stiffer competition from those who did not enter. An additional complication was the desire to include Belgium, which had a debt ratio of 130 percent of output, which undermined the case for rejecting Italy, whose debt ratio was 120 percent. In the end, supported by a range of special measures and generous statistical interpretations, all of the potential entrants were admitted into monetary union starting on January 1, 1999.

* * *

The Flawed Single Currency

The drive to create a single European currency unexpectedly succeeded largely due to a dose of sheer luck and two underlying dynamics. The good luck was the unexpected fall of the Berlin Wall that created a need to bind a unified Germany more fully to the rest of the European Union, an imperative used to create the single currency. One dynamic was the understanding between Mitterrand and Kohl on the need for progress on greater European monetary integration that allowed crucial decisions to be made without the process getting bogged down in bureaucratic niceties. The other dynamic was that the detailed planning for the single currency was done by technocratic central banks rather than more politicized finance ministries, which allowed the plan to overcome the Economist/Monetarist split that had bedeviled previous efforts to create a single currency.

Part of the reason that the flaws in the Maastricht Treaty were missed was that neither of the two major drivers, Mitterrand and Kohl, were comfortable with, or interested in, economics. This is in stark contrast to their predecessors, Giscard d'Estaing and Schmidt. Schmidt said of Mitterrand "we were able to cooperate personally and politically, [but] in economic and *particularly in monetary matters*, Mitterrand didn't have great knowledge or judgment" (emphasis added), while Giscard said that Mitterrand was "not very interested in monetary or financial affairs".[37]

Similarly, Kohl's grasp of economics was weak, as shown by decisions over German unification such as supporting the former East Germany through subsidies to investment, when the objective was to encourage jobs.

The outcome of this tortuous process was an early but extremely narrow and compartmentalized monetary union. With political decisions tending to ensure agreement at the lowest common denominator, the monetary union made much more political than economic sense. In particular, it provided no effective macroeconomic support in respond to large shocks to the finances of individual members. The central bank was prohibited from supporting governments; fiscal policy was almost entirely national; and so was banking supervision and support. In the final analysis, the French and Germans fought each other to a bloody draw. The Germans obtained an independent central bank that was prohibited from bailing out countries in fiscal difficulties, a no-bailout clause for other members of the union, and strict rules on fiscal deficits—provisions that only made sense in an area that was already highly economically integrated. The French, on the other hand, achieved an early monetary union in a region with limited economic integration.

Rather than the old adage "hope for the best but plan for the worst", economic and monetary union could be characterized as "hope for the best and plan for the best". The Maastricht Treaty essentially plonked a single currency and an independent European Central Bank into the middle of a region where almost all other economic decisions were national. In addition, plans for tough rules on member states' deficits and debts were largely undermined by the absence of serious surveillance on members' behavior, which subsequently allowed the Greek government to easily circumvent them. When the Euro area crisis came, the lack of an effective backstop for member governments put the entire Euro area project at risk through a self-reinforcing cycle in which questions about the viability of banks increased fiscal strains even as questions about fiscal solvency increased strains on banks.

Understanding the process by which this flawed union came about is important for the future as it explains why it continues to be so difficult to change the structure laid down in the Maastricht Treaty. The underlying tension between the Germans and the French was never resolved. As the country with the soundest economy and finances as well as a federal system backed by binding rules, the Germans naturally revert to the view that monetary union should work without the need for new mechanisms to share risk, consistent with their view that such a union should have only occurred after adequate economic integration. Countries that got into crisis did so by breaking the rules, so that offering them bailouts would only encourage further bad behavior. The French and other weaker currency economies with their tradition of a powerful, flexible central government maintain the view that bailouts of crisis countries are needed to limit the macroeconomic damage to the Euro area as a whole.

Given these different starting positions and the associated suspicions, it is unsurprising that there is little appetite for a major renegotiation of the Maastricht Treaty. Indeed, even changes that were envisaged by the Treaty, such as the potential need for centralized supervision of banks, took a long time to agree even after the crisis. Moving forward, the underlying tensions are unlikely to be solved by technicians, as occurred within the Delors Committee, since views on the future of EMU are highly politicized. More generally, in the absence of a priority as compelling as the need to create a single currency to bind a unified Germany to the rest of western Europe, it is difficult to see any Euro area leader being prepared to accept changes to EMU that are not in their economic interest, as Chancellor Kohl believed he did at the 1990 Strasbourg summit that set the EMU process in motion.

Combining an early move to monetary union with an independent central bank and decentralized fiscal arrangements was always going to be tricky. While such an arrangement would work smoothly in a boom, in the absence of rapid economic integration it was always going to be tested by the limited ability to provide macroeconomic support to countries in a slump. It was efficient but not robust. The North Atlantic crisis came close to splitting the monetary union so painstakingly assembled over the late 1980s and 1990s. The crisis led to an improvement in the institutional framework, but the crucial test for EMU going forward will be the ability to deliver the rapid economic integration predicted by the French, so as to create an integrated monetary union of the type envisioned by the Germans. This subject is left to a later chapter.

Chapter 5

INTELLECTUAL BLINKERS AND UNEXPECTED SPILLOVERS

The 2008–12 North Atlantic financial crisis was so destructive in part because it was so unexpected, and hence the recipients were unprepared to absorb the blow. In early 2008, most economists and policymakers still felt that the excesses becoming apparent in US subprime mortgages were a minor financial hiccup that would soon be overcome. A few months later, when the extent of the problems in US financial markets became apparent after the rescue of the investment bank Bear Stearns, European policymakers remained confident that the fallout would be limited to the United States. This erroneous belief that the two regions were not closely linked was tellingly illustrated when the European Central Bank (ECB) hiked rates in July 2008 on fears of rising inflation, consciously moving in the opposite direction to the easing by the US Federal Reserve on concerns over decelerating output. The ECB was in for a rude awakening.

This lack of preparation mattered as policymakers faced unexpected challenges, resulting in responses that were improvised, piecemeal, and included a good number of mistakes. In the United States, this included the fateful decision to allow the US investment bank Lehman Brothers to go bankrupt despite the fact that it stood outside of the procedures to limit the resulting financial fallout available to insolvent regulated banks. It was the chaos from the sudden closing of Lehman Brothers that led to a generalized market panic. In the Euro area, the lack of preparation for a crisis was evident in the rules that severely limited the support that could be given to troubled banks or governments. The absence of such support led to destructive cycles in which questions about the solvency of banks strained government finances even as questions about government finances put pressure on banks. The resulting upward cycle in borrowing costs almost destroyed the currency union.

Why did nearly all policymakers and economists miss the warning the signals of a future financial crisis?[1] The answer lay in the growing belief that financial and economic shocks were limited in scope and temporary in nature, supported by a view that, even in the unlikely event that there was a large shock, astute policy responses would be able to contain the resulting economic fallout. Three separately derived beliefs—the efficient markets hypothesis, the great moderation, and benign neglect—intertwined to create the intellectual blind spots that led policymakers to the Panglossian belief that the unsustainable boom of the early 2000s was a new normal that reflected a permanent improvement in economic understanding, information, and policies.

The outcome was that central banks, finance ministries, and other key economic institutions became increasingly inward–looking. An outsized belief in the self-healing properties of the economy led policymakers to create a system that appeared efficient but was not robust. There is a reason that human beings have the failsafe of a second kidney despite the fact that one is sufficient most of the time. If one kidney fails, then the second one can function on its own. The intellectual overconfidence that preceded the North Atlantic crisis led to a fragile system that was incapable of responding effectively to the shock waves generated by the bankruptcy of a second-order US investment bank. The North Atlantic lacked a second kidney when the first one failed.

* * *

How The Efficient Markets Hypothesis undermined Bank Regulation

The efficient markets hypothesis is a powerful concept that caused policymakers to underestimate financial risks. Economic theories are valuable because they bring clarity to a complex world, allowing people to organize and make sense of incoming information. However, if they result in overly simplified mental structures then major mistakes can be made. The efficient markets hypothesis lulled economists and policymakers into thinking that financial markets were self-correcting and hence unlikely to be an independent source of major economic disruption despite a plethora of historical evidence to the contrary.[2] It was the victory of a convenient theory over historical experience.

The efficient market hypothesis essentially states that financial prices aggregate all available information, and hence that there is no investment strategy that can consistently beat the market. Put differently, if it is known to investors that (say) shares in General Motors are undervalued and will go up soon, then investors will bid up the price immediately until it reaches this fair value. While the theory and its tests come in softer and harder forms, the idea is that no individual investor or policy institution can beat the wisdom of crowds. This has implications for short- and long-term behavior. The short-term prediction is that day-to-day movements in prices of stocks and bonds are unpredictable except to the extent that they reflect new information. Clearly, if General Motors announces profits that are higher than investors expect then the price of its shares will increase. However, it is equally likely that the profit announcement will disappoint and shares will go down. Hence, *before* the announcement, the direction of the share price is unpredictable—it is as likely to rise as to fall.

This is often called the random walk theory, as the same properties are exhibited by a random walk in which, while taking a step forward, a person—usually assumed to be drunk—is as likely to also lurch to the left as to the right. Because the left-right movement is unpredictable, the best guess as to where the drunk will be at the next step is straight ahead. While there are some modest deviations from the prediction that markets are as likely to surprise on the upside as on the downside, as a whole it stands up pretty well. For example, it is extremely difficult to find mutual funds that consistently beat the short-term returns seen in the overall market. Asset prices do indeed seem to be essentially unpredictable from day-to-day and month-to-month.

The more powerful and controversial element of the efficient markets hypothesis is the prediction that markets also accurately foretell asset values over longer periods. This implies that the market is essentially omnipotent, in that not only is the price of General Motors unpredictable tomorrow and next week but that it is unpredictable at any point in the future. There is no point in trying to outguess the market as prices reflect all of the available information about General Motors. The share price in the middle of a recession, when investors seem to have lost heart and General Motors appears cheaply valued on measures such as the ratio of the price of a share to profits, is actually an accurate assessment of the current situation. A more sophisticated version of this argument, used before the crisis by the US Federal Reserve, was that market valuations can on occasion deviate from their long-term fundamentals, but that such outliers are so difficult to iden-tify that it is best to assume financial markets are always right.

The view that markets are good predictors of the future rests on the assumption that economists commonly make that the likelihood of different future paths for the economy can be calculated. In other words, that investors can assess what is likely to happen. By contrast, at least one well-known academic and policy maker—Mervyn King, the former governor of the Bank of England—has persuasively argued that in the face of "unknown unknowns" the future may not be calculable because of the uncertainty is fundamental and does not have well defined probabilities.[3] For example, even fifteen year ago it may have been impossible to foresee the changes to our lives coming from smart phones, so that it would have been impossible to "predict" the future that actually transpired. In this world, rather than trying to calculate the most likely future, investors may rationally lock into (relatively) synchronized narratives about the path of the economy that can remain stable for long periods but can also change rapidly in the face of unanticipated events. Such narratives have many similarities to Keynes's famous likening of the stock market to a game in which contestants try to guess which female image most other contestants will pick as the most attractive. From the point of view of the efficient markets hypothesis, the important implication is that investors cannot be omnipotent since it is (literally) impossible to accurately assess the future.

In the run-up to the crisis, the conviction that market prices were (almost) always right even in the long-run led to a gradual downgrading of the importance of financial risks and regulation. As financial markets became more sophisticated and complex, it became common to assume that they were also becoming better at assessing risks. This attitude led the US Federal Reserve to believe that investors were better at monitoring the risks being taken by investment banks than were government regulators. As Alan Greenspan stated in his memoirs (sent to press in mid-2007 just before the financial warning signs started to appear): "Markets have become too huge, complex, and fast-moving to be subject to twentieth-century regulation . . . oversight of these transactions is essentially by means of individual-market-participant counterparty surveillance."[4] This view led to the disastrous 1996 decision by the Basel Committee to allow banks to use their own internal risk models to calculate the capital buffers required to offset risks in investment banking. It was also a powerful factor in the decision by the United Kingdom and Ireland to adopt light–touch regulation. If financial market prices could not be usefully questioned, then regulation is not needed.

The mental block on the risks posed by financial markets was also a property of the economic models used by policymakers. Financial markets are messy, different across countries, and ever-changing in focus, making them unsuitable candidates for universal models. By contrast, the macro-economic models that were used to assess policies, while incorporating complex assumptions about the behavior of consumers and producers, almost uniformly exhibited extremely basic financial sectors which used simplifying assumptions such as that all financial assets were perfect substitutes for each other. They also embodied the efficient markets hypothesis, in that all changes in asset prices reflected "rational expectations" of the future.

The result was that policymakers failed to focus on the consequences of the huge expansion of financial activity and private debt over the 2000s. Financial regulation was focused on ensuring that individual institutions were sound (called micro-prudential regulation) with little regard for risks to the system as a whole. Easy financing conditions were seen as a result of changes in the behavior of households and producers, and the role of lax regulation in the expansion of bank lending was largely ignored. This lack of attention to financial regulation and risks associated with bank leverage also manifested in an uncritical belief in the benefits of free international capital flows, so that the rapid expansion of core European banks into the United States and the Euro area periphery was seen as a benign development. Over the North Atlantic crisis, the losses inflicted on poorly capitalized core European banks and their withdrawal from the US and Euro area periphery amplified and internationalized the initial shock. This important intellectual dynamic is discussed in more detail in the next chapter.

The strong belief in the efficient markets hypothesis by macroeconomics was particularly striking as it was out of step with the concurrent trends in financial economics. Within academic finance, models of asset pricing based only on efficient markets had been found wanting. Empirical work had increasingly added variables that reflected market inefficiencies, such as the observation that smaller and relatively less liquid firms attracted higher returns. More generally, skeptics of the efficient markets hypothesis such as Professor Robert Shiller of Yale University argued that consistently following simple strategies such as investing in firms with low share prices compared to their earnings could achieve long-term returns modestly above the average without taking on more risk (the trading philosophy used by Warren Buffett). Against this, however, was always the rejoinder that this could be a statistical fluke and that if such models worked then why was the proponent not rich?

The lack of attention to financial risks was also out of step with the historical role played by central banks. While the original central banks, for example the Bank of England and the Banque de France, had initially been set up to handle government finances, by the latter half of the nineteenth century it had become clear that there was also a need for the central bank to maintain financial stability. Walter Bagehot, the celebrated editor of *The Economist* magazine and father of modern central banking, wrote after the 1866 financial crisis in England that the Bank of England held, should hold, and should be responsible for holding "the sole banking reserve of the country".[5] In 1890, when Baring Brothers was threatened with collapse, the Bank of England organized a rescue in the form of a guarantee fund to which more than £17 million was pledged, mostly from other banks. This demonstrated the responsibility the Bank of England had come to feel for the stability of the banking system. The link to financial stability was even clearer for the Federal Reserve, which was formed in 1913 in large part as a response to the financial panic of 1907, whose widespread economic losses would have been worse but for a personal intervention by John Pierpont Morgan that stabilized markets. Indeed, it is symptomatic of the importance of financial instability in nineteenth-century economics that the common name for what is now called recessions was panics.

The role of the central bank in supporting financial markets was codified in the phrase "lender of last resort". It gradually became common practice for central banks to lend at a penalty rate to private banks that were unable to secure funding elsewhere to provide breathing room to arrange more organized support. If needed, the central bank would act as a last port of call. In the pre-crisis boom, such facilities covered most of the financial sector in bank-dominated Europe. In the United States, by contrast, it only covered regulated banks that accepted federally insured deposits. Importantly, it did not cover the independent investment banks and rest of the shadow banking system that grew rapidly in the 1990s and 2000s. This explains why a financial institution of the size and centrality of Lehman Brothers was not able to use the bankruptcy proceedings for regulated banks that allowed insolvent institutions to function for a while in order to limit the financial shock waves from an unexpected cessation of activity. It was the sudden disruption in markets following the abrupt closure of Lehman Brothers that sparked a global market panic.

The belief in the efficient markets hypothesis also led to an underestimation of the risks from the pre-crisis rapid economic and financial expansion in the Euro area periphery. Once the members of the Euro area had been agreed, the borrowing rates of the member governments converged downwards towards those of Germany. For example, at the time of the introduction of the Euro in January 1999, the Portuguese government was borrowing for ten years at an interest rate of 3.9 percent compared to 3.7 percent for the German government. Three years earlier, well after the Maastricht Treaty had been signed but before the members of the currency union were known, the gap had been over 3 percentage points. A similar process happened with Italy and Spain, as well as Greece when she joined the Euro area in 2001.

The lending boom that accompanied these dramatically lower borrowing costs was ascribed to economic convergence within the monetary union. Economic convergence is the process by which incomes in poorer countries catch up with those in richer ones. This occurs because poor countries have less capital—machines and the like—per worker, so that the benefit of adding an extra machine is greater in a poorer country than in a richer one. This higher return means that the poor country is able to attract more investment, which allows its income to gradually converge to that of the richer country. The general view at the time was that this process had been accelerated by the introduction of the Euro, as the single currency had made it easier and cheaper for less wealthy members of the monetary union to borrow from their richer brethren.

Careful analysts were aware of some of the oddities of the Euro area convergence process but viewed them as self-correcting.[6] For example, the additional borrowing was often used to buy houses rather than machines, so that productivity was not improving in the periphery despite more borrowing. In addition, higher inflation in the periphery was eroding the competitiveness of the exports needed to service the costs of higher foreign debt. However, none of these warning signs were seen as particularly urgent. The Euro area was viewed as a success in which lower borrowing costs and deeper financial markets had allowed greater investment by the periphery that would generate gradual convergence. In fact, little or no fundamental convergence seems to have been achieved over the boom of the 2000s.

In sum, the efficient markets hypothesis reinforced the view that financial markets were largely self-regulating, blinding policymakers to the importance of careful financial market supervision. If asset prices were always correctly priced, then there was no need for such oversight. This point of view, for example, led the Federal Reserve to advocate using internal models to calculate risk buffers, to leave the US investment banks under the light supervision of the Securities and Exchange Commission, and to soft-pedal consumer protection for mortgage borrowers. More generally, the result was that policymakers on both sides of the Atlantic missed the growing financial and economic imbalances, including in the Euro area periphery. As a result, they had to scramble to provide adequate support to the financial sector when the crisis hit. Similar blinkers were leading to an underestimation of macroeconomic risks, but through a different process.

* * *

The Great Moderation and Overestimation of Monetary Policy's Effectiveness

If the efficient markets hypothesis was a theory, the "great moderation" was an observation. More precisely, the phrase the great moderation came from the observation that the volatility of US output had fallen markedly after the mid-1980s.[7] This shift is sufficiently large and rapid that it stands out clearly in a graph as growth becomes noticeably less jagged after 1985 (Figure 40). What was (and remains) so striking is the speed with which growth shifted from high- to low-volatility. The instability of 1960–85 suddenly switches to relative stability. Formal tests across a range of measures confirmed the impression that that there was a sudden improvement in economic stability. By contrast, there was no noticeable increase in growth, explaining why this observation is dubbed the "great moderation" rather than (say) "the great acceleration". It was the inferences from the great moderation that led to policy makers to overestimate their ability to response to macroeconomic shocks.

More stable output implied a smoother business cycle, the regular process by which extended periods of economic expansion are interrupted

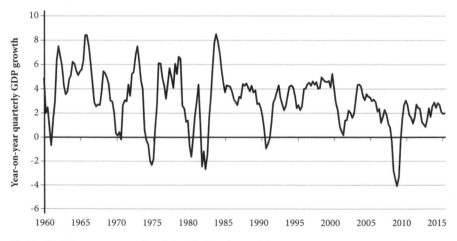

Figure 40: US output growth stabilized after the mid-1980s.
Source: US National Accounts.

by short recessions in which output drops. As growth became less volatile, it became less likely that the severe shocks required to create a recession would occur. Similarly, even if a recession did occur it was likely to be shallow. Indeed, these predictions appeared to be coming true. In the twenty years from 1985 to 2005 the US experienced two mild recessions, in comparison to the four generally deeper recessions in the previous twenty years.

As the reality of lower volatility came to be accepted, the debate moved to explaining this moderation. Three main explanations were put forward: structural changes in the US economy, good luck, or better monetary policy. Investigators generally placed some weight on structural changes coming from the adoption of "just in time" delivery as a result of the information technology revolution. The timing worked, as such techniques were introduced in the early 1980s. In addition, the fall in output volatility was accompanied by a reduction in the variability of production relative to sales, consistent with the view that firms were able to use technology to better synchronize production with the demand for their goods. By contrast, the role of the switch toward production of less volatile services (think restaurant meals versus cars) and deeper financial markets that made it easier for firms to ride out bad times by borrowing, were generally discounted. These were gradual trends, so why did output volatility fall so rapidly in the mid-1980s? In addition, the fall in volatility included sectors that would not have benefited from either trend.[8]

Good fortune was also acknowledged to play a role. Analysis indicated that most of the reduction in output volatility came from smaller shocks rather than from changes in behavior over the business cycle. Further support for the role of good luck came from the observation that the reduction in output variability seemed to occur equally over the short-, medium-, and long-run. This was what would be expected if good luck was the driving force, as the effects would be uniform regardless of the length of the interval being examined.[9]

As time went on, however, it became conventional wisdom to attribute the bulk of the great moderation to better monetary policy.[10] The timing worked as the rapid reduction of US output volatility occurred soon after Paul Volcker was appointed Chairman of the Federal Reserve and abruptly diverged from the relaxed approach to inflation taken by the Federal Reserve in the 1970s. More generally, the synchronous fall in inflation and output volatility occurred at different times in different countries. Since tighter monetary policy was the driver of lower inflation, this provided strong evidence for a causal link between tighter monetary policy and the great moderation. In response to the observation that there was no change in behavior over the business cycle, proponents of the tighter monetary policy explanation argued that the earlier work looking at the business cycle had not included measures of inflation expectations. They argued that it was the anticipation of low and stable future inflation that was the main conduit through which tighter monetary policy had lowered inflation and reduced output fluctuations.

Under this view the surprise was less that a different monetary policy altered the business cycle, but that it could simultaneously improve outcomes for growth and inflation. It was already well established that the conduct of monetary policy could affect the business cycle. Indeed, a growing body of evidence measured how much the Federal Reserve and other central banks hiked or lowered policy rates in response to higher or lower inflation and growth. The associated theories concluded that if a central bank focused on reducing inflation volatility then this would be offset by an increase in output volatility.

The concurrent improvement in growth and inflation variability over the great moderation was ascribed to the fact that earlier monetary policies had been fundamentally flawed. In the 1970s, central banks had made the mistake of ignoring the impact of changes in expectations of future inflation on wages.[11] As a result, the Federal Reserve and other central banks had reacted weakly to increases in inflation as they believed that they could permanently run a hotter economy with higher inflation and lower unemployment. In reality, however, this had proved to be a chimera as it assumed that workers' expectations of future inflation remained unchanged. As inflation rose during the 1970s, however, workers anticipated that inflation would remain high and upped their pay demands beyond what the Federal Reserve predicted. The Federal Reserve thus presided over an upward spiral in wages and prices. When Paul Volcker took over the helm of the Fed in the early 1980s, his strong anti-inflationary stance had broken this spiral as workers realized that inflation would start to fall back to previous levels.

The lesson that policymakers took from this experience was to be skeptical of apparently stable empirical relationships, such as the trade-off between inflation and output that the Federal Reserve had tried to exploit. This was because such "reduced form" relationships that relied on data rather than on economic theory might change unexpectedly since they embedded implicit assumptions such as that inflation expectations were stable. This observation, made forcefully by Robert E. Lucas in 1988 and hence dubbed the Lucas critique, put the onus on developing more complex models in which relationships between (say) a household's income and its spending were identified through sound theoretical models where households sought as much satisfaction as possible for a given income stream.

The resulting "dynamic stochastic general equilibrium models" (mercifully dubbed DSGE models for short) became an increasingly important part of how academics and more academically inclined policymakers thought about the economy. The models were, and remain, an impressive intellectual feat that combine deep theory with empirical evidence to create workable models of the economy. While more traditional empirical models based on estimated relationships with less theoretical support continued to be used, the smaller DSGE models were increasingly the preferred choice for policy analysis in the United States and Europe. The increased sophistication of the theory-based models led to a growing view that monetary policy was becoming more scientific, characterized by predictable responses to changes in inflation and economic slack that stabilized current activity by providing confidence that the economy would remain on an even keel. This is not to say that central bank committees literally used these models or the mechanical rules that they assumed policymakers followed. Rather, predictability and consistency were seen as increasingly important virtues for monetary policy.

The dark side of DSGE models, however, was that they tended to make policymakers complacent about risks to the stability of the economy. This partly reflected the limitations required to put together so many parts of theory—on the behavior of households, firms, financial markets, and governments—into a single model. Tractability often required specific behavioral assumptions to make the edifice work. More basically, however, these models almost uniformly assumed that households and firms were extremely far-sighted. They not only peered into the future, they peered into the far, far future. So, for example, most DSGE models assumed that tax cuts that boosted take home pay would not result in higher spending because lower taxes today would have to be paid for by higher taxes in the future. Understanding this, individuals choose to save the entire tax windfall in order to have the money to pay higher future taxes. This hyper-rational response, which assumed that everyone in the model understood how the economy worked, how policymakers reacted, and hence could rationally predict where the economy was headed in the future, was clearly out of step with reality. As discussed in the section on the efficient markets hypothesis, it is not clear that in a world of "unknown unknowns" such a predictable future even exists. If it does not, then the DSGE apparatus may be built on quicksand as people decide to use rules of thumb to navigate a complex and unpredictable world.

The flip side to the assumption that far-sightedness made tax cuts ineffective was that it made monetary policy extremely powerful. Monetary policy changes that were anticipated to occur even several years in the future fed back strongly onto current spending and activity. The implication was that as long as the central bank promised to respond gradually and sensibly to developments, it was extremely difficult to generate large booms or recessions even in the face of major shocks. A specific example in which a relatively standard DSGE model was used to analyze the impact of the Euro area crisis may help illustrate this point.[12] In the model, the promise of easy future monetary policy created a sufficiently robust recovery that the European Central Bank started raising its policy rate above zero after a year or so. At the time that this paper was written, the ECB had kept policy rates at zero for six years. The stark contrast between the robust recovery in the simulation and the slow one in reality illustrates how DSGE models helped to mislead monetary policymakers into thinking that they had more influence over the economy than they actually did.

This belief in the efficacy of monetary policy was reinforced by the limited economic costs of the collapse of the technology bubble in global stock markets in 2001. The US Federal Reserve, in particular, ascribed the limited impact on the US economy to its swift monetary response. Consequently, rather than viewing the collapse in prices of overvalued equities as a warning sign of the risks from financial instability, the Fed came to believe that financial risks were limited. To quote from a speech given by vice-chair Kohn in 2006:

> The health of the US financial system remained solid after the collapse of the high-tech boom ... Moreover, the financial sectors of most other developed economies also weathered the worldwide drop in corporate equity values fairly well ... I do agree that market corrections can have profoundly adverse consequences if they lead to deflation ... but it does not follow that conventional monetary policy cannot adequately deal with the threat of deflation by *expeditiously mopping up after the bubble collapses* (emphasis added, double negative in the original).[13]

Symptomatic of this overconfidence in the effectiveness of monetary policy was the Fed's attitude to the boom in house prices. In early 2006, in response to an article by the European Central Bank (ECB) suggesting that there were benefits from monetary policy responding aggressively to perceived house price bubbles, vice-chairman Kohn presented an extremely high bar for any additional monetary policy response to financial risks over and above the impact on inflation:

> To wrap up this critique, I summarize as follows: If we can identify bubbles quickly and accurately, are reasonably confident that a tighter monetary policy would materially check their expansion, and believe that severe market corrections have significant non-linear adverse effects on the economy, then extra action may well be merited. *But if even one of these tough conditions is not met*, then extra action would lead to worse macroeconomic performance over time than that achievable with conventional policies that deal expeditiously with the effects of unwinding bubbles when they occur (emphasis added).[14]

The message was clear. The Fed thought that it could cope with a major downturn in house prices on its own and without the need to respond preemptively to potential bubbles.

The North Atlantic crisis demonstrated that this assessment was wrong. The limited impact of the collapse of the tech bubble in 2001 reflected the nature of the financial shock rather than the relative sophistication of financial markets. In the global tech bubble investors mainly bought shares with their own money so that, while painful, the resulting losses could be absorbed by the buyers. Things got much more complicated in 2008 because home buyers had typically only put down a small part of the purchase price of the house and borrowed the remainder using a bank mortgage. This "leverage", where initial seed money (or, on occasion, no such money) was augmented by bank loans meant that if the borrower was unable to pay the loan, the problems cascaded back to the bank. The knock-on effects of leverage to undercapitalized banks amplified and widened the losses from the housing collapse to the entire North Atlantic economy.

A second feature of DSGE models that led policymakers astray was that they assumed that excess spending would be reflected in inflation and slack. For all of the complexities of the DSGE models, the regular waxing and waning of spending and activity over the business cycle was basically ascribed to the slow response of inflation to changes in economic slack. As a result, all that was needed to stabilize activity was for monetary policy to respond in an appropriate manner to changes in current and future inflation.

Unfortunately, the imbalances that were building up in the United States and the Euro area periphery over the 2000s were not seen primarily in inflation. The booms primarily involved excessive borrowing, much of which was used to buy houses. The resulting increase in house prices, however, had little impact on the measures of consumer price inflation that the central banks focused on. In the United States, the consumer price index used rents rather than new house prices to estimate the cost of housing as this is (correctly) seen as more direct measure of the price of shelter. As rents did not take off in the same way that house prices did, the impact of the housing bubble on consumer price inflation was muted. In the European Union, house prices had no direct impact on consumer price inflation as, in the absence of a uniform way of measuring dwelling costs across the member countries, the consumer price index used by the ECB excluded any measure of housing costs. In addition, much of the additional spending on goods was satisfied by higher imports. This manifested itself in rapid increases in trade deficits rather than in higher domestic inflation. Central banks underestimated risks from the growing financial imbalances because they were focusing on inflation and slack rather that financial imbalances due to excess borrowing. They were looking under the wrong lamppost.

As a result of this intellectual myopia, policymakers were forced to improvise when activity remained in the doldrums in the wake of the North Atlantic crisis even after monetary policy rates had been lowered to zero. The great moderation convinced central banks that they could stabilize the economy on their own. As a result, macroeconomics largely devolved into the analysis of conventional monetary policy, while the analysis of fiscal, financial, and structural policies, as well as unconventional monetary policies, were given much less attention as they came well down the academic and policy totem pole. Monetary analysis begat more monetary analysis, to the detriment of a wider view of macroeconomics. When the crisis came, this framework proved wanting, a deficiency compounded by a loss of interest in international policy cooperation.

* * *

How Benign Neglect Undermined International Policy Cooperation

While the efficient markets hypothesis was a theory and the great moderation was an observation, benign neglect illustrated yet another way to get things completely wrong, namely a framework. Benign neglect was not a phrase initially coined by economists, in contrast to the efficient markets hypothesis and the great moderation. It was first used in a January 1970 memo from Senator Daniel Patrick Moynihan to President Richard Nixon when Moynihan was serving as Nixon's Councilor for Urban Affairs.

It reflected a rejection of the free-spending approach of the Great Society program as a way of solving US racial problems. In Moynihan's somewhat cynical view, what was needed was an organic progress without rhetoric.

In the realm of international economics, benign neglect refers to the view that countries should look after their own internal affairs and that the benefits from cooperating with other countries are too small to be worth the trouble. In particular, exchange rates across countries and resulting trade balances are better determined by private markets. In many ways, it is an extension of Adam Smith's insight that markets and competition can create an efficient economy, but extended to countries rather than individuals. It had its intellectual roots in the resurgent belief in market economics in the 1980s associated with President Reagan and Prime Minister Thatcher.

Benign neglect represented a major shift from the thinking of the earlier postwar period. With the memory of the international instability of the 1930s Great Depression in mind, economic cooperation and the avoidance of negative spillovers from exchange rate devaluations was central to the design of the Bretton Woods exchange rate system. In this system, described in more detail in the next chapter, countries kept their exchange rates fixed against the US dollar, which itself was fixed against gold and (at least in theory) any changes in parity against the dollar needed to be discussed with the international community via the International Monetary Fund.

The system was supported by an intellectual framework in which countries could use a combination of fiscal and monetary policy to achieve full employment and a desirable trade balance. The key insight was that, in response to excess economic slack, either a looser monetary policy or a larger government deficit could be used to achieve full employment ("internal balance"), but that the two policies had contrasting effects on the trade balance. Cutting short-term interest rates to stimulate activity via monetary policy would tend to lower the exchange rate, increase exports, and create a larger trade surplus. By contrast, running a larger government deficit for the same purpose would raise interest rates, appreciate the exchange rate, reduce exports, and lower the trade balance. A judicious use of the two instruments allowed policymakers to keep the domestic economy in sync while also achieving a desired trade balance. The two macroeconomic policies (monetary and fiscal) could combine to achieve the two objectives (full employment and a desirable trade balance).

Support for this integrated policy framework started to fray soon after the break-up of the Bretton Woods system in the early 1970s as belief in the active use of fiscal policy waned. This came in large part from a backlash against the increased size of government and rapid rise in government debt in the 1960s and 1970s. The focus of fiscal policymakers switched from fine-tuning the government deficit so as to achieve full employment to longer-term objectives such as reducing the size of government and the associated tax bill. This was accompanied by a revival of the "Ricardian equivalence" hypothesis in economics, which held the view that if people could lend and borrow easily, tax cuts or hikes had small effects on spending as households and firms would simply save the money from (say) a tax cut to pay the resulting higher future taxes. As discussed earlier, this type of thinking was embodied in DSGE models.

Questions about the efficacy of fiscal stimulus was accompanied by an erosion in the belief that policymakers needed to worry about the trade balance. Coming immediately after the financial turmoil of the 1930s, the Bretton Woods system had been sympathetic to government-imposed constraints on the transfer of money across borders. As time went on, however, these constraints started to be lifted and money flowed more freely, particularly across rich and financially advanced economies. More open international financial flows made it easier for countries to borrow to finance trade deficits and lend the money required to maintain trade surpluses. As access to international markets became more routine, concerns about the risks from trade deficits began to wither. In particular, the growing US trade deficit remained easily financed.

Another element driving the popularity of "benign neglect" was the growing conviction that spillovers between countries were small. The limited role of financial shocks in policy models left trade as the main economic link across economies. Trade is a substantial part of economic activity—in the Euro area, for example, exports and imports each comprise almost 40 percent of output, although it is a more modest 15 percent in the United States. Even in Europe, however, apart from some specific close trade relationships (such as Dutch exports to Germany), trade between any given pair of countries is much smaller. For example, even if exports to another country comprise a hefty 5 percent of output, a fall in activity in the foreign country would only cause a domestic output loss of some 5 cents in the dollar. This is not large enough to transmit significant shocks, which weakened the perceived need for messy and complex international negotiations.

The lack of attention to financial market spillovers left many of the risks to the international system undiagnosed. For example, financial globalization was seen as beneficially linking international borrowers and lenders rather than creating potentially dangerous financial booms and busts across countries. As a result, policymakers in the Euro area core spent little time worrying about the rapid increase in international exposures of their large banks. The lack of attention to financial spillovers also explains why the European Central Bank decided that it could safely ignore the growing problems in US financial markets and hike rates in July 2008.

Benign neglect gained in popularity even though an initial experiment by the Reagan Administration had to be reversed. Soon after the 1980 election, the new Reagan Administration adopted an aggressively *laissez faire* approach to international economic policy. However, the steep appreciation of the dollar between 1980 and 1985, buttressed by an expansionary fiscal policy and tight monetary conditions, triggered protectionist pressures in the US Congress that forced a change in course. This resulted in what many regard as an apogee of international policy coordination, the September 1985 Plaza Agreement, in which the five largest advanced economies agreed to intervene to lower the value of the dollar.[15] While the dollar had already started to gradually depreciate over the spring and summer of 1985, the Plaza Agreement led to a much more rapid fall.

Indeed, by early 1987 the dollar was back around its 1980 value and seemed destined to continue depreciating. In response, the same five countries plus Canada negotiated the Louvre Accord of February 1987 to stabilize exchange rates. Unlike Plaza, the Louvre Accord included explicit macroeconomic policy commitments including tax reforms by the German government, monetary and fiscal stimulus by the Japanese government, and a trimming of the US fiscal deficit. However, these relatively loose policy commitments started to create tensions among the signatories. These tensions overflowed when US policymakers did little to oppose renewed dollar depreciation after the stock market crash later in 1987. Support for benign neglect rose as this discord ended the last significant attempt at international policy coordination before the North Atlantic crisis.

The decline in importance of economic cooperation after 1987 is vividly illustrated by the communiqués of successive G7 leaders' summits.[16] The communiqués summarized the views expressed in the most important forum for discussing international economic cooperation. The 1987 Venice G7 summit, held at around the time of the Louvre Accord, produced an Economic Declaration of thirty-five paragraphs of which the first twenty paragraphs were devoted to the global economy. Paragraph 3 stated: "Since Tokyo, the Summit countries have intensified their *economic policy coordination* with a view to ensuring internal consistency of domestic policies and their international compatibility" (emphasis added). The three noneconomic declarations were all much shorter (the longest was eight paragraphs). By contrast, at the 2008 Hokkaido Toyako G7 summit, held in the hiatus between the rescue of the US investment bank Bear Stearns and the collapse of Lehman Brothers, only ten of the seventy-two paragraphs in the leaders' declaration were devoted to broad economic issues, and the only policy commitment was to "promoting a smooth adjustment of global imbalances through sound macroeconomic management and structural policies in our countries as well as in emerging economies and oil producing countries". As these quotes make abundantly clear, over the intervening twenty years the leaders of the seven most powerful rich nations had essentially given up on organized economic cooperation.

Benign neglect can also be seen in the lack of interest in updating the international monetary system in response to changing realities. For example, the resources of the International Monetary Fund (IMF)—the cornerstone of the international financial safety net—did not keep up with the increase in world trade and (in particular) the expansion of global financial flows. In addition, despite some attempts to recognize the growing economic clout of poorer emerging markets, the most important global economic clubs remained the province of rich nations. The Hokkaido Toyako G7 summit did include a joint statement by the leaders of Brazil, China, India, Mexico and South Africa and there were regular meetings of the finance ministers of the G20, a more representative group that included the major emerging markets including China. But the main forums for international macroeconomic and financial dialogue remained the province of rich countries, be it the G7, the Basel Committee on Banking Regulation, or the Financial Stability Forum.

Trade was a major exception to this pattern but also illustrated the limitations of universal membership. In 1995, the loosely organized General Agreement on Tariffs and Trade (the GATT) was replaced by the World Trade Organization (WTO), whose wide membership was further enhanced by the accession of China in 2001 and Russia in 2002. The WTO proved a useful venue for dispute settlement, one of the most formalized parts of global economic cooperation. However, the complexities of a near-universal membership were exposed in the tortuous negotiations of successive rounds of international trade liberalization. This culminated in the seemingly never-ending wrangling over the 2001 "Doha" round. While Doha negotiations were advertised as being about supporting developing countries, they floundered on disagreements on the relative roles of advanced economies and emerging markets in improving the trading system.

The loss of interest in policy cooperation was particularly unfortunate as it played out against the rapid growth in the importance of emerging markets in the global economy. As measured by the IMF, the size of the

European Union, home to four of the seven members of the G7, contracted from 30 percent of world output to 20 percent between 1980 and 2007, even as the clout of emerging Asia, unrepresented in the G7, expanded from less than 10 percent of the world output to over 20 percent. In particular, the spectacular rise in China as a global economic force was treated as a threat by the western nations, with the United States focusing on countering their fixed exchange rate and rising trade surplus. Indeed, in 2007, with strong US backing, the IMF approved a new framework for surveillance that was seen by virtually all outside commentators as an anti-China move.

Benign neglect also had an impact on European policymakers. Enforcement of the fiscal rules embodied in the Stability and Growth Pact had already started on the back foot, as the major economies allowed a lax approach to the choice of the initial members of the European Monetary Union. However, the lack of attention to cross-country spillovers fostered by benign neglect further eroded the desire to strictly supervise the rules. The 3 percentage points of output cap for government deficits and 60 percent of output ceiling for debt embodied in the pact gradually moved from an upper limit to more of a target. The European Commission was given few powers to enforce the rules. These deficiencies were highlighted in 2009 when the Greek government's admission of much higher deficits and debt than had earlier been reported led to a Euro area fiscal crisis.

On the eve of the North Atlantic crisis, global economic governance remained the province of rich economies. The global safety net had been allowed to wither while emerging markets felt that their legitimate interest in playing a more important role had been largely ignored and China, the most important member of this group, saw the system as rigged against it. Meanwhile, the Euro area did not really have the kind of solid surveillance that might have spotted increasing fiscal malfeasance. Across the North Atlantic, the main consequence of benign neglect was that policymakers missed the implications of increasing external financing of the US and Euro area periphery housing booms.

* * *

How Economic Models Distorted Policymaking

The properties of economic models have come up repeatedly in this account of how prevailing macroeconomic views lulled policymakers into missing growing risks to the North Atlantic economy. This is intentional as in many ways these models reflected the conventional orthodoxy of the time among policymakers, academics, and pundits.[17] This is not to say that policymakers and commentators necessarily understood the detailed structure of these models, or relied heavily on the results they produced. The point is rather that these models embodied and reinforced views about the economy that created intellectual blinkers, that both allowed imbalances that generated the North Atlantic crisis to build and produced inflexible policy structures that amplified its costs.

Part of the problem was that the DSGE models that were used extensively by economists had only a limited relationship to the underlying data. As has been emphasized by others, this deficiency was obscured by the use of complex estimation techniques. The end result was that these models tended to reflect the perspectives of their creators—so, for example, monetary policy turned out to be extremely powerful in the models built by central banks but less so in those built by academics.[18] More generally, DSGE models reflected the characteristics of the underlying economic models on which they were built, including an emphasis on sophisticated and hyper-rational responses to anticipated future events. This contrasts to more eclectic approaches that assume that people develop simple stories and rules of thumb to guide them through the complexities of the modern economy. As discussed earlier, such behavior may be rational if "unknown unknowns" make accurate calculations of the future impossible.

An important consequence was the growing belief that the economy was largely self-correcting and that policymakers could safely specialize in their own macroeconomic compartments. Monetary policymakers focused on keeping inflation and economic growth steady, fiscal policymakers on keeping debt sustainable, while financial stability and underlying growth were largely taken for granted and the need for international cooperation heavily discounted. The narrow focus of policymakers provides another perspective on how the growing financial risks and imbalances of the 2000s were missed, why the bursting of the financial asset bubbles later in the decade came as such a surprise, and why the policy response was so muddled.

Another consequence was that fiscal policy came to be seen as largely ineffective, shifting the focus of policy to central banks. The consensus in the Bretton Woods era that both monetary policy and fiscal policy had a role to play in stabilizing the economy was increasingly replaced by a view that monetary policy should be the main instrument to stabilize economic fluctuations. Fiscal policy might assist monetary policy by providing "automatic stabilizers", the process by which, during a downturn in activity, government spending automatically increases while tax revenues decrease, thereby pumping more money into the economy. Active use of fiscal policy, however, was seen as largely ineffective and, to the extent that it was effective, potentially dangerous, given a political process in which fiscal support took a long time to plan and was often difficult to reverse.

In addition, predictability became a cardinal virtue for monetary policy-makers since this reduced financial market uncertainty. The possible impact of predictability in encouraging more risk-taking in the financial system was recognized but largely discounted. While there was some debate about the risks from the "Greenspan Put", whereby the Fed's prompt easing in response to negative news might encourage investors to think they would always be bailed out and hence start taking larger risks, such concerns about the incentives of investors were not analyzed in depth as they did not fit into the mental structure associated with macroeconomic models.

The design of European Monetary Union in the early 1990s provides a good example of how the intellectual weaknesses affected the policy architecture. As discussed in the last chapter, the plan for monetary union was produced by the Delors Committee that was dominated by central bankers, and hence closely followed the prevailing orthodoxy in macroeconomics. Monetary policy was to be run by an independent central bank whose only mandate was to stabilize inflation and whose actions were free from political interference. Day-to-day financial regulation was left in the hands of decentralized national supervisors so that it would not interfere with the central bank's independence. Fiscal policy was also national, and flexibility was crimped by rules aimed at lowering debt and constraining deficits. This structure, which looked so good on paper, proved completely inadequate in the face of the financial and fiscal crisis that enveloped Europe from 2009 to 2012.

More generally, DSGE models provided powerful subliminal messages that fed the belief that government intervention and regulation were generally harmful. It has already been noted that most of these models found that cutting taxes or increasing transfers (such as welfare payments) had no impact on private spending. Rather, taxes led to inefficiencies by distorting prices while direct government spending on roads and such like was generally modeled as having no value. The implicit message was that government should be limited, in line with the prevailing intellectual climate after the Thatcher/Reagan revolution in the early 1980s. To take another example, the representative household and firm structure that was predominant in DSGE models was blind to issues of inequality. Since all households acted in the same manner there was no role for welfare payments to the poor to have a different impact than tax cuts to the rich.

The crisis has led to an acknowledgement of importance of financial risks, but policymakers are still struggling to put these risks into an effective overarching framework. It is striking, for example, that the DSGE models that are being currently used in policy analysis have most of the blind spots of their predecessors. To be fair, some more complex versions of these models have made progress in incorporating financial markets.[19] However, even in these cases it is not clear that the true essence of financial markets have been captured. By their nature, these models generally involve smooth transitions—the central bank raises rates and the rest of the economy responds gradually to the new incentives. By contrast, financial markets are by their nature unpredictable and volatile. This is because the traders who dominate transactions are always looking for new ways to see the future that will give them an edge over the competition. This forward-looking focus leaves financial markets in a constant state of flux.

A parallel with physics may be useful here. For almost a century physics has been dominated by two theories that have yet to be reconciled. On the large scale, the world is characterized by Einstein's theory of general relativity in which changes in one variable create smooth transitions elsewhere. At the micro scale, the world is characterized by quantum mechanics in which particles jump from one state to another in a jerky fashion as they gain or lose quanta. Both theories are excellent descriptions of their particular areas, but attempts to unify them have fallen foul of fundamental differences in their structure.[20]

In many ways, standard macroeconomics, with its predictable and smooth changes in behavior, can be seen as similar to relativity while financial markets, which can change abruptly from calm to panic, are more like quantum mechanics. Just as physics has learned to live with these two views of the world, it may be helpful for economists and policymakers to do the same and accept that there are insights from conventional macroeconomics, and that there are different but equally valid insights from the analysis of financial markets, so that a balanced policy requires giving both aspects due attention.

This has obvious implications for the structure of policymaking. For example, central bank committees should be populated by a mixture of macroeconomists and those with financial expertise, while the chair should remain neutrally placed between the two camps and assess the merits of both points of view. It also implies a much greater focus on testing how robust the economic system is to large, unexpected financial shocks and the potential role of monetary, fiscal, financial, and structural policies in limiting vulnerabilities and responding to unanticipated events. The adage "hope for the best but plan for the worst" comes to mind.

Macroeconomic theory and practice has come a long way since the early 1980s. Most of these changes have been beneficial—for example, the lower volatility of output seen during the great moderation appears to be continuing after the crisis, suggesting that better monetary policy has indeed provided lasting benefits to the economy. But there is a very real issue as to how the North Atlantic crisis could have come as such a surprise to the vast majority of observers and policymakers—the rare exceptions being those who saw financial imbalances as a clear and present danger either because of their background in emerging markets (such as Professor Nouriel Roubini of New York University) or their belief that markets were often irrational and needed to be closely supervised (such as Bill White of the Bank of International Settlements, Professor Robert Shiller of Yale, and IMF Economic Counsellor Raghuram Rajan).

The inadequate intellectual apparatus was not simply unfortunate in the sense that it allowed the crisis to build. It also meant that policymakers needed to respond hurriedly to unexpected challenges within badly designed structures. This led to policy missteps such as the bankruptcy of Lehman Brothers and the premature tightening of fiscal policies in the Euro area. Most worrying of all, many of the implicit beliefs contained in the great moderation, efficient markets hypothesis, and benign neglect remain important components of conventional macroeconomic models and thinking. As discussed in a later chapter, a more radical overhaul of macroeconomics is overdue that accepts the fundamental role of policy cooperation, uncertainty, rules of thumb, and inclusiveness.

Chapter 6

A HISTORY OF THE INTERNATIONAL MONETARY SYSTEM IN FIVE CRISES

A strong belief in the virtues of open global capital markets amplified and—in particular—globalized the costs of the North Atlantic crisis. As discussed previously, outflows from the core Euro area banks helped feed growing housing and financial bubbles in the United States and the periphery of the Euro area over the 2000s. By pumping more oxygen into the system, this financing amplified the bubbles and the associated losses when they burst. In addition to generating deep recessions, the financial turmoil blew back onto the undercapitalized banks in the Euro area core, widening the collapse in output to the entire North Atlantic region. And it did not stop there. The recession rapidly became global, as investors withdrew indiscriminately from risky assets regardless of where they were located and global trade was battered by a sudden stop in spending on investment and durable goods as well as a drying up of trade finance—a segment of the market where the European mega-banks had become dominant. The retreat from international finance generated a global recession.

The strong support for open international capital flows among North Atlantic policymakers was linked to the growing belief that financial markets were self-regulating and stable. Financial globalization was seen as smoothly funneling money around the world as savers seeking the highest returns (adjusted for risk) channeled money into the most productive investments. Indeed, international investors were seen as providing welcome discipline to national policymakers as they would ferret out unwise policies and gradually stiffen borrowing terms, providing increasing incentives for policymakers to pursue a more advisable course.

The belief in the benefits of free international capital flows was by no means universal, with emerging market policymakers, in particular, often questioning them. Rather than the smooth and efficient system envisaged in theory, emerging markets had been battered by a series of crises in which foreign money had first flooded into their economies and then even more swiftly ebbed away. The largest of these events was the Asian crisis of the late 1990s which started in Thailand but quickly spread to Indonesia, Korea, Malaysia, and even Hong Kong. North Atlantic policymakers, however, generally ascribed this instability to the less developed financial systems and policy regimes of the recipient countries. Emerging markets needed a policy upgrade to take full advantage of the benefits of global capital markets. The prevailing view in the United States and Europe was that the problem was not with global capital markets, but rather with the way that countries behaved within them.

Strikingly, this faith in the benefits of unfettered international debt flows has largely survived the crisis. There has been no wholesale reform of the international financial system in its wake. To be sure, funds available to the International Monetary Fund and similar regional bodies to combat crises have been boosted and there is somewhat more sympathy for countries using capital controls to limit the ebbs and flows of international money. However, the focus of post-crisis financial reforms has been squarely on improving domestic financial regulation. Indeed, while the need for tighter regulation of *national* financial markets to reduce risks is generally acknowledged, the equivalent argument for *international* financial market regulation is not. Echoing the ethos of benign neglect and the resulting disdain for international policy cooperation discussed in the last chapter, proposals to more closely police international flows of money to limit risks remain controversial.

The strong consensus on the benefits of open capital markets is surprising for a couple of reasons. Evidence on the benefits of open capital flows has never been as clear-cut as for international trade. The long-term benefits and limited short-term risks from trade openness are well documented, although even these benefits are currently being questioned, given rising inequality and the difficulty of supporting those who lose jobs.[1] For international capital markets, on the other hand, the potential longer-term growth benefits have to be set against the losses from possible future financial crises. A recent survey by the International Monetary Fund has described the empirical evidence of the benefits from more open capital markets as "mixed" because of potential financial disruption coming from surges and reversals of international flows, and emphasized that liberalization is "more conducive to economic growth in countries that are more financially developed, have greater human capital, or have greater absorption capacity"—in other words more advanced economies gain more from financial liberalization.[2]

The consensus across advanced country policymakers on the benefits of international capital flows is also surprising as the period since 1970 has seen a regular and highly destructive succession of international financial crises. These have occurred around every ten years and have alternated between advanced and emerging regions. Most importantly, the crises have been becoming steadily more destructive. This longer historical assessment contrasts with the prevailing orthodoxy that financial crises are largely limited to emerging markets and the weakness of their policies.

The first of these crises was the break-up of the Bretton Woods fixed exchange rate system in the early 1970s as debt flowed from the United States to Germany and Japan, countries whose economic policies were considered more stable. In the early 1980s, the crisis pendulum swung to the emerging markets of Latin America as inflows of petrodollars channeled through US banks suddenly reversed, resulting in a "lost decade" of stagnant growth. In the early 1990s it was western Europe's turn, as speculative attacks shook the Exchange Rate Mechanism designed to limit currency fluctuations against Germany. Italy and the United Kingdom were forced to leave the Mechanism in 1992 and France only avoided the same fate in 1993 because of a face-saving widening of intervention bands. In the late 1990s, international financial instability engulfed Asia, as outflows of debt from Thailand rapidly widened to create a regional crisis. The last, and by far the largest, was the North Atlantic crisis, where the rapid reversal of inflows from northern European banks into speculative ventures in the United States and Euro area periphery led to a meltdown.[3]

* * *

Why International Debt Flows Are So Skittish

These crises have followed a strikingly similar pattern in which foreign debt (in the form of bank loans or bond purchases) initially flows into a region and then rapidly reverses course. The emphasis on debt is vital, as this unstable pattern of inflows followed by rapid outflows is not seen for equities. This is clear from the much more jagged behavior of US debt outflows (the sum of bank loans and bonds) versus equity outflows (small "portfolio" investments plus foreign direct investment that involves buying a major stake in a firm) (Figure 41).[4] While the dotted line that represents equity

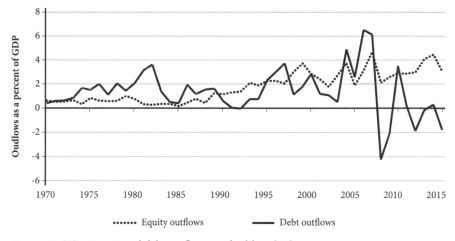

Figure 41: US international debt outflows are highly volatile.
Source: US External Accounts.

flows shows a stable upward trend due to financial globalization, the black line that represents debt flows also shows increasing volatility.

The instability of international debt flows is particularly striking as debt is generally regarded as a safer investment than equity. In a debt contract, a borrower (a government, a firm, or an individual) agrees to pay back the face value of the loan plus interest, so repayments are fixed unless the borrower defaults. By contrast, an equity investment involves taking a share of the future profits of a company. Since future profits are much less predictable, equity prices are less stable. Why, then, are international debt flows more unstable than equity flows?

The key difference between international debt flows and their domestic equivalents is risks from changes in exchange rates. In addition to the usual assessments about the risks of a bond or loan in local currency, foreign investors also need to evaluate prospects for the exchange rate. If (say) a US investor buys a bond priced in British pounds, he or she accepts the risk that the investment will lose value should the pound depreciate against the dollar even if the borrower repays in full (this is not true of foreign equities as, at least in theory, they represent future profits whose value does not depend on the chosen currency). An alternative is to lend the money in dollars, but this merely transfers the exchange rate risk from the investor to the borrower. A depreciation of the pound against the dollar raises the cost of repayments in pounds, making it more likely that the borrower will default. Either way, the foreign investor faces risk linked to the exchange rate.

Exchange rate risk creates the potential for contagion across foreign investors since their expected returns all depend on expectations about the future value of the currency—in the example above for the pound. If foreign investors get nervous about (say) UK mortgages and consider pulling their money out of the market, the risk that this outflow will lower the value of the pound provides incentives for other foreign investors to leave.[5] This is different from domestic investors, since the value of debt in pounds in other markets is not directly affected by outflows from the mortgage market. International debt is thus inherently more unstable than domestic debt.

Exchange rate policies can also create distortions that limit how much international investors discipline policymakers. For example, consider a country following an expansionary monetary policy that is creating inflation, a risk that leads domestic investors to charge higher and higher interest rates for loans over shorter and shorter time periods. If policymakers also promise to fix the exchange rate, however, foreign investors will enjoy the benefit of higher interest rates without their returns being eroded by higher domestic prices. They will continue invest as long as they believe that they will be able to convert their money back into dollars at the fixed rate. However, this is clearly a double-edged sword, as any devaluation will impose major losses on dollar investors. As a result, there is a risk of a sudden outflow of foreign money if investors decide that a devaluation is likely to occur.

Models in international finance have formalized the dynamics of such exchange rate crises.[6] In the initial "first generation" of these models, a country following a fixed exchange rate experiences a crisis once the vulnerabilities cause inflows of foreign money to hit a limit. Within this framework, the timing of the exchange rate crisis is (at least in theory) predictable. If foreign debt reaches the threshold, then foreign investors flee and an exchange rate crisis occurs. One obvious difficulty with this approach is that it is not clear why foreign investors would wait passively for the threshold to be reached, rather than anticipating the crash and pulling out earlier. In response to this concern, the second and third generations of these models make the timing of the crisis also dependent on exchange rate expectations of investors. In this approach, foreign debt can continue to flow into a country even after the threshold has been met as long as investors expect the exchange rate peg to be maintained. The crisis only happens once a sufficient number of investors switch to expecting a devaluation—the exact timing of a crisis depends on the mood of investors.[7]

If fixed exchange rate regimes create risks of a currency crisis, then why not simply adopt a floating exchange rate regime where the value of the currency is left to market forces? While a floating exchange rate solves the problem of investors rushing in on the assumption they will be able to leave before the inevitable devaluation of a fixed exchange rate, it has its own potential problems. Like other asset prices, exchange rates can experience excessive swings as a result of herding behavior by investors. For example, the appreciation of the US dollar in the early 1980s is a case where market psychology drove the dollar to excessive levels from which it corrected only after the Plaza Agreement changed investor sentiment.[8]

Fundamentally, large and unstable international capital flows as a result of the ebb and flow of investor sentiment can be destructive regardless of the exchange rate regime. Large inflows can loosen domestic financial conditions and spark domestic lending booms that can lead to asset price bubbles.[9] If they cause an appreciation of the exchange rate they can also discourage exports and encourage imports. On the other side of the coin, rapid outflows can generate exchange rate crises. The impact of foreign debt inflows and outflows are more potent for countries such as emerging markets with smaller and less liquid domestic financial markets, which explains why they worry more about international financial instability.

* * *

International Debt and Its Discontents

Exchange rate risks make foreign investors more skittish than domestic ones. The result has been a series of five ever larger international crises in which large inflows of foreign debt are followed by rapid and destabilizing outflows. While each crisis has its own idiosyncratic elements, the underlying similarities are striking. Since the outflows at the end of one crisis have been rapidly followed by the start of inflows into the next one, the history of the international financial system since 1970 can be told through the lens of footloose international debt flows that have ebbed and flowed across regions.

The Center Cannot Hold: Collapse of the Bretton Woods Fixed Exchange Rate System

The collapse of the Bretton Woods fixed exchange rate system in the early 1970s was a watershed event.[10] It marked the end of international efforts to maintain fixed exchange rates across major currencies that had characterized the century since the advent of the classical gold standard in the 1870s. The classical gold standard had broken down during World War I and the

gold exchange standard that replaced it between World Wars had found-
ered because the parities across currencies were too rigid, creating
constraining "golden fetters".[11] In response, the 1944 Bretton Woods conference created a new and more flexible fixed exchange rate system in which
countries could adjust their parities in the face of persistent trade deficits.
In addition, while the new system encouraged international trade it allowed
countries to limit flows of assets between countries so as to reduce potentially disruptive speculative flows that had bedeviled the interwar gold
exchange standard.[12]

The Bretton Woods system comprised a two-tier exchange rate system
in which the dollar was fixed to gold and other currencies were fixed against
the dollar. More precisely, individual currencies such as the pound sterling,
the Deutsche mark, and the yen were only allowed to fluctuate by plus or
minus 1 percent of a fixed parity against the dollar, while the value of the
dollar to gold was fixed at $35 an ounce. The advantage of this special status
for the dollar was that international reserves could be held in either gold or
dollars, solving the issue of limited amounts of gold reserves that had been
a problem in the interwar period. Parities could be altered if a country
experienced "fundamental external disequilibrium" and International
Monetary Fund loans were available for short-term support as the economy
adjusted. To avoid abuse of this flexibility, countries were expected to
consult with the International Monetary Fund before any change in parity.
This outcome was a compromise between the views of John Maynard
Keynes from the United Kingdom, a debtor nation that sought relatively
automatic financing of external deficits, and Harry Dexter White of the
United States, a creditor nation that sought more constrained access to
funds.[13]

The system became gradually less flexible as the size of international
capital flows increased. The neat distinction envisioned by the founders of
Bretton Woods between trade-related "current account" transactions and
"capital account" transactions in which financial assets were bought
and sold became increasingly leaky over time. For example, in the face of an
expected change in an exchange rate parity, importers and exporters could
speculate by deliberately over- or under-invoicing their foreign currency
needs.[14] More generally, as rules on which international financial transactions were and were not permitted became increasingly complex, the system
became more difficult to control and international capital flows increased.
Small changes in parities became less attractive because rather than stabilizing the situation they could create destabilizing expectations of further
future devaluations. This problem was exacerbated because adjustments in

parities were only permitted if an exchange rate was "fundamentally" misaligned, an approach that discouraged preemptive responses to growing market concerns. In addition, market pressures worked in an asymmetric manner. There was limited pressures for countries that were running trade surpluses to revalue their parity as the surplus could be easily financed by accumulating more international reserves. By contrast, market pressures were much larger on countries running trade deficits that had to defend the parity by selling their finite stock of international reserves.

In addition, expansionary US fiscal policies were putting pressure on the core of the system, the dollar parity with gold. The steady expansion of the stock of US government debt relative to gold led to questions about whether the United States was prepared to follow the restrained domestic policies required to maintain the gold parity. In 1961, the major central banks established a Gold Pool to assist the United States by sharing the burden of intervening in the gold market to maintain the parity. However, as the 1960s wore on enthusiasm for the Gold Pool faltered as the United States showed little interest in constraining its fiscal deficits and debt to ensure the survival of the gold parity. France left the pool in mid-1967, having earlier converted much of its reserves into gold because it felt US policymakers were abusing the "exorbitant privilege" (in the words of French Finance Minister Valéry Giscard d'Estaing) of being able to issue dollar assets at low cost because of the additional demand for US assets coming from its status as a reserve currency. Soon after, the devaluation of the pound sterling intensified doubts about the dollar peg against gold and the pool was forced to sell $800 billion worth of gold in a month, a very large sum by the standards of the day. By the next spring the pool had disbanded, and soon after the United States allowed the price of gold for private transactions to float away from $35 an ounce, although the old parity continued to be respected for transactions between central banks.

The separation of the private and official gold parities sealed the fate of the Bretton Woods system since it took away its underlying logic. The unwillingness of the United States to run the policies necessary to maintain the gold parity undermined the reason for other countries to fix against the dollar. For lack of an alternative, however, the system limped along for the next few years. This was supported by increasing use of capital controls by the United States to limit outflows, combined with the unwillingness of other countries to allow a dollar devaluation since this would worsen the competitiveness of their products against US ones.

The next jolt to the system occurred in the spring of 1971. It started when Germany stopped intervening and allowed the Deutsche mark to

appreciate against the dollar. The problem for Germany was that speculative inflows from the United States were increasing the money supply and
threatening to spark inflation. The appreciation of the Deutsche mark was
supposed to discourage these inflows, but it only set up expectations for
further appreciation and the flight from the dollar to the Deutsche mark
continued. The resulting downward pressure on the dollar led the Nixon
administration in the United States to take its own drastic action to force
changes in the system. In the week of August 13 the administration (without
consulting the IMF) imposed a surcharge of 10 percent on foreign imports
and stopped exchanging gold with foreign central banks. Following four
months of negotiations, the major countries agreed to a major overhaul of
the Bretton Woods system at the Smithsonian Conference in Washington.
The dollar was devalued by 8 percent against gold, the currencies of the
other major countries were revalued against the dollar, and intervention
bands around dollar parities were widened from 1 to 2¼ percent. In return,
the US import surcharge was abolished. However, gold transactions were
not reopened and the core problem of excessively expansionary US fiscal
policies was not addressed. This laid the seeds for the third and final speculative attack against the dollar in early 1973. When a further devaluation of
the dollar against gold failed to stem speculative outflows to the Deutsche
mark and the yen, Germany and her European partners floated their
currencies against the dollar and the Bretton Woods fixed exchange rate
system finally expired.

The felling of the Bretton Woods system came from the unwillingness
of the United States to subordinate its domestic priorities to the need to
maintain a fixed parity. This led successively to the abandonment of the
dollar–gold parity for private transactions (1968), for official transactions
(1971), and finally the dollar–Deutsche mark parity (1973). Since other
countries had a stake in the system, a significant part of the costs of the
interventions to support the dollar were borne by others through mechanisms such as the Gold Pool. With the benefit of hindsight, however, what is
most striking compared to subsequent crises is the small size of the speculative flows, trade imbalances, and international disruption when the system
toppled. Much more destructive international financial crises were to come.

Petrodollars Looking for a Home: The Latin American Debt Crisis

The seeds of the Latin American debt crisis came from the need to recycle
oil producers' rising holdings of dollars to new borrowers.[15] Soon after the
collapse of the Bretton Woods system in 1973 came the 1974 quadrupling

of the price of oil, followed by a further doubling in 1979. Since oil was priced in dollars, the hikes generated huge inflows of dollars to the Arab oil producers. Given a paucity of domestic investment opportunities, these petrodollars were mainly deposited at the major US banks at a time when the interaction of rising inflation and limits on deposit and lending rates were constraining domestic lending. Consequently, the petrodollars were mainly recycled as international loans that were protected from changes in exchange rates since they were made in dollars and protected from fluctuations in US interest rates as the rate was changed twice a year using the six-month London Interbank Offering Rate (LIBOR).

Most of the money went to developing countries, particularly in Latin America, a part of the world that was growing rapidly and whose economic prospects appeared bright. Concerns were expressed by some about the rapid increase in foreign lending by the major US banks. For example, in 1977 the Chair of the Federal Reserve, Arthur Burns, said that "commercial and investment bankers need to monitor their foreign lending with great care" and the US regulators issued warning letters and started monitoring overseas borrowing more closely.[16] But this was a minority view and most policymakers were unworried, including the administration of President Ford. US equity markets were also unfazed, with the price of major bank equities rising rapidly along with the bull market.

The latter stages of the Latin American lending boom were given a further boost by favorable interpretations of US bank regulations. As the boom continued, loans by US banks were increasingly running up against rules that limited exposure to a single borrower to 10 percent of a bank's capital. The key issue was how to define a single borrower. In early 1978, the US Office of the Comptroller of the Currency (OCC) proposed that all loans to public sector corporations and agencies within a country be counted as a single borrower, an interpretation that would have significantly limited further lending. In its final ruling in 1979, however, the OCC determined that public sector borrowers were not a single entity if each borrower had the "means to service its debt" and "the purpose of the loan involved the borrower's business".[17] Since such assessments were left to the banks, this decision effectively ended regulatory constraints on further lending.

The lending boom was particularly focused on Mexico and Brazil— hence the descriptor the Latin American debt crisis. The external debt of both countries rose by about half between 1975 and 1982 as a ratio of output, from slightly over 20 percent to slightly over 30 percent. Furthermore, because Mexico and Brazil were relatively closed to international trade, the cost of servicing this debt increased to an astonishing half of exports. In the early 1980s, Mexico and Brazil were hit by an economic triple-whammy comprising of lower commodity prices, higher US interest rates, and dollar appreciation.

The second oil shock in 1979 led to a recession in the advanced countries that lowered the demand for, and the price of, commodities, thereby hurting export earnings. On top of this, the new Chairman of the Federal Reserve, Paul Volcker, hiked US interest rates aggressively in order to tame inflation. The six-month LIBOR rate tripled from 6 percent in 1976 to 18 percent by mid-1981 and remained in double digits through most of 1982. Finally, the combination of loose US fiscal policy and tight monetary policy led to a long appreciation of the dollar that eventually culminated in the Plaza Agreement in 1985. This left developing countries with a choice between pegging to the dollar and losing competitiveness to Europe and Japan, or depreciating against the dollar and seeing the local cost of dollar loans soar. Given their high levels of dollar debt, Mexico and Brazil chose to maintain their parities by imposing increasingly tight policies that led to recessions even before the crisis.

The Latin American debt crisis proper started on August 12, 1982, when Jesus Silva-Herzog, the Finance Minister of Mexico, told the chairman of the Federal Reserve Board, the Secretary of the US Treasury, and the Managing Director of the International Monetary Fund that Mexico would not be able to make its debt payment on August 16. He then announced a ninety-day moratorium on debt payments together with a renegotiation of existing loans and a request for new loans. The Mexican default led to a sudden stop of new loans across the developing world and by October 1983 twenty-seven countries owing a total of $239 billion had, or were in the process of, rescheduling their international debts. Four Latin American countries—Mexico, Brazil, Venezuela, and Argentina—accounted for three-quarters of this total. This included $37 billion owed to the eight largest US banks, which was considerably larger than their combined capital and reserves and reportedly risked insolvency for seven or eight of the ten largest US banks.[18] In response, the "US bank regulators, given a choice between creating panic in the banking system or going easy on requiring our banks to set aside reserves for Latin American debt", chose the latter course.[19]

With the United States government unwilling to bail out either the borrowing countries or their own banks, the outcome was a prolonged period of economic stagnation. Latin America, in particular, went through a lost decade of sluggish growth as the overhang from unpayable debts corroded the ability and incentive to invest for the future. After several years in which the major US banks restructured loans and accumulated reserves to cover losses, starting in 1987 the banks eventually began to acknowledge the true extent of their developing country loan losses. Finally, the 1989 Brady Plan (named after US Secretary of the Treasury Nicolas Brady) provided permanent reductions in debt and debt service in return for economic reforms by the borrowers. Latin America gradually recovered and the lost decade came to a close.

The Latin American debt crisis showed the perils of international lending through banks. The recycling of petrodollars was left in the hands of the US money center banks on the assumption that they would do a better job at lending money than governments. In practice, however, the banks lent recklessly to developing countries that were equally reckless in their willingness to accept large debts and the associated interest and exchange rate risk. When regulation threatened to limit the boom, the banks successfully persuaded the regulators to reinterpret the rules. The unsustainable loans deteriorated rapidly in the face of an admittedly unlucky combination of a global recession, lower commodity prices, higher US interest rates, and an appreciation of the dollar. With the US government unwilling to bail out their banks' foreign debts, there was a need to maintain the fiction that most of the loans were serviceable, which led to prolonged problems for Latin America as well as the US money center banks. Just as the Latin American crisis came to a close in the late 1980s, the international debt pendulum was swinging back to the advanced countries.

The Outskirts Cannot Hold: The European Exchange Rate Mechanism Crisis

After the collapse of the Bretton Woods fixed exchange rate system, the European Economic Community (EEC, later the European Union) tried to maintain fixed exchange rates across its membership even as the United States and Japan switched to floating exchange rates. There were good reasons for Europe to choose a different approach. The United States and Japan were large economies that were relatively closed to international trade. As a consequence, while the value of the exchange rate mattered, it was not regarded as a central policy issue. By contrast, the members of the Community had deliberately fostered much closer trade ties through a customs union that made exchange rate fluctuations between them more important. In addition, the commitment to "ever closer union" and eventually to a single currency embodied in the 1957 Treaty of Rome provided further incentives to stabilize exchange rates. Finally, and more prosaically, exchange rate stability was also important for the smooth functioning of the EEC's Common Agricultural Policy.

The initial arrangement to foster exchange rate stability was the European snake, set up in 1971 as part of the failed attempt to salvage the Bretton Woods system at the doomed Smithsonian Conference.[20] The conference agreed to widen the band of fluctuations around dollar parities from 1 to 2¼ percent. This implied that European currencies could fluctuate by up to 4½ percent against each other if one currency was at the top of the dollar band and the other was at the bottom. Such a range was seen as too large by European policymakers, who agreed to limit their bilateral fluctuations to plus or minus 2¼ percent backed by various regional financial facilities. The arrangement was called the "snake in the Smithsonian tunnel", while the smaller 1½ percent fluctuation bands of the exchange rates among Benelux countries (the Netherlands, Belgium, and Luxembourg) with Germany was often referred to by the even less appealing tag of "the worm". These animals survived the collapse of the Bretton Woods system. However, faced with the financial turbulence of the 1970s and the fact that most of the onus to maintain the parity was on the weaker currencies, whose governments were already under the greatest financial pressures, the snake gradually lost members. By 1977, it had essentially become a small Deutsche mark zone with only the Netherlands, Belgium, Luxembourg, and Denmark participating. The other European currencies floated, including the French franc, the Italian lira, and pound sterling.

In 1979, the snake was replaced by the Exchange Rate Mechanism (ERM). The ERM started as a bold initiative hatched between French President Giscard D'Estaing and German Chancellor Helmut Schmidt involving a new European unit of account, some pooling of reserves, and a more symmetric system for intervention between strong and weak currencies.[21] However, the final result was basically a snake with wider membership. It operated under the same plus or minus 2¼ percent intervention bands (although wider 6 percent bands were permitted for weak members), while plans for reserve sharing and an associated European Monetary Fund never materialized. In addition, the formal commitments for countries with strong currencies to intervene in an unlimited fashion was undermined when Chancellor Schmidt entered into an agreement with the Bundesbank that this provision could be waived if intervention threatened German financial and economic stability. This deal that was not made public as Schmidt explained that its disclosure would have ended any chances of an agreement at the European level.[22]

As with Bretton Woods, the ERM gradually hardened and realignments became less common. With the system becoming less flexible and more politicized, investors became less worried about unexpected changes in parities and started to move their money into members with higher interest rates but less strong policies. The recipients of this "convergence play" included Italy (particularly after it moved to the narrow ERM band in early 1990) and new entrants Spain (1989), Portugal (1992), and, most importantly, the United Kingdom (1990). These governments myopically viewed such inflows as signaling that markets approved of their policies. Over time, however, these seemingly supportive foreign inflows became a trap as countries became dependent on the kindness of strangers. It became increasingly difficult for the recipients to contemplate parity realignments or lower interest rates for fear of triggering destabilizing outflows by international investors.

Tensions within the ERM escalated as the economic consequences of the unexpected fall of the Berlin Wall and associated unification of the two halves of Germany became apparent. Unification led to a rise in the German fiscal deficit as a result of subsidies to the former East Germany, especially given the generous fixing of exchange rate between the East German Ostmark and West German Deutsche mark at unity. While this made East Germans richer it left East German industry uncompetitive within the newly unified country. The Bundesbank responded to the fiscal largess and the associated threat to price stability by tightening monetary policy, hiking the base rate by 2¾ percentage points between unification in late 1990 and July 1992.

This tightening occurred at a time when ERM membership was becoming more important to other countries as it was woven into criteria for entrance in the new single currency. The realization that Germany would soon reunify resulted in a tacit agreement between President Mitterrand of France and Chancellor Kohl of Germany to bind the new Germany to the rest of western Europe through monetary union. The 1989 Delors Report was dusted off and used as the blueprint for the negotiations. These culminated in the 1992 Maastricht Treaty that promised a single currency by 1999. One of the convergence criteria for entry into the monetary union was that a country had maintained unchanged ERM parities for the previous two years. The increased incentives to maintain existing ERM parities meant that partners had little choice but to tighten monetary policy as Germany did so, leading to a debilitating slowdown in output.

The trigger for the 1992 ERM crisis was the change in investor sentiment caused by the rejection of the monetary union by Denmark. On

June 2, 1992, a Danish referendum narrowly rejected the Maastricht Treaty—with 50.7 percent against and 49.3 percent in favor. In France, where President Mitterrand promised a similar vote on September 20, the outcome was also uncertain. With the future of the single currency in doubt, foreign investors increasingly questioned commitments to maintaining existing ERM parities, especially for recipients of convergence play funds. Market pressure on the pound sterling and the Italian lira mounted rapidly. Policy disagreements at emergency European discussions short-circuited a coherent response. With the French opposed to a general ERM realignment because of the upcoming referendum, and the United Kingdom unwilling to agree to a realignment without France, a last-ditch lira devaluation announced on Sunday, September 13 was too little too late.

On the morning of September 16, 1992 ("black Wednesday"), the Bundesbank invoked its secret exit clause and stopped intervening to support the pound and the lira. When two UK interest hikes failed to end speculative attacks, the pound was forced to leave the ERM that evening; the lira followed the next day. With markets smelling blood, massive Franco-German intervention was needed to stave off intense pressure on the French franc over the next few weeks. However, the tensions reappeared the next summer. In July 1993, there was a renewed speculative attack on the ERM aimed mainly at the French franc. Over the weekend of July 31–August 1, at a meeting of the European Commission Monetary Committee, countries blocked various potential solutions, including a French franc devaluation (vetoed by France), a general realignment (vetoed by others), and a German float (vetoed by the Netherlands). At the last minute, a face-saving compromise to widen the ERM intervention bands to plus or minus 15 percent was proposed and agreed, allowing currencies to find their own value while retaining the fiction of an ERM with wide participation.

The lesson from the ERM crisis was that financial instability and contagion could strike advanced economies just as potently as emerging markets. The future participants of the Euro area had already decided that the solution to exchange rate instability was to tie themselves to the mast of a single currency on the assumption that eliminating the possibility of exchange rate adjustments would force countries to run mutually consistent policies. This was the economic equivalent of assuming that people in glasshouses do not throw stones. The North Atlantic crisis showed that the plan was insufficient. In the face of stone throwing (in the shape of excessive Greek borrowing) in a glasshouse (in the shape of a badly designed currency union) the Euro area ended up suffering a prolonged existential crisis that it only narrowly survived. Turning back to our narrative, as money flowed out of western Europe, debt inflows switched back to emerging markets, this time in Asia.

Too Much of a Good Thing: The Asian Crisis

The Asian crisis arose out of a similar set of miscalculations to the Latin American debt crisis, namely rapid foreign inflows into a fast-growing region with seemingly strong future prospects.[23] In the decade before the crisis, output growth in Thailand, Indonesia, South Korea, and Malaysia was consistently above 5 percent and was often in double digits. Expectations that rapid growth would continue emboldened domestic firms to borrow and foreign investors to lend. Success was assumed to breed more success.

Financial deregulation by the Asian countries also played a role in the crisis by providing domestic banks and others with greater freedom to borrow from abroad. For example, the Thai government created the Bangkok International Banking Facility in 1992 with the aim of making Bangkok into an international financial center.[24] The plan was for overseas money to come into Bangkok and then be lent out to other countries— "out-out" loans. In practice, however, the foreign money was mainly used to finance local Thai loans—instead of "out-out" the loans became "out-in". Financial deregulation allowed this "out-in" pattern to be repeated across the region as banks borrowed short-term in foreign currencies to make domestic loans, making local banks increasingly vulnerable to withdrawals by foreign investors.

The returns being made by companies on local loans deteriorated gradually over the 1990s, a shift that happened slowly enough for lenders and borrowers to miss the growing risks. As already high domestic savings were supplemented by foreign borrowing, investment spending rose to 30 percent or more of output. These ample funds were increasingly channeled into low value projects. Examples included semi-conductor factories, where increasing global overcapacity made it difficult to make money, or real estate where returns depended on rising house prices.

Within this basic picture, the experiences of individual Asian crisis countries were diverse.[25] Thailand and Malaysia experienced classic foreign-financed bubbles over the early 1990s, running large current account deficits accompanied by high levels of foreign borrowing, domestic investment, and unsustainable booms in property and equity prices. By contrast, in South Korea most of the excess investment was financed domestically, at least until 1996 when there was a rapid rise in foreign borrowing by firms. The main issue in South Korea was that the local industrial conglomerates—called Chaebol—were borrowing short-term money at interest rates well above the rate of return they were obtaining on their investments. Indonesia was an intermediate case, involving a mixture of international and domestic vulnerabilities. This diversity in experience extended to exchange rate policies. While Thailand, Malaysia, and Indonesia maintained increasingly uncompetitive dollar pegs, South Korea had a more flexible exchange rate policy. The example of South Korea is particularly striking as it is a case in which it was primarily domestic problems that triggered the sudden exit of international investors.

Adverse economic shocks played a much more minor role in the creation of the Asia crisis than they did in the Latin American or the ERM crises. A depreciation of the yen against the dollar in the middle of the 1990s put some pressure on the export-driven growth model of the region. The depreciation of the Chinese renminbi against the dollar in early 1994 may have also played a role, although analysts differ as to whether China was a significant competitor to the crisis countries at this time. Prospects of US monetary tightening may have also led foreign investors to re-examine the attractiveness of their loans to Asia. That said, there was no equivalent of the rapid tightening of US or Germany policies that helped precipitate the Latin American and ERM meltdowns, respectively, or the multiple speculative attacks at the end of the Bretton Woods system.

As in earlier crises, financial markets gave few warnings signs of growing imbalances. Instead of the gradual building of investor concerns about the region and a tightening of loan conditions envisaged by believers in efficient markets, the crisis was more consistent with the exchange rate crisis models in which a sudden Gestalt Switch in investor confidence turned steady foreign inflows into panicked withdrawals.

The crisis proper started on July 2, 1997, when the Thai authorities were forced to float the baht in the face of sustained speculative pressure. While on paper the Thai government had significant international reserves, in reality most of them were already committed to defending the currency in forward markets. After this wake-up call about the risks of devaluations and the unreliability of official data on reserves, foreign investors rapidly exited the region. Malaysia, the Philippines, and Indonesia were all forced to float their currencies within a few weeks of the Thais. The most startling impact, however, was on South Korea, which was forced to devalue its currency the won gradually at first but then increasingly rapidly. At the height of the fire sale in early 1998, the won had sunk to half of its pre-crisis value.

The main lessons from the Asian crisis is that crises can come from switches in financial market sentiment rather than policy shocks and that contagion can jump to countries with quite different underlying fundamentals. Indeed, the Asian crisis raised the perceived risk of lending to all emerging markets, helping trigger the subsequent exchange rate collapses in Russia in 1998 and in Brazil in 1999. These were the last major emerging market countries to experience financial disruptions as the boom of the 2000s led to another wave of easy financing that ended abruptly with the North Atlantic crisis.

A Global Shock: The North Atlantic Crisis

In many respects the 2008 North Atlantic crisis was an amalgam of these earlier experiences. As in the case of the Bretton Woods break-up, unsustainable imbalances in the United States (in this case driven by private financial flows) led to global disruptions. In the Bretton Woods episode, these disruptions were limited because of the controls on private capital flows so that most of the losses were on holdings of dollar reserves. Open capital markets amplified the destructive power of the later North Atlantic crisis, as problems in US markets led to a global pullback from risk that in turn led to a worldwide recession.

Petrodollar lending flowing through US money center banks to Latin America in the 1970s was similar to the unsustainable expansion in lending by core Euro area banks to the United States and the Euro area periphery in the 2000s. The basic forces were the same. Banks with cash to spare, limited options in their domestic markets, and facing compliant supervision pushed money into rapidly growing parts of the world where investment opportunities appeared attractive. Even more importantly, an unwillingness to admit the size of the banking problems associated with the crisis led to excessive regulatory forbearance and a prolonged period of economic stagnation in the Euro area. Just as occurred in Latin America, the Euro area suffered a lost decade.

Misplaced confidence in the stability of a fixed exchange rate regime links the ERM crisis with the Euro area part of the North Atlantic crisis. In the face of unexpectedly large speculative outflows from Italy and the United Kingdom in 1992 and on France in 1993, Germany was not prepared to put its macroeconomic stability at risk to save the system. Similarly, when speculative flows erupted across the monetary union in 2009, German reluctance to bail out the periphery countries allowed their problems to fester.

Finally, the Asian crisis demonstrated how a crisis could erupt in the absence of major policy shocks and contagion could transfer to other countries with rather different underlying conditions. The North Atlantic crisis also erupted in a seemingly stable policy environment in which central banks were fretting over policy interest-rate changes of one-quarter of a percentage point. And just as in Asia, where the exit of foreign investors jumped from the internationally exposed Thailand to less exposed Indonesia and Malaysia and finally to South Korea, (whose problems were largely home-grown), the Euro area crisis jumped from unsustainable foreign-financed borrowing by the Greek government, to Ireland, Portugal, and Spain—countries where the private sector was responsible for excess foreign borrowing—and then to Italy, whose financial problems reflected low growth rather than excessive foreign borrowing.

On the other hand, the popular view that the North Atlantic crisis was brought about by "too big to fail" banks exploiting implicit government guarantees for their own ends finds little support in the historical record. While moral hazard can be important in misdirecting financial flows, there do not seem to be earlier cases where banks deliberately financed a crisis on the assumption that they would be bailed out. Banks were not important drivers of the collapse of Bretton Woods or the ERM crises. Bank flows played a more important role in the Asia crisis, but excessive optimism about future growth seems to be a more convincing explanation for the boom in foreign financing than expectations of a bailout. Even in the case of the Latin American debt crisis, where bad loans by large US banks were the driving force, there was no explicit bailout of the major US banks and their profits suffered, just as occurred over the North Atlantic crisis.[26] It seems odd to assume that banks are perceptive enough to anticipate government support but cannot also anticipate low profits and tighter regulation. "Too big to fail" primarily matters because it exacerbates the costs of government support and losses in output, rather than because it drives banks into financing crises, something they appear perfectly capable of doing of their own volition.

A more promising view about the origins of international crises is the tendency of all investors, including banks, to herd. If lending to a particular region is generating profits for some investors, others follow suit on the assumption that the risks have been carefully assessed. Banks follow this behavior as much as other investors. The importance of herding helps to explain why it is difficult to find evidence of widespread market jitters in the run-up to a crisis. Rather than explanations in which banks deliberately lend into a crisis because of anticipated bailouts—greed and cunning—it is much simpler to believe that crises are caused by collective greed and fear, with the latter translating into sudden panics.[27]

* * *

Charting International Financial Crises

How destructive were these crises to the countries themselves and to the world economy? A simple way of comparing the size of the crises across countries involved is to calculate a "misery index" that sums up the fall in growth and the compression in the trade deficit as a ratio to output. The misery index provides a simple way of measuring the fall in overall spending across crises and to separate this fall in spending into that part borne domestically through lower growth and that part borne by the rest of the world through a lower trade deficit.[28]

The misery index finds that crises have been becoming more destructive over time, and that for the countries themselves crises in emerging markets are more destructive than those in advanced economies. Figure 42 reports the average misery index across the countries most affected by each of the five crises described earlier, while Figure 45 at the end of this chapter reports the results for every major country involved in each crisis.[29] In the case of the Bretton Woods break-up (the earliest of the advanced country crises) the misery index for the United States is just one, implying a reduction in spending of 1 percentage point of US output, with half of this modest shock transferred to the rest of the world through a lower trade deficit (the gray segment versus the black segment). The average misery index for the countries involved in the ERM crisis, the next shock to the advanced countries, jumps to 5½ percent of output. The recent North Atlantic crisis involved another major leap in the size of the shock to spending, with an average index of 12. The emerging market shocks are even larger, with an average misery index of 18 percent of output for the Latin American crisis, rising to over 30 for the subsequent Asian crisis. This is over thirty times the shock to spending created by the Bretton Woods break-up on the United States, with half of the fall in spending being borne by the crisis countries. It is easy to understand why emerging markets are more concerned about international capital flows and potential crises than advanced countries.

An alternative approach is to scale the misery index by world output, which gives a sense of the size of the shock to global spending (Figure 43). Strikingly, the shock to global spending from crises increases steadily over time because the larger shocks to emerging markets are offset by their smaller weight within the world economy. The impact on global spending rises steadily from around ¼ percent for the Bretton Woods crisis of the late 1960s/early 1970s to 1 percent by the time of the Asia crisis of the late 1990s. It then jumps massively to over 2½ percent of global output for the North Atlantic crisis of 2008–12. The pattern of steadily rising losses also holds

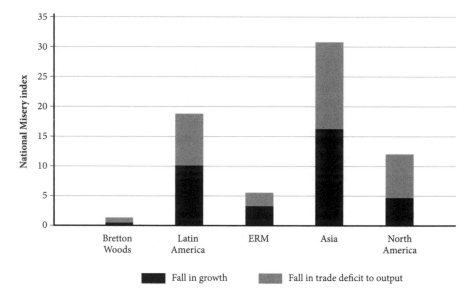

Figure 42: Crises are more costly for emerging markets.
Source: World Economic Outlook Database.

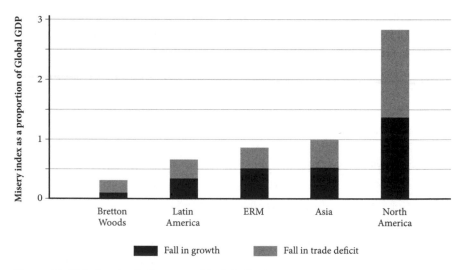

Figure 43: Global costs of crises rose with globalization.
Source: World Economic Outlook Database.

separately for the impact on the domestic economy through growth and the rest of the world through the trade deficit.

In addition, the financial outflows during these crises have consistently come from debt holdings rather than equities, underlining the more destructive nature of debt flows (Figure 44). By contrast, the composition of debt seems less important, as the relative role of bank and bond finance varies widely. In the case of the break-up of Bretton Woods and the Latin American debt crisis, most of the flows came from banks. By contrast, for the ERM crisis, bond and bank outflows were of a similar magnitude as investors such as George Soros bet on a devaluation, a pattern that also holds for the Asia crisis. Finally, in the North Atlantic crisis the form of the debt outflows reflected the manner in which the bad loans were bundled. In the United States the largest outflows were from bonds as foreigners sold securitized assets, while in the European periphery the outflows were driven by banks.

These are illustrative calculations and questions could be raised about the time windows that are used and the inclusion or exclusion of specific countries. In addition, these calculations look at outcomes, which can be affected by the effectiveness of the policy responses rather than the underlying shocks. That said, it would take a large number of adjustments to overturn the basic, and intuitive, result that the destructiveness of international financial crises has risen over time along with increasingly open international debt flows. So how can debt flows be constrained?

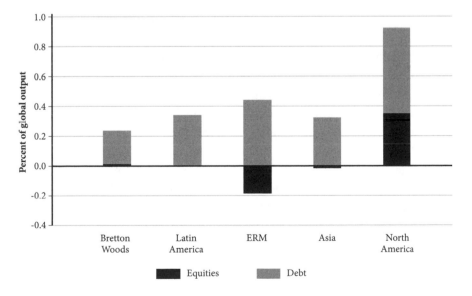

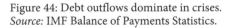

Figure 44: Debt outflows dominate in crises.
Source: IMF Balance of Payments Statistics.

* * *

Taming International Debt Flows

Policymakers should promote policies that preserve most of the benefits of open international capital markets while minimizing the associated risks. In particular, international equity flows should be encouraged as they are relatively stable and typically provide long-term benefits to both sides of the transaction. By contrast, as this chapter has documented, there is a strong case for some discouragement of international debt flows. Such flows have been associated with ever larger shocks to the international monetary system in which excessive earlier lending is abruptly reversed. This does not imply stopping all debt flows. There is clearly a role for debt in the financial system since such loans require much less oversight of the borrower than an equity stake. But there are equally good reasons to be careful about such flows given their inherent instability. In this context, three basic approaches have been proposed to increase the stability of the international financial system: Expanding the global financial safety net, allowing countries more leeway in responding to inflows, and improving the mix within capital flows from lending countries. Which is the best solution?

Expanding the Global Financial Safety Net

The communiqué to the first ever G20 leaders' summit, convened at the height of the crisis in November 2008, emphasized the importance of expanding the global financial safety net with a commitment to "ensure that the IMF, World Bank, and other M[ultilateral] D[evelopment] B[anks] have sufficient resources to continue playing their role in overcoming the crisis".[30] Five months later, at the London summit, the G20 leaders followed up on this commitment when they agreed to triple the IMF's resources (to $750 billion), together with other reforms to make IMF voting shares more representative of the changing global economy and to provide additional support to other multilateral institutions. Although the process took longer than anticipated, this commitment has been more or less achieved with the passage of the IMF's 14th quota increase in early 2016.

The record, however, suggests that a larger global safety net is unlikely to solve the problem of sudden reversals of unsustainable debt inflows. The IMF committed significant resources in past crises, for example providing loans of about 1½ percent of output to Thailand and South Korea in 1997. These loans provided a major increase in reserves available to counter capital flight. However, they represented only about one-tenth of the change in trade balance over 1996–98. A larger global safety net could help cushion the blow further, but in any realistic scenario the available resources will remain small compared to potential outflows. In addition, IMF loans are designed to restore external viability, an objective that is generally associated with painful policy adjustments.

An alternative way of boosting the global safety net is to expand central bank swap lines—agreements to let one central bank borrow currency from another one. Swap lines were used extensively over the North Atlantic crisis. The general experience was that the initial amounts pledged were too small to provide a significant counterweight to capital flight by investors. While emerging market swap lines remained relatively ineffective, lines across the major advanced country central banks were steadily augmented and eventually became unlimited. Clearly, an unlimited swap line can counter any speculative flow, but such arrangements are only open to a few countries and are thus a limited panacea. And even for the countries with unlimited swap lines, the commitment could be tested if such loans threatened macroeconomic stability at home, as demonstrated by the pullback by the Bundesbank from support for Italy and the UK in the ERM crisis.

Encouraging Intervention or Capital Controls by Recipient Countries

An alternative is to encourage countries to protect themselves from the risks caused by international debt flows by building international reserves or by imposing controls on capital flows. While ample reserves can be useful, it is difficult to see this as a game-changer for similar reasons to the global financial safety net. Larger reserves provide countries with a buffer, but it is a folk theorem among international finance analysts that reserves are most useful when they are not used. Selling reserves can be viewed by investors as a sign of trouble that can increase rather than limit the scramble for the exits. Indeed, the evidence suggests that selling reserves to defend an overvalued exchange rate is generally ineffective, although once the exchange rate has fallen to a sustainable level such intervention can break market momentum and avoid "overshooting" of the exchange rate to excessively depreciated values.

Capital controls are another self-insurance mechanism. They work best as a preemptive device, countering excessive inflows of debt from the rest of the world. However, such foresight is not a characteristic of past international financial crises. Rather, in the crises discussed in this chapter, policymakers and investors alike believed that the capital inflows reflected high returns combined with bright prospects for future growth. Imposing capital controls after a crisis has started is clearly much less effective. In addition, there is an issue of timing. Malaysia imposed capital controls in 1998 but most commentators agree that this only occurred after most of the foot-loose international money had already left.[31]

Discouraging Debt Outflows from Source Countries

The most promising approach to making international capital flows safer is for source countries to encourage investors to use safer instruments. While there are good reasons for investors to use debt contracts in a financial system, in practice many government policies have encouraged debt over equity. For example, interest and principal repayments on debt are typically treated more favorably in tax systems than dividend payments or capital gains on equities. Similarly, required capital buffers for investors tend to be lower for debt which is seen as being less risky for the individual lender. Strikingly, for example, bank purchases of rich country debt is given a zero risk weight within the Basel capital rules, a provision that encouraged loans to Euro area governments such as Greece.

Given the systemic costs from recurring international financial crises, regulatory reforms to make global capital flows safer should be given a high priority. As large debt inflows are generally financed from advanced countries, it is particularly important for "source" countries in take the lead in such an initiative. Changing tax laws that favor debt over equity promotes financial stability domestically and well as internationally. In addition, the added systemic risk coming from international bank loans and bond purchases should be acknowledged by increasing the risk weights on such activities, just as has been done since the crisis for domestic markets such as repossession agreements and securitizations. The risk weights should be higher for short-term loans than longer-term ones and should rise steadily as inflows into a country increases compared to (say) the size of its financial system. The rising costs of these capital buffers would cause investors to consider the wisdom of blindly following others into a country. It would also provide regulators in source countries with a market-based lever to discourage such outflows, avoiding the ineffectiveness of the warnings provided, for example, by the Federal Reserve about US bank lending to Latin America in the 1970s.

These additional charges for the systemic risk coming from international debt flows would complement domestic macroprudential policies that have been widely adopted in the wake of the North Atlantic crisis. Such policies are now an important feature of the financial landscape as countries have shown an increasing willingness to use tools such as higher capital buffers or restrictions on (for example) loan-to-value ratios to restrain potential excesses within the housing market. The extension of such a macro-prudential approach to international lending is an obvious corollary given the regularity and growing size of the associated crises. Putting some judicious sand in the wheels of debt-creating international flows would have limited costs for the allocation of saving and investment around the world through equities flows while promoting a significantly less risky international financial system.

	Growth	Trade Deficit/GDP	Misery Index
Bretton Woods 1967–73			
US 70–75	-0.4	-0.6	-1.0
Latin Am+AC8:American Debt 1981			
Mexico 80–82/81–83	-10.0	-10.1	-20.1
Brazil 80–82/82–84	-8.6	-9.1	-17.7
Average	-9.3	9.6	-18.9
ERM 1992–93			
France 89–93	-5.0	-1.5	-6.5
UK 89–92	-2.1	-2.9	-4.9
Italy 89–92	-2.6	-3.1	-5.7
Average	-3.2	-2.5	-5.7
Asia 1997			
Thailand 96–98	-13.3	-21.9	-35.2
Malaysia 96–98	-20.9	-5.8	-26.8
Indonesia 96–98	-17.4	-19.2	-36.6
Korea 96–98	-13.1	-14.9	-28.0
Average	-16.2	-15.5	31.6
North Atlantic 2008–2011			
US 07–09	-4.6	-1.5	-6.1
Italy 07–13	-3.2	-2.7	-5.9
Spain 07–13	-5.4	-9.2	-14.7
Ireland 07–13	-4.1	-10.6	-14.7
Portugal 07–13	-3.6	-9.2	-12.8
Greece 07–13	-6.5	-9.1	-15.6
Average	-4.6	-4.8	-9.4

Figure 45: Misery index for the major players in the crises.
Source: IMF World Economic Outlook database except US 70–75 which is from national sources.

PART III

COMPLETING THE CURE

Chapter 7

WILL REVAMPED FINANCIAL REGULATIONS WORK?

The need for a thorough revamp of financial regulation was recognized from the outset of the North Atlantic crisis. The first ever G20 leaders' summit, convened in November 2008, just weeks after the collapse of Lehman Brothers in Washington, pledged to "implement reforms that will strengthen financial markets and regulatory regimes so as to avoid future crises". A few months later at the April 2009 London G20 summit the leaders issued a Declaration of Strengthening the Financial System that promised extensive changes, including expanding the clubby Financial Stability Forum into the more formal Financial Stability Board whose membership includes every G20 country.

The result has been a massive overhaul of international and national financial regulations and supervision. This has responded vigorously to the immediate problems laid bare by the North Atlantic crisis, including stronger international rules on capital buffers, tighter definitions on what comprises bank capital, and new liquidity standards that have decreased reliance on potentially unstable wholesale funding. At the same time, EU leaders have endorsed the principle of a full banking union while in the United States the Dodd–Frank legislation involved a thorough tightening of regulations, including on shadow banks. Indeed, the current conjuncture may well be a high water mark for bank regulation as the political landscape has started to turn against tougher rules. Some proposed reforms may well not go forward or be watered down and others that have been passed could be rolled back or weakened. This is therefore a good time to assess how far the regulatory revamp has solved the long-term weaknesses that drove the North Atlantic into crisis discussed earlier in this book, rather than simply responding to immediate symptoms.

The initiatives taken internationally, in Europe, and in the United States all have the same aim of making the banking system sounder using the principles articulated by the G20. However, despite the similarity in purpose, each set of initiatives basically deals with different aspects of a common problem. As such, it is easiest to explain the content and implications of each set of reforms in turn.

* * *

Upgrading the Basel Rules

The crisis laid bare the inadequacy of the Basel 2 international regulatory rules, as numerous banks that adhered to them had to be rescued or given major government support in response to severe market pressures. Rescues included IKB Deutsche Industriebank (Germany), Dexia (France/Belgium), Fortis (Belgium/the Netherlands), Banco Português de Negócios (Portugal), Anglo Irish Bank (Ireland), Bankia (Spain), as well as Citi and the independent US investment banks Bear Stearns (sold to JP Morgan Chase) and, most famous of all, Lehman Brothers (whose post-bankruptcy remnants were sold to Barclays Bank). In addition, many of the Euro area mega-banks came under sustained market pressure, including Deutsche Bank (the largest), ING (which accepted a capital injection from the Dutch government), and several French banks, while in the United States the two largest independent investment banks (Morgan Stanley and Goldman Sachs) saved themselves by becoming regulated banks which gave them access to emergency Federal Reserve funding. The failure of the existing Basel regime could not have been plainer.

The ensuing reforms comprised an emergency fix followed by a new framework. The awkwardly named Basel 2.5 system was an emergency fix that shored up capital charges for market risk. One reason that the internal risk models used in Basel 2 had generated inadequate capital buffers was that they used historical patterns of shocks and correlations across asset prices. Basel 2.5 moved the system from these value-at-risk models (VaRs) to stressed value-at-risk models (SVaRs) which incorporate the larger financial shocks, higher correlations across asset prices, wider margins between the buy and sell prices of assets, and the higher default risks seen in times of market panic. Some specific provisions for securitized assets, whose markets had largely seized up in the immediate aftermath of the

Lehman Brothers bankruptcy, topped off this emergency revamp of capital buffers for market risk.

The 2011 Basel 3 agreement was a more fundamental overhaul of international rules on bank safety. Given that the preamble to the new guidance describe the goal as providing a "comprehensive reform package addresses that the lessons of the financial crisis", it is worth critically assessing the Basel Committee's assessment of what had gone wrong.[1] The Committee ascribed the crisis to the build-up of excessive financial leverage (both on- and off-balance sheet), an erosion in the quality of the capital base, and insufficient liquidity buffers. These weaknesses meant that banks were unable to ride out the temporary trading and credit losses, so that banking problems were rapidly transmitted to the rest of the financial system and the real economy, resulting in unprecedented injections of liquidity, capital support, and guarantees that exposed taxpayers to large losses as well as spillovers to the rest of the globe. Notably absent from this assessment was the manipulation of risk weights by large banks using internal risk models. The Basel Committee was not willing to acknowledge that the switch to internal risk models had been a mistake. That rather than improving bank regulation, the switch had been driven by a view that regulation was not needed as market discipline was more effective, a flawed approach that had allowed the emergence of undercapitalized mega-banks on both sides of the Atlantic.

Based on this diagnosis, the Committee's new capital rules aimed to "improve the banking sector's ability to absorb shocks from financial and economic stress, whatever the source", with subsidiary objectives to "improve risk management and governance as well as strengthen banks' transparency and disclosures" and "to strengthen the resolution of systematically significant cross-border banks". Given the size of the changes, provisions are being phased in gradually, so that the entire Basel 3 package will not be in place until 2019, although in practice the impact on banks is quicker as market analysts are already comparing bank performance with these future requirements.

The Committee proposed a major strengthening of the existing risk-based capital framework. The definition of bank capital was tightened, with common equity (the most effective type of capital) raised from one-half to three-quarters of core capital and less effective hybrid instruments that had crept into the definition gradually eliminated. In addition, rules on supplementary "Tier 2" capital were tightened, and the even more supplementary "Tier 3" capital eliminated.

These improvements in the quality of capital were accompanied by an increase in the size of the capital buffers that banks had to hold against risk-weighted assets. Banks are required to hold common equity of at least 7 percent of risk-weighted assets (a baseline figure of 4½ percent is augmented by a 2½ percent "capital conservation" charge that provides an additional buffer than can be eroded in the face of a shock). Regulators can also choose to add a further counter-cyclical charge of up to 2½ percent if they are worried that bank lending is rising too fast during an economic boom. Should a bank allow its capital to fall below the minimum it faces steadily increasing constraints on how much of their profits can be distributed to shareholders. This compares with a pre-crisis requirement to hold only 4 percent of risk-weighted assets in core capital, only half of which had to be common equity.

Large "systemic" banks face a further charge of 1 to 2½ percent, implying a minimum common equity buffer of 8 to 9½ percent of risk-weighted assets. This charge is aimed at offsetting the wider risks that they pose and the funding advantages associated with being viewed by markets as too big to fail. In addition, globally important systemic banks will be subject to holding further capital buffers of 16 to 20 percent of risk-weighted assets (the precise figure has yet to be determined) comprising capital and unsecured bonds, adding a further layer of capital buffers, with the objective of ensuring that there are ample private lenders who can participate in any bank rescue.

To further protect tax payers from bearing the brunt of the costs of bank rescues, the EU has augmented these provisions with rules that require private lenders to participate in bank rescues to discourage generous government bailouts (US rules already required that the Federal Deposit Insurance Corporation choose a rescue plan that minimizes the costs to the federal government).

In a partial acknowledgement of the problems posed by internal models, the Committee also introduced a leverage ratio based on total assets. The acknowledgement of the need for a leverage ratio using total assets is an important step forward by the Basel Committee. However, the Committee made clear that the leverage ratio was only a backstop to the risk-weighted calculations. It requires banks to hold 3 percent of assets as core capital, a looser definition of capital than the common equity required for risk-weighted assets, and there is no supplement for systemic banks. While the Committee will revisit the size and definition of the leverage ratio in 2018 based on the experience to that point, the current pushback against stronger bank regulation does not bode well for a tougher approach.

Basel 3 also introduced two new liquidity standards aimed at ensuring that banks are protected against market contagion. The liquidity coverage ratio requires banks to hold enough saleable assets to survive a severe financial shock, in other words that investment banking operations are sufficiently backstopped with ready money. The net stable funding ratio (NSFR), on the other hand, limits the degree of maturity mismatch by constraining the degree to which long-term lending (loans of a year or more) can be financed through short-term and potentially volatile wholesale funding.

Basel 3 likely reflects the apex of tougher bank regulation and the accompanying burden on banks. Recently, attempts to further toughen the Basel 3 rules with an additional package known colloquially as "Basel 4" that was championed by the US Federal Reserve is now in limbo after it was postponed due to strong European objections, particularly from the Germans. This difference in views partly reflects long-standing differences in the philosophy on the role of banking in the economy. The US and the UK, who rely more on direct finance of companies via bond markets, are less concerned about abrupt changes in bank regulation than their French and German counterparts where banks are the major source of finance for firms.[2] The "Basel 4" initiative has also been weakened by the resignation of the Federal Reserve official who took the lead in the Basel negotiations and by the Trump administration's less stringent view on bank regulation.

While the Euro area and the United States have both adopted the Basel 3 framework, there are important and revealing differences that loosen the rules for Euro area banks while tightening them on US banks.[3] The most important difference is that the European Central Bank decided not to adopt the leverage ratio as a binding constraint, which means that large Euro area banks remain only subject to capital charges based on internal risk models. While it seems likely that the European Commission proposal to make the leverage ratio binding in 2018 will come into effect despite the current backlash against stricter regulation, the devil will be in the details. It is quite possible that the final implementation of the leverage ratio will include tweaks of rules that make it less stringent, as has occurred with other elements of the Basel 3 package. By contrast, the US has embraced the leverage ratio for its banks and, for the eight globally significant US banks, it increased the requirement to a more meaningful 5 percent of assets (6 percent for regulated banking backed by deposit insurance).[4] In addition, as discussed further below, the US-specific Dodd–Frank Act imposed a further backstop on the way that banks can calculate risk-weighted assets that also constrains the ability of US banks to manipulate risk weights using internal risk models.

There are also important differences in the types of banks covered by Basel 3 rules on either side of the North Atlantic. In the Euro area, the framework applies to all banks, and hence continues to favor the competitive position of large banks that can use internal risk models to calculate their capital buffers versus small banks that have to use standardized weights. By contrast, in the United States, Basel 3 applies only to large banks. Smaller banks are subject to older rules that fit more easily with US accounting rules, including the US version of the leverage ratio. Overall, the subtractions from the Basel guidance led the Basel Committee to assess that the European Union was "materially noncompliant" with Basel 3 while the additions by the United States left them with a "largely compliant" status. By contrast, most of the rest of the world adopted the suggested package without significant changes and hence are simply "compliant".

The key question is how well these changes in the Basel framework have addressed the pre-crisis weaknesses in bank regulation. The first part of this book argued that the fundamental flaw in the system was that large European and US investment banks could manipulate internal risk models to gain a competitive advantage over the rest of the system. This advantage was especially potent in boom times when high asset prices justified extremely thin capital buffers. Looked at from this perspective, the Basel reforms provide only a partial solution to the underlying issues. On the positive side are more stringent rules on capital buffers, including surcharges for systemic banks, and the new rules on liquidity. In addition, the introduction of the leverage ratio is a useful acknowledgement of the deficiencies of only monitoring risk-weighted assets. All of this makes the North Atlantic financial system safer against a new crisis even if some analysts still worry that capital buffers should be still higher.[5]

On the negative side, however, the fact that at this time Euro area banks remain only subject to internal risk models perpetuates some of the pre-crisis distortions. It provides the large Euro area banks with a competitive advantage over smaller banks, and hence perpetuates mega-banks. Indeed, it is striking that an assessment of the leverage ratio by the European Bank Authority (EBA) found that, in contrast to smaller banks:

> The quantitative benchmarking results give indications of a potentially elevated exposure to REL [risk of excessive leverage] in the case of *the largest and most complex credit institutions, in particular those that operate the business model of a 'cross-border universal bank' and that are, at the same time, GSIIs [Global Systematically Important Institutions]* (emphasis added).[6]

This implies that capital remains thin compared to total assets despite additional capital charges for systemic banks, and the EBA goes on to recommend a higher leverage ratio for such institutions. Recent market jitters with regard to Deutsche Bank also suggest that capital buffers for large Euro area banks remain problematic. The fact that the Euro area banks are not subject to the leverage ratio also gives them a potential competitive advantage over their international competitors, especially systemic US banks that are under additional constrains over and above baseline Basel 3 rules. At present, the advantage conferred by internal risk models is limited since depressed asset prices imply a more pessimistic assessment of credit worthiness and higher capital charges. With asset prices starting to recover, however, these models could again promote a cyclical boom in bank lending based on an inappropriate thinning of capital buffers. This risks restarting the cross-Atlantic financial drift that helped to fund the US housing bubble. How far can better supervision coming from moves to a Euro area banking union offset these risks?

* * *

Moving Toward a Euro Area Banking Union

In June 2012, even as the Euro crisis continued to rage, European heads of state agreed in principle to move to a banking union in which all Euro area banks would be overseen and supported by the European Central Bank (ECB) rather than national governments. This decision holds the promise of eliminating competition across national regulators and hence solving a major weakness in the design of the Euro area. Indeed, the announcement had an almost immediate dramatic effect on the Euro area crisis although in a somewhat indirect way. This was because it paved the way for President Draghi of the ECB to pledge that he would do "what it takes" to preserve the Euro, a move that rapidly ended the acute phase of the European crisis. Indeed, the promise of ECB support was so successful in calming market fears that the central bank was never required to activate the associated new Outright Monetary Transaction program designed to provide support to stressed Euro members.

The agreement to move towards a banking union reflected frustration at the failure of national regulators to "break the vicious circle between banks and sovereigns". Over the crisis, uncertainty over the costs of bailing out banks led to questions about the financial stability of the governments of Euro area members in crisis. Simultaneously, questions about the ability of these governments to provide banking support raised the riskiness of banks. The result was a vicious circle as the two processes reinforced each other and borrowing costs spiraled upwards. Much of the problem stemmed from the fact that markets assumed the worst because national regulators were unable to paint an accurate picture of the true state of the Euro area banking system. In particular, nationally led European stress tests in 2009, 2010, and 2011 were not deemed credible by the markets because individual national regulators were seen as providing low estimates of the true problems in their banking system since they did not want to disadvantage their own banks and sovereigns compared to those in other members. The failure of the European stress tests to calm market jitters over the state of the banking system was in sharp contrast to the success of the US stress tests of May 2009 conducted by the Federal Reserve Board and thrift supervisors that almost immediately calmed markets as they were seen as a realistic assessment of the amount of capital needed by US banking system.

The agreement to move to a banking union resulted in centralized supervision of Euro area banks at the European Central Bank. ECB supervision could be implemented relative easily because it had been contemplated as part of the Maastricht Treaty, and hence did not involve opening the Pandora's Box that a major treaty revision would entail. While Maastricht clearly gave the prudential supervision of credit institutions and the stability of the financial system to the "competent national authorities", a clause allowed the European Council to transfer these functions from national regulators to the European System of Central Banks if it voted unanimously on a proposal coming from the Commission, after having consulted the ECB, and if the European Parliament agreed. The inability of national regulators to ensure the stability of the banking system by providing credible stress tests over the crisis allowed these hurdles to be overcome.

The ECB now directly supervises 129 significant Euro area banks that include over 80 percent of regional assets.[7] Inspections of these banks occur through Joint Supervisory Teams headed by a coordinator from the ECB (who cannot be a national of the country involved) plus a sub-coordinator (who is such a national). These two lead a team comprising ECB staff and supervisors from the home country as well as any other Euro area countries in which the bank has major operations. This team reports to the ECB's Supervisory Board, comprising a chair and vice-chair from the ECB Executive Board, four more ECB employees, and representatives from all countries. The remaining three thousand-odd Euro area banks are supervised at the national level under the oversight of the ECB, whose job is to maintain consistency and provide technical support.

The 129 significant Euro area banks supervised by the ECB can be stratified into three groups depending on their international reach. Three Euro area banks are truly international—Deutsche Bank of Germany and Santander and BBVA of Spain—with over 30 percent of their assets outside of the EU, so that effective supervision implies the need for close collaboration with non-EU supervisors. A further seven banks can be thought of as pan-European, in that more than 30 percent of their assets are in the rest of the European Union. These are the banks whose supervision benefits most from the switch from national to centralized banking supervision since it allows European supervisors a fuller assessment of their overall operations. The remaining 119 banks are primarily national, with over 70 percent of their assets in their home country. Strikingly, while the ten international/ European banks are owned by private shareholders, many of the 119 nationally orientated banks are owned by less transparent cooperatives or by the government. These arrangements create a strong national bias that limits their ability to expand overseas or to be acquired by other banks, and suggest that there remain major institutional limits on how much further the integration of the European banking system can proceed.

How do these changes in the Euro area banking system compare with its pre-crisis deficiencies? As outlined in the first part of this book, the combination of universal banks (as a result of the single market program), regulatory competition (as a result of the Maastricht Treaty), and internal risk models for investment banking (as a result of the Basel market risk amendment) created a small number of nationally oriented mega-banks that were large as a proportion to their own economies and generally had bloated investment banking operations. Over the boom, these mega-banks manipulated the flexibility of the internal risk models to thin their capital buffers, and reallocated the capital that was freed to make increasingly unwise loans that led to a banking crisis. The move to ECB supervision clearly solves the problems associated with competition across national supervisors, including the incentives of national supervisors to support national champions, discourage foreign entry, and undermine stress tests of the European banking system. Indeed, banking union holds the promise of creating a truly integrated Euro area banking system.

Crucially, however, the banking union remains only half formed.[8] This is because responsibility for bank rescues remains largely with national governments. Bank deposit insurance is still the province of individual members within European Monetary Union and, while a European-wide bank resolution system was agreed in July 2014 funded from charges on banks, it will take seven years to mature and even when complete will be too small to cope with any major bank rescues. In theory, there is also a (limited) option to provide centralized support for Euro area banks using

European Stability Mechanism (ESM), a bailout fund for countries in crisis. Indeed, in 2012 there was an expectation that EU funds would be used to directly recapitalize and restructure the Spanish banking system. If the EU had indeed taken the lead, this would have cemented the use of centralized funds to support Euro area banks and would have been a major move toward banking union. In the end, however, funds were only lent to the Spanish government, which bore responsibility for the actual bank restructuring. In practice, therefore, bank support currently remains in essence a national responsibility within the Euro area. Since the mega-banks are so large compared to national output, this also implies that some banks remain too big to fail.

The split between centralized bank supervision and national responsibility for bank rescues risks undermining the effectiveness of centralized ECB supervision of Euro area banks. This is because it replaces one set of misaligned incentives with another set. The problem with the pre-crisis system was that national regulators were responsible for both bank supervision and support, creating incentives for a regulatory race to the bottom. The new system generates a new misalignment of incentives since national regulators, who have responsibility for bank support, will generally want to minimize their assessment of banking problems and the associated costs which will put them at odds with the ECB, which is responsible for supervision. Indeed, this already seems to be occurring in the case of the Italian banks where the ECB is keener on a comprehensive approach to cleaning up the problems of the system than the Italian authorities. Unless this dichotomy is resolved by creating a Euro area bank rescue fund, the gap between the centralized responsibility for supervision and national responsibility for the costs of bank cleanup will continue to create unhelpful tensions between the ECB and national authorities. This underlines the importance of completing the half-formed Euro area banking union. We now turn to the quite different imperatives involved in US financial reform.

* * *

Taming the US Shadow Banks

US financial reformers faced a fundamentally different issue from those in Europe. Banks in Europe were under a flawed single system. The issues in the United States, on the other hand, centered on the dual nature of the pre-crisis banking system that contained a relatively tightly regulated core and a loosely regulated shadow banking system. Post-crisis changes in US regulation were thus focused on revamping the regulation of shadow banks and altering the dividing line between the two sectors.

The most important reform since the crisis has been to move the investment banks into the regulated banking sector. Most of this change largely occurred by necessity over the crisis, as the independent US investment banks were either rescued and absorbed by regulated banks (Bear Stearns, Merrill Lynch, and Lehman Brothers) or voluntarily converted to regulated banks to gain access to Federal Reserve emergency funding (Morgan Stanley and Goldman Sachs). There was also one deliberate action, which was the decision to bring foreign-owned investment banks into the US safety net by forcing them to become bank holding companies.

The conversion of the investment banks into regulated banks has largely tamed the pre-crisis shadow banking system since the lightly capitalized investment banks were at its core. Bringing the investment banks into the regulated banking system with its much more stringent capital buffers has made the investment banks themselves safer. Equally important, however, is that it has largely eliminated the funding advantage of the rest of the shadow banking system. The investment banks were the main providers of funds to other parts of the shadow banking system such as hedge funds. The additional costs of higher capital buffers in the investment banks have been passed on to their clients in the shadow banking sector through higher interest rates on loans.

Bringing the investment banks into the regulated banking sector leveled the playing field between the two halves of the banking system. However, the broker-dealers at the heart of the investment banks are still subject to some differences in regulation compared to commercial banks, although how these procedures would work in the case of a new crisis is unclear given the creation of a system-wide oversight council which can label firms as systemic. In addition, while the FDIC can extend support to broker-dealers in the face of a crisis, it may take a more cautious approach to such nonbanks compared to its traditional bank clients.

This major change in the US dual banking system has been reinforced by numerous other tweaks, most of them contained in the 2010 Dodd–Frank Wall Street Reform and Consumer Protection Act.[9] Among its many provisions, the Dodd–Frank Act ended the silos across regulators that had allowed the rapid pre-crisis expansion of shadow banking system. More specifically, the act created the Financial Stability Oversight Council (FSOC), chaired by the Secretary of the Treasury and including all major financial regulators, with a mandate to oversee the entire US financial system for systemic risks and regulatory gaps. For example, the FSOC can require Fed oversight of nonbanks that are viewed as posing a potential risk to financial stability and facilitates information-sharing across agencies. While there are concerns about how effective the somewhat large and unwieldy FSOC would be in the event of a crisis, its creation clearly signaled a desire to end the destructive pre-crisis compartmentalization across US financial regulation.

Another important aspect of the Dodd–Frank Act was the Collins amendment, which limits the ability of large US banks that adhere to the Basel rules to use internal risk models to manipulate risk weights. The amendment requires these banks to calculate risk-weighted assets using the standardized risk weights designed for smaller banks as well as their own internal risk models and use whichever risk-weighted asset calculation is larger. The large US banks are thus subject to three regulatory capital approaches: The opaque internal risk model calculations of risk-weighted assets, the simpler and more verifiable standardized approach to risk weighted assets, and the Basel 3 leverage ratio on total assets discussed earlier. The use of standardized weights and the leverage ratio largely elim-inates the ability of large US banks to use their internal risk models to reduce capital buffers, just as before the crisis the simple leverage ratio protected the US regulated banks from the erosion of capital buffers seen in the Euro area and US investment banks.

Numerous other aspects of US financial regulation were strengthened by the Dodd–Frank Act. Among the most important is the Volcker rule, which disallows banks from most trading in markets on their own behalf and raised the capital buffers on the reminder. Capital requirements were also tightened on repurchase agreements (repos) and securitizations, the latter of which has essentially ended private securitizations. In addition, complex institutions such as universal banks are also required to create living wills that specify how they will be resolved in the event of bank-ruptcy, many shadow banks such as hedge funds are now registered with the Securities and Exchange Commission (SEC), which also now oversees the credit agencies, and the Consumer Financial Protection Bureau was created. On the other hand, the international effort to move trading of derivatives to centralized platforms to make the market more transparent and avoid the confusion associated with the pre-crisis spaghetti bowl of bilateral trades has met with only partial success. In particular, while the US repo market has shrunk and the length of the typical loan has been extended, a lot of trading has moved from the more transparent and more easily regulated trilateral market, in which a third party holds the collateral, to the hazier bilateral market in which the lender and borrower dispense with third-party assistance.

A final major element of US regulatory reform was the nationalization of the two major housing government-sponsored enterprises (GSEs), Fannie Mae and Freddie Mac. Before the crisis, the status of these institutions was ambiguous as they were private institutions with a public purpose. The markets treated them as having a pseudo-government guarantee, on the (accurate) assumption that in the event of a crisis the federal government would take control of them. With the private mortgage-backed asset markets moribund, essentially all new mortgage-backed securities are now being issued through Fannie and Freddie, and hence have federal guarantees on the quality of the underwriting. In short, the US mortgage-backed securities market has in effect been nationalized.

How do these changes respond to the problems observed in the pre-crisis US financial system? Three major trends created the US financial crisis. The first was the expansion in securitization of mortgages as higher capital buffers for regulated banks provided incentives for them to sell such loans to shadow banks with lower capital buffers. The second was the accompanying expansion of the lightly regulated shadow banking system centered on the investment banking groups, including their broker-dealer operations that borrowed wholesale funds from those with large pools of cash and lent them out to other parts of shadow banking such as hedge funds. Finally, the widening of repo collateral to mortgage-backed securities and foreign bonds led to an increase in private label securitizations based on questionable mortgages and an increase in dollar borrowing and purchases of such US assets by foreign banks.

The US regulatory revamp has largely negated these underlying weaknesses, although future changes in regulation could undermine this progress. Bringing the investment banks under Federal Reserve supervision has eliminated the differences between the capital buffers that provided the regulated banks with strong incentives to sell loans to investment banks and the rest of the shadow banking system. In addition, higher capital charges on securitized assets and repurchase agreements led to a dramatic decrease in the size of investment banks, including their loans to the rest of the shadow banking system. The result has been the effective elimination of private securitizations even in areas such as car and credit cards where private securitizations had always dominated. On the other hand, while differences in the size of capital buffers between US regulated and shadow banks have been eliminated, there remain significant gaps between the capital buffers required for Euro area and US banks. As discussed earlier, this risks the reappearance of trades based on this gap.

Recent moves by the Trump administration suggest a willingness to reduce the burden of financial regulation. While most of this effort is directed at small banks, these include moves to curtail the powers of the FSOC and of the Consumer Financial Protection Bureau and to weaken provisions such as the Volcker rule. In addition, talk about passing a twenty-first century Glass–Steagall law opens up the possibility that investment banks will again face less stringent regulation than regulated banks, potentially reopening the differences in regulation that helped drive the crisis.

On a wider level, the difference between the European regulators' past and present focus on risk weights based on internal models and the US preference for including an unweighted leverage ratio leads to the question of the relative merits of the two approaches. Clearly, a risk-weighted measure would be more sensible if risk could be accurately measured, as bank capital buffers are held to offset potential losses that should vary with the type of loan. On the other hand, several studies have found that the leverage ratio based on total assets was a better predictor of bank failures than risk-weighted ratios in both the US and Euro area over the crisis, suggesting that an unweighted measure of assets is safer despite its apparent bluntness.[10] The evidence about which banks were hit hardest over the crisis, however, may reflect the nature of this particular crisis, which involved a prolonged period of market turmoil. Such turmoil would naturally have its largest effect on banks with large investment banking operations. In addition, leverage ratios create their own distortions, particularly by lowering the incentive to keep low-risk loans on the books, implying that either fewer safe loans will be made or that banks will sell them to institutions under less onerous capital charges.

Ultimately, it is difficult to determine whether a generic risk-based capital standard based on standardized risk weights is better or worse than an unweighted one. This suggests aiming for a regime in which both matter by making sure that capital buffers are adequate using both the leverage ratio and the risk-weighted approach. Most basically, however, it is difficult to see why regulators continue to let banks use individual internal risk models to calculate risk-based capital charges rather than using standardized risk weights determined by supervisors. These models were introduced as a method of reducing the role of bank regulation on the assumption that market discipline would create the needed constraints on bank behavior. The crisis amply demonstrated that this approach was a mistake, and that using proprietary models to calculate capital buffers can create powerful incentives for a regulatory race to the bottom in search of short-term competitive advantage.

* * *

Charting the Post-Crisis Changes in the Financial System

It is useful to take a snapshot of the impact to date of financial reforms of the US and Euro area banking systems. While financial reforms remain a work in progress, with parts of Basel 3 only fully implemented in 2019, market analysts are already comparing bank performance with the eventual standards, which suggests more adjustment may have been made in practice than on paper. In addition, the data indicates that there have been limited changes in both systems between 2014 and 2016, suggesting that they are no longer experiencing radical structural shifts. At the same time, it needs to be recognized that the macroeconomic situation remains highly abnormal, with negative policy rates in the Euro area, some periphery banking systems still facing major problems from nonperforming loans, and banks continuing to hold large reserves at the central bank. Even in the United States, where economic recovery and bank cleanup are more advanced, interest rates remain low and reserves high.

There is also a question about the appropriate benchmark to compare the current situation with the past. Since the Euro area and US financial systems had become unsustainably large by 2008–09, the simple fact that they have subsequently shrunk says little about how far the system has been healed. This snapshot assumes using 2002 as a year in which the two systems were still relatively stable. This is the year before the SEC decision to widen the collateral eligible for repos. The first part of this book argued that the banking systems in the Euro area and the United States were relatively stable before this decision, and that it was after 2002 that the financial boom that led to major domestic and international financial imbalances gained steam. Consistent with the policy discussion earlier in this chapter, the results suggest that the Euro area banking system is much further away from being repaired than the US system.

Euro Area Banking Repair Remains Work In Progress

The Euro area banking system has shrunk since 2009 but remains much larger in proportion to the economy than it was in 2002 (Figure 46). Since peaking at well over 300 percent of output in 2009, the Euro area banking system has shrunk about one-third of the way back to its 2002 size. Within this overall pattern there is a significant difference between the core and the periphery. Assets in the Euro area core banks have shrunk about half way back to their 2008 values while in the periphery the equivalent shrinkage is one-fifth (although the core banks remain considerably larger in absolute terms and more dependent on investment banking). This suggests that major further Euro area bank restructuring is needed, particularly in the periphery where banks have limited the shrinking of their assets by increasing their holdings of zero risk-weighted government debt which has further linked the financial fortunes of banks with the government.[11] This is also consistent with other assessments that suggest that the Euro area banking system remains overbanked with low profitability.[12]

The compression in the size of the Euro area core banks largely reflects a pullback from foreign ventures in the United States and the periphery (Figure 47). Assets of Euro area core banks in the periphery, the United Kingdom, and the United States have approximately halved since 2008 as a ratio of output to below their 2002 levels. The pullback from the periphery may help explain some of the difference in the size of the contraction in banking systems between the two halves of the Euro area. The shrinkage of the UK/US operations reinforces the evidence of a significant pullback from investment banking. In additions, commercial loans have risen in

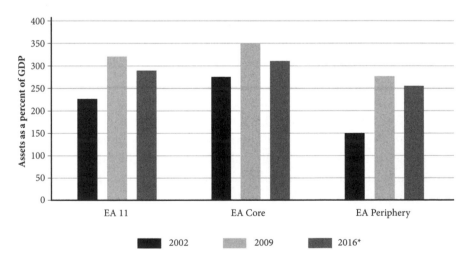

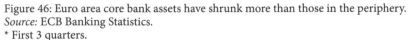

Figure 46: Euro area core bank assets have shrunk more than those in the periphery.
Source: ECB Banking Statistics.
* First 3 quarters.

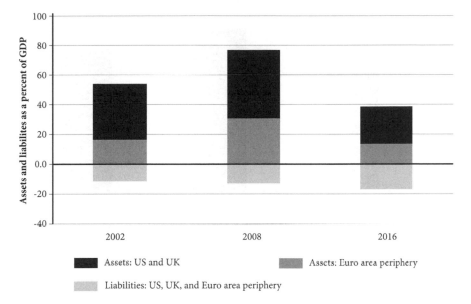

Figure 47: Euro area core banks have pulled back from the periphery and the US/UK.
Source: BIS banking statistics and EU national accounts.

importance to around their 2002 level when the data are adjusted for continuing large holdings of central bank reserves.

The twelve Euro area mega-banks have shrunk as a proportion of the overall banking system, but remain more important than in 2002 (Figure 48). Most of the mega-banks survived the crisis with varying types of support, the exception being the French/Belgian bank Dexia which has been broken up. The pullback has been more marked for the eight banks headquartered in the Euro area core such as Deutsche Bank of Germany and BNP Paribas of France, plausibly associated with the retreat from investment banking that was always a much more important part of their business. By contrast, assets of the more commercially orientated periphery mega-banks have shrunk by much less. Indeed, the assets of the two Spanish mega-banks, Santander and BBVA, have expanded as a ratio of output.

Tighter regulation has improved capital buffers for the Euro area mega-banks. Figure 49 updates the relationship between the risk-weighted Basel capital ratio (on the horizontal axis) and the unweighted ratio of equity to assets (on the vertical one) earlier reported in Figure 25 in Chapter 3. Euro area bank capital buffers have improved compared to 2008 (and 2002). Risk-weighted capital ratios have leapt and the tail of banks with exceptionally low ratios of equity to assets has been eliminated. In addition, the clear

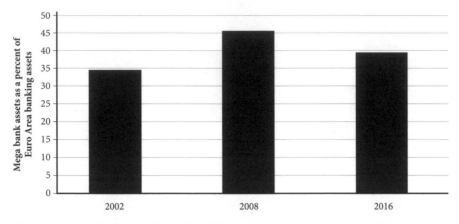

Figure 48: Mega-bank assets have shrunk but remain a large component of the Euro area banking system.
Source: Bloomberg and Euro Area Banking Statistics.

negative relationship between the two measures of bank soundness seen in 2008 has disappeared as banks with large investment operations have been forced to raise more capital, but the positive relationship seen in 1996 has not been restored. In addition, as discussed earlier, capital buffers will likely thin as asset prices recover.

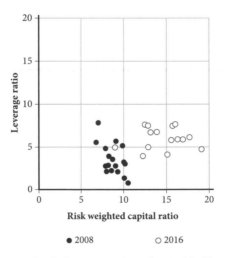

Figure 49: Euro area mega-banks have strengthened capital buffers.
Source: Bloomberg.

US Reforms Seem More Complete

Tougher post-crisis regulation has changed the structure of the US financial system more fundamentally than the European one. Assets of regulated banks have expanded slightly compared to output while those of investment banks have fallen by almost a half (Figure 50).[13] This reflects the leveling of the regulatory playing field between the regulated and investment banks compared to the much looser regulation of investment banks before the crisis. As a result, despite the expansion in regulated banking since 2008 as a ratio to output, the size of the overall dual banking system has shrunk back close to its 2002 value. This suggests that most of the excesses in US banking have been redressed.

The private securitization market effectively disappeared after the regulatory playing field was leveled, underlining that the market was driven by pre-crisis differences in capital buffers between the regulated and investment banks rather than fundamentals (Figure 51). The eclipse of private label securitized assets can be seen most clearly in the market for consumer loans (credit card debt and car loans). One-quarter of this debt was sold to markets using private securitized assets in 2008 (a similar proportion to 2002), while by 2016 such securities were negligible. There are still some private mortgage-backed securities in the market, but this reflects the

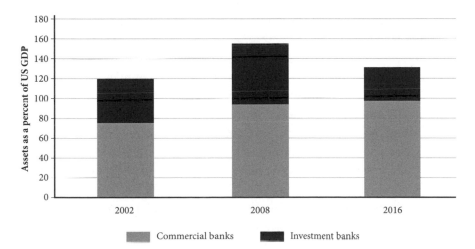

Figure 50: US commercial bank assets rose after the crisis, investment bank assets contracted rapidly.
Source: US Flow of Funds.
Note: Investment bank assets are calculated as twice the size of broker-dealers.

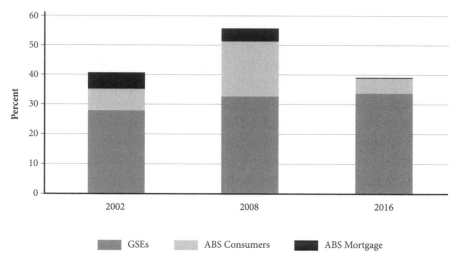

Figure 51: Private securitization has dwindled.
Source: US Flow of Funds.

remnants of pre-crisis issuance rather than new activity, and the stock of assets continues to fall. The flip side to the disappearance of the private mortgage-backed securities has been a larger role for those issued by the GSEs. Around 60 percent of US mortgages are now guaranteed by the federal government through Fannie Mae and Freddie Mac, 10 percentage points higher than in 2002. This outsized federal role in the mortgage market is likely to likely to continue as reform of the GSEs has been put on the political back-burner.

Tougher regulation of the investment banks can be seen in the enormous rise in their capital buffers. Figure 52 compares the average leverage ratio for the independent US investment banks versus the US commercial and universal banks. At its pre-crisis nadir in 2007, the investment banks had a leverage ratio of just over 3 percent, only one-third of those at regulated banks and modestly lower than in 2002. By 2016, with the independent investment banks having been converted into bank holding companies and hence under the same regulatory regime as other banks, the capital buffers for the two remaining independent investment banks had almost tripled to 8 percent of assets. There is still a gap with the rest of the banking sector, whose capital buffers had also increased modestly as a result of tougher regulations. However, the limited size of this gap suggests it could plausibly reflect difference in underlying risk due to business models.

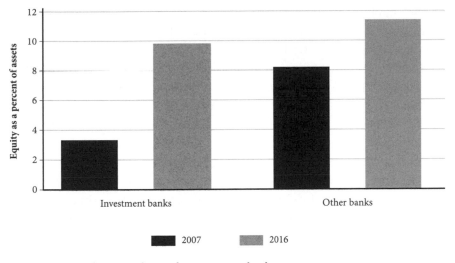

Figure 52: Capital increased most for investment banks.
Source: SNL.

* * *

The Road Ahead

The post-crisis period has seen the largest rejigging of the North Atlantic and global financial system since 1988 when Basel 1 imposed (relatively) consistent capital charges across countries. In the process, capital buffers have been increased, particularly for investment banking, rules on liquidity have been introduced, and the use of short-term wholesale funds has been reduced. While legacies of the crisis, including disappointing output growth and a volatile trading environment, have delayed the return to financial normality, particularly in the Euro area, it is clear than the North Atlantic financial system is more stable than it was before 2008.

Many of the weaknesses within the Euro area and the United States banking systems have been tackled. Within the Euro area, the major banks are under the centralized supervision of the ECB, which has put an end to the supervisory competition that initiated a pre-crisis race to the bottom as national regulators supported the expansion of their own national champion banks at the expense of sound supervision. In the United States, the remaining investment banks are now under federal supervision and support rather than being allowed to operate with inappropriately thin capital buffers. While other, less systemic parts of the shadow banking system remain largely outside of the regulatory framework, they have shrunk as short-term funds from investment banks have become more expensive and as the supply of complex financial instruments driven by differences in regulation has withered. The financial market place has become simpler and the corresponding trading strategies less obscure.

Looking ahead, the Euro area and United States face different banking challenges. In the United States, the priority is to ensure that legitimate simplification of red tape faced by smaller banks does not morph into a rollback of needed tougher regulation of large banks. In particular, any new version of the Glass–Steagall Act separating banks into investment and commercial banks should not be used to lower the stringency of regulation on the former.

The Euro area needs to complete its planned regulatory revamp and shrink banking assets to eliminate the overbanking that is crimping profits and setting the stage for future banking problems. The major priorities are twofold. First, introduce a meaningful leverage ratio above the Basel minimum of 3 percent ratio on the mega-banks, as well as a floor that limits the abuse of risk weights through internal risk models, such as the US approach of forcing large banks to also calculate risk-weighted assets using the standardized approach. Currently, the capital buffers for the Euro area mega-banks are still calculated using internal models whose properties are not well understood or closely policed. As asset prices recover, there is a risk that capital buffers of the mega-banks will erode further as models interpret high asset values as meaning lower risk. Even now, the advantage from internal risk models have meant that the European banking system continues to be dominated by "too big to fail" mega-banks despite post-crisis talk of cutting down the size of banks by raising capital buffers on systemic banks. Ensuring that Euro area banks are under similarly tough regulation to those currently in place in the United States will also avoid the risk of restarting "North Atlantic financial drift" trades created by looser regulation in the Euro area rather than competitive advantage, and which allowed a US housing crash to create a Euro area banking crisis.

Second, the Euro area banking union needs to be completed by setting up a centralized Euro-area-wide system of bank support. At present there is a risk that the new misalignment of incentives in Euro area bank regulation will slowly erode the advantages of centralized ECB banking supervision. The pre-crisis misalignment was that individual national bank supervisors were in competition with each other and allowed banks to expand too fast. The new misalignment is that supervision is centralized but the costs of banking problems remain national. Unless bank deposit insurance and support is also centralized, there is a risk that the national supervisors, who are a crucial component in making centralized supervision work, will begin to start gaming the central supervisors.

Chapter 8

MAKING MACROECONOMICS MORE RELEVANT

The North Atlantic crisis represents a massive failure for macroeconomics and policymakers. Macroeconomics was basically created after the Great Depression so that governments could limit economic cycles. After an unsustainable boom, the North Atlantic crisis generated the deepest global recession since the Great Depression and a tepid subsequent recovery. Talk of a "new mediocre" in growth and the rise in populism and associated rejection of expertise by political systems underlines the degree to which the optimism of the early 2000s has evaporated and been replaced by stagnant economic prospects and associated populist political tensions.

Before the crisis, North Atlantic policymakers missed the growing imbalances and overestimated the potency of policies. This reflected the increasing dominance of a market-based framework in which private sector activity was assumed to be fundamentally stable. As a result, policymakers focused on narrow objectives that provided support for such activity that allowed a series of financial, macroeconomic, and structural strains to fall under the radar. The policy parts did not sum to a whole and an apparently efficient system turned out not to be robust. A deep lesson from the crisis is that a robust economy requires a more integrated approach to policies based on a more realistic view of macroeconomics in which nobody is all-knowing, no institution is all-powerful, and instability can come from many sources, including financial markets.

The immediate response to the crisis in the United States and the Euro area illustrates the advantages of an integrated policy approach. The initial US policy response involved a cohesive mix of rapid monetary easing, fiscal expansion, and effective stress tests on the banks that avoided a repeat of the Great Depression. However, as the crisis has receded the imperative to pursue integrated policies has faded. As policies started to focus on differing goals, the anticipated rapid recovery never materialized and the US economy has settled into modest growth. The story in the Euro area is bleaker. With policy integration constrained by a badly designed monetary union, the initial banking crisis was extended by the revelation of fiscal mismanagement in Greece—a country that represents about 3 percent of Euro area output. The interaction between concerns about banks and government finances generated severe strains in Italy, Spain, Greece, Portugal, and Ireland. Indeed, at one point the crisis threatened the existence of the currency union itself, before a more aggressive stance to preserving the union by the European Central Bank diffused growing negative feedback loops.

* * *

The Way We Were

The pre-crisis macroeconomic orthodoxy had a precise and relatively narrow view of policy challenges. It focused on business cycle fluctuations around a slowly evolving path for underlying output (underlying output was determined by technology and was thus not part of the analysis). These fluctuations were primarily ascribed to wages and prices being sticky in the sense that they responded slowly to changes in economic slack. The challenge for policymakers was to minimize these temporary deviations from a slowly moving baseline.

The central bank of each country was viewed as the main institution responsible for responding to such business cycle fluctuations. Its policies were ideally guided by an inflation target, since an overheating economy would generate upward inflationary pressures while an economy with too much slack would exhibit downward inflationary pressures. Most advanced country central banks tried to keep inflation at around 2 percent, which was seen as low enough to mean that the general public would not worry about the rise in prices (particularly as measured inflation is upwardly biased due to difficulties in measuring technological change) while allowing the nominal interest rate to stay well above its lower bound of zero. If the economy was overheating and inflation was starting to rise, the central bank would raise its short-term policy rate, tightening financial conditions through higher costs of borrowing and by appreciating the exchange rate. This would gradually lower demand and bring the inflation rate back to its target. Symmetrically, if there was too much slack in the economy, the central bank would lower the short-term policy rate and boost demand and inflation.

Fiscal policy was primarily tasked with long-term objectives such as ensuring that government debt was low and sustainable and limiting the size of government. Active use of spending and taxes to dampen the business cycle was discouraged for several reasons. Political interference was thought to make it difficult to reverse any stimulus, leading to a larger government, fiscal deficit, and public debt. In addition, the delay involved in implementing a fiscal package meant that any fiscal stimulus (or consolidation) might occur after the cycle had already turned and end up amplifying fluctuations rather than cushioning them. Rather, automatic stabilizers (the natural increase in the government deficit in a slump as taxes fall and spending on the unemployed increases) were viewed as a more reliable way of stimulating the economy during slumps since its effects were immediate and were automatically reversed in a boom. Finally, economists had doubts about the effectiveness of fiscal deficits in stimulating private spending as tax cuts would lead to higher saving in anticipation of higher future taxes.

Financial and structural policies were handled by behind-the-scenes specialists. Financial stability was delegated to regulators who focused on the safety and soundness of individual institutions—so-called microprudential supervision. Similarly, the task of maintaining robust underlying growth was delegated to specialists in structural policies aimed at improving the functioning of specific areas of the economy, such as labor markets.

The pre-crisis orthodoxy elegantly compartmentalized policies by assigning specific goals to each institution. Central banks were responsible for taming the business cycle and delivering low and stable inflation, while other policymakers and institutions were primarily responsible for maintaining stability and efficiency in their areas of specialization—fiscal, financial, and structural. Clearly, this highly stylized system was a long way from the reality facing policymakers, even in major advanced countries, let alone the emerging markets that were prone to larger and more varied economic and financial shocks. This stylized vision of macroeconomics did, however, hold an important sway on thinking. This was particularly true for more analytically inclined policymakers such as Ben Bernanke, Chairman of the US Federal Reserve; Timothy Geithner, Head of the US Treasury; Jean-Claude Trichet, President of the European Central Bank; and Mervyn King, Governor of the Bank of England—the first and last being ex-academics, the middle two being trained economists with extensive policy experience.

Crisis and Consequences

The North Atlantic crisis called into question almost every element of this pre-crisis orthodoxy. The major economic shock came from the financial sector, a risk that had been largely discounted in mainstream models. It generated such a large shock that it rapidly overwhelmed the micro-prudential buffers required of individual firms. The resulting recession was so large that policy interest rates in the United States and Europe were rapidly driven down to zero. With no more room to cut rates and the economy still weakening, central banks were forced to experiment with "unconventional" monetary policies such as quantitative easing, in which central banks buy large amounts of assets such as government bonds by printing money. This eased financial conditions by reducing the supply of assets available to private investors, forcing them to either accept a lower interest rate on government bonds or move their money into riskier assets such as equities or foreign paper, thereby lowering long-term interest rates, raising equity prices, and depreciating the exchange rate, all of which supported activity. Tellingly, such policies were dubbed "unconventional" because they were inconsistent with conventional macroeconomic theory which implies that buying and selling assets would have no impact, as investors were assumed to be indifferent about holding different assets, despite the fact that before the crisis central banks controlled short-term interest rates by exactly this mechanism.

In another deviation from pre-crisis orthodoxy, in the immediate aftermath of the crisis the G20 successfully used fiscal stimulus to support activity. This largely reflected the initiative of Dominique Strauss-Kahn, then the head of the International Monetary Fund. At the conclusion of the first-ever G20 leaders meeting in Washington in November 2008, the final communiqué included a relatively innocuous pledge that leaders would "use fiscal measures to stimulate demand to rapid effect, as appropriate, while maintaining a policy framework conducive to fiscal sustainability". In a press conference later that day, however, Mr. Strauss-Kahn provided a much more concrete vision when he said: "What we're trying to organize is this coordinated action plan to have a boost in growth starting from a fiscal stimulus of 2 percent [of output]. Some measures have already been taken by some countries, and we are looking for a result of an increase in growth of also 2 percent."[1] In the face of concerns about a new depression, the idea of an internationally coordinated fiscal stimulus rapidly caught on, and the G20 did indeed achieve a fiscal expansion of around 2 percent of output over 2009 and 2010 that boosted growth temporarily.

Finally, the deep global recession and slow recovery (after the fiscal stimulus wore off) have led to an increasing recognition that structural policies can support the recovery by boosting medium-term growth. The key insight here is that the debt burden facing a country depends not only on the level of debt but also on how fast an economy is expected to grow. Debts that were regarded as easily repayable in an era of high growth expectations can become much more problematic in a low growth environment. This creates the risk of a self-reinforcing downward spiral in which it becomes harder to borrow, which constrains future growth, thereby making it still harder to borrow. In an attempt to break this cycle, in 2014 the G20 leaders committed to structural reforms that would add 2 percentage points to global potential over the next five years. Sadly, the effort was half-hearted as most of these commitments were to policies that were already planned.

In the light of the broad challenges that the crisis posed for the existing orthodoxy, post-crisis changes to macroeconomic thinking have been surprisingly limited. The recognition that financial shocks can be systemic and generate major recessions has been acknowledged by elevating "macrofinancial" policies as a new policy tool. Macrofinancial policies are regulations designed to avoid systemic risks to the financial system, such as capping the amount of debt that a mortgage borrower can assume compared to the value of a house. This reduces financial risks by constraining banks from providing high-risk loans in which the home owner makes little or no downpayment, so that even a small fall in house prices can create defaults and losses for banks. Another example of a macrofinancial policy is to limit the size of the mortgage compared to the borrower's income, which again seeks to curb banks from providing outsized mortgages which are more likely to be defaulted upon.

Macrofinancial policies are macroeconomic in two senses. First, they focus on the risk to the financial system as a whole, as opposed to the pre-crisis attention on the soundness of individual institutions though rules on capital buffers and the like. In addition, responsibility for macroprudential policies generally involves the central bank either on its own (as in the case of the United Kingdom) or as part of a wider committee (such as in the United States and the Euro area). The logic of linking macroprudential policies to central banks is that systemic financial shocks have major macroeconomic consequences, and hence decisions on macrofinancial policies should include the institution primarily responsible for macroeconomic stability.

In most other respects, however, macroeconomic orthodoxy has reverted to something surprisingly close to its pre-crisis normality as the immediate shock of the crisis has faded. For example, there appears to be an increasing consensus that financial stability and macroeconomic stability should be treated as separate objectives and assigned to separate policies—macro-prudential policies for financial risks and monetary policy for the business cycle. This reflects an evolving belief that monetary policy is too blunt an instrument to support financial stability, which is better left to more focused and specialized policies and policymakers.[2] Hence, while macroprudential policies have been elevated to new macroeconomic instrument, the basic pre-crisis assignment that financial regulators should take care of financial risks and that monetary policymakers should focus on stabilizing the business cycle has been largely maintained. Equally strikingly, central banks continue to use inflation targets as their basic framework, even though in the run-up to the crisis it was asset prices and trade deficits rather than inflation that most clearly pointed to overheating in the United States and the Euro area periphery. There are certainly macroeconomists who take a more eclectic view and think that monetary policy should also focus on financial imbalances, most notably in the Bank for International Settlements. But this seems to be becoming a minority view.

A similar reversion to pre-crisis orthodoxy has occurred with fiscal policy. Short-term fiscal stimulus was used by the G20 to boost output in the immediate aftermath of the crisis. In addition, many pundits continue to argue that fiscal stimulus should be used more aggressively to support the recovery given low borrowing costs for funds. However, the reality is that after the G20 boost ended in 2010, fiscal policymakers rapidly switched back to the pre-crisis mode of concentrating on longer-term objectives. These involve either ensuring that debt remains on a smooth and sustainable path, the objective behind the rules in the Euro area and the budget consolidation of President Obama's administration, or on reducing the tax burden and the reach of government, the motive behind the tax cuts proposed by President Trump's administration. After a brief flowering over the crisis, the idea that fiscal policy should be used to actively support demand has again fallen out of fashion.

With fiscal policy focusing on longer-term objectives, monetary policy has again become the primary instrument to stabilize the economy. This explains the reliance on "unconventional" monetary policies to boost lack-luster economic growth by buying long-term bonds and reducing the short-term policy rate below zero. It also led to calls for central banks to play a wider catalytic role in policymaking, including by encouraging a fiscal boost by promising easy money or even by sending out checks to individuals (so-called "helicopter money"). The desire to use the central bank as a way of inducing a fiscal expansion illustrates the abiding prefer-ence of experts for interacting with "technical" independent central banks rather than more "politicized" governments, a preference closely linked to memories of the inflation of the 1970s. More recently, pledges of tax cuts in the United States have led to the Federal Reserve potentially playing its more traditional post-1980 role of offsetting the stimulus to the economy coming from ideologically driven tax cuts, as occurred under the earlier administrations of Presidents Reagan and George W. Bush.

The story on structural policies is similar to that for fiscal policy, namely an initial burst of enthusiasm followed by a reversion to type. The initial burst of enthusiasm was centered around strengthening financial regulations and involved national initiatives, most notably the Dodd–Frank legislation in the United States, banking union in the Euro area, and tougher international standards, as embodied in revamped Basel 3 regulations. This has not, however, been followed by a wave of broader structural reforms. In most countries, including the United States and Euro area, reforms remain the province of particular departments, with labor reforms being covered by the labor department, product reforms by the commerce departments, tax reforms by finance departments, and so on. Only in Japan has "Abenomics" provided the clear commitment to wide-ranging structural reforms earlier embodied in Thatcherism and Reaganomics, although the recent election of strongly pro-European President Macron in France may change the situation.

A deep lesson from the crisis, however, is that policy compartmentalization runs the risk of tunnel vision and major mistakes. As the 2008 meltdown demonstrated, an environment in which policymakers focus on their own narrow mandates can result in missing threats that can create massive shocks to the system as a whole. A more inclusive view of macroeconomics and macroeconomic policies would be more robust as it would be less prone to such miscalculations. Specifically, a more inclusive view of macroeconomics is needed along three dimensions: Expanding the focus of macroeconomics to include topics such as potential growth as well as financial stability; widening interactions between institutions so macroeconomic policies can be decided in a more cooperative manner; and extending the frame of macroeconomic models beyond "homo economicus", the self-seeking individual at the core of most theories, to acknowledge the importance of group dynamics and rules of thumb.

* * *

Expanding the Focus of Macroeconomics

The rapid switch back to giving central banks the primary responsibility for combatting macroeconomic fluctuations after fiscal stimulus ended in

2010 is particularly striking given the lackluster economic performance subsequently. Over the following years, inflation remained well below US and Euro area targets and growth was substandard. In addition, central banks across the advanced world have yet to start shedding the assets they bought as part of quantitative easing. Equally importantly, assigning macroeconomic stability solely to the central bank is not intuitive. Indeed, before the 1980s the macroeconomic orthodoxy embraced an integrated approach in which monetary and fiscal policies were used simultaneously achieve full employment ("internal balance") and a desirable trade position ("external balance"). In this macroeconomic scheme there were two objectives (full employment/ stable inflation and a sustainable external position) and two instruments (monetary and fiscal policy). Currently, there are four objections—stable inflation/low slack, high underlying growth, low government debt, and financial stability—as well as four instruments—monetary, fiscal, structural, and financial policies. Since there are as many policies as objectives, it is possible (at least in principle) to achieve each objective independently. But there is clearly much more flexibility and many more options if policies assist each other rather than each being assigned to a specific task, just as was done in the 1960s for full employment and the trade balance.

The integrated approach of the 1960s in which monetary and fiscal policies were used to achieve full employment and a desirable trade balance fell out of favor in the wake of the rise in inflation of the 1970s. The loss in monetary control was diagnosed as coming from a slowing in underlying growth that governments and central banks failed to recognize. Politically motivated attempts to push the economy above its new sustainable underlying potential created overheating and inflation. This left an abiding distrust of government attempts to fine-tune the economy, which was part of a wider rejection of a "mixed" economy in which the government had a central role in promoting economic growth and private sector activity. It also left central banks with a strong view that cooperating with more politicized fiscal policymakers could skew their judgment, leading to an increasing belief that central banks should operate completely independently of governments.

The new paradigm in the 1980s emphasized a market-orientated approach in which the role of the government was to provide a stable backdrop against which the private sector could flourish. This approach, associated with the pro-market philosophy of Prime Minister Margaret Thatcher of the United Kingdom and President Reagan of the United States, envisaged a limited role for government policies. The desire to get the government out of the way of private enterprise meant that independent central banks limited themselves to achieving the narrow objective of an inflation target. Similarly, other policy instruments were focused on providing a predictable environment in their own areas of expertise—government debt, financial stability, and potential growth.

The North Atlantic crisis challenged this paradigm as a lightly regulated private sector turned out to be at least as capable of generating macroeconomic crises as government activism. If the economic instability and low growth of the 1970s was a product of overly active government policies, then the even more destructive crisis that erupted in 2008 was a product of too much confidence in the self-stabilizing properties of private financial markets. The immediate response has been a renewed interest in active financial policies comprising stricter regulation and a new willingness to use macroprudential policies to reduce signs of financial overheating.

The early response to the crisis also involved a healthy dose of policy integration. In 2009 and 2010 the G20 provided concerted fiscal stimulus to support monetary easing at the same time that the most affected financial sectors were stabilized with government backing. The mix worked, as global growth climbed from zero in 2009 to over 5 percent in 2010. It then gradually slowed to its current rate of slightly over 3 percent as fiscal policymakers refocused on reducing the ratio of government debt to output and structural policies remained on the sidelines. With unconventional monetary policies unable to revive demand on their own, the North Atlantic saw a prolonged period of mediocre growth and low inflation.

This pattern is similar to the pre-crisis experience of Japan. After the bursting of a major property price bubble in the early 2000s, Japan fell into a prolonged depression characterized by a gradual fall in prices accompanied by low growth and serial recessions. All of this occurred despite policy rates that remained stuck at zero and various bouts of central bank asset purchases and fiscal stimulus, the latter increasing government debt to a precarious level. The conventional wisdom at the time was that this inability to revive the Japanese economy reflected insufficiently robust macroeconomic policy implementation and that more consistent monetary and fiscal stimulus could have raised the economy out of the doldrums. The North Atlantic crisis is causing this to be reassessed given the similarities between the problems of Japan and the post-crisis experience of other parts of the world, most notably the Euro area where growth forecasts remain lackluster, inflation stubbornly below target despite monetary stimulus, and debt high.

Meanwhile, Japan is experimenting with a more integrated policy approach to resuscitate its economy. In late 2014, Prime Minister Shinzo

Abe was elected on a platform based on reviving the economy through a combination of monetary and fiscal stimulus as well as structural reforms to raise potential output. This approach, dubbed "Abenomics", had initial success as monetary and fiscal stimulus pushed inflation towards the central bank's target of 2 percentage points and supported output. However, the limited focus on structural reforms meant that the economy relapsed after the initial macroeconomic stimulus wore off.

The Abenomics approach in which monetary, fiscal, and structural reforms are (in theory) being marshaled in reviving activity and inflation is a welcome departure from prevailing macroeconomic orthodoxy. It embodies a more integrated view of macroeconomic challenges, as several policies are used to support a recovery rather than the usual and inefficient approach of assigning each target to a specific policy. This allows much more firepower to be used on pressing policy needs, such as the desire to reinvigorate the Japanese economy after twenty years in the doldrums, resume growth and convergence in incomes in the Euro area, and recharge US economic vitality.

Despite its attractions, however, transferring the integrated Abenomics policy philosophy to the North Atlantic region will not be easy. The constraints on greater policy integration are particularly evident in the Euro area, where the European Central Bank remains committed to pursuing low and steady inflation, fiscal policies are the preserve of national governments, Stability and Growth Pact rules limit the degree of fiscal flexibility, and structural policies are also decided at the national level. The result has been a disjointed policy response that has been unable to overcome low growth and substandard inflation. While some crisis countries such as Spain and Ireland have successfully used structural reforms of labor markets and banks, respectively, to help overcome their macroeconomic misery, other crisis countries such as Italy, Portugal, and Greece remain mired in low growth.

In the United States, an initial burst of policy coordination in the immediate aftermath of the crisis seems to have faded. In response to the economic and financial crisis, stimulus was jointly applied by the central bank and the fiscal authorities using emergency funding. In addition, a combination of easy financial conditions, government support, and tough stress tests encouraged banks to raise their capital buffers. These additional funds allowed banks to deal with their bad loans, most notably through a wave of foreclosures on mortgages that was accompanied by considerable short-term macroeconomic and financial stress. The final result has been a stronger recovery than in the Euro area, where nonperforming loans have not been fully written down. Over time, however, interest in monetary and fiscal cooperation has dwindled. While the new Trump Administration advocates fiscal stimulus, this reflects ideology (a desire to boost growth through lower taxes and a smaller government) rather than a plan to provide an integrated approach to reviving growth.

Only at the international level have policymakers been happy to support an integrated approach to reviving growth and inflation. At a meeting in Chengdu, China in July 2016, the G20 finance minsters reiterated their

> determination to use all policy tools – monetary, fiscal and structural – individually and collectively to achieve our goal of strong, sustainable, balanced and inclusive growth. Monetary policy will continue to support economic activity and ensure price stability, consistent with central banks' mandates, but monetary policy alone cannot lead to balanced growth. Underscoring the essential role of structural reforms, we emphasize that our fiscal strategies are equally important to support our common growth objectives . . . while enhancing resilience and ensuring debt as a share of GDP is on a sustainable path.[3]

Sadly, the admittedly short history of the G20 suggests that this lofty rhetoric is unlikely to significantly alter domestic policy priorities. Part of this skepticism reflects the inclusion of caveats such as "consistent with central banks' mandates" and "ensuring debt as a share of GDP is on a sustainable path". In addition, however, earlier and more ambitious attempts at policy cooperation through the G20 have failed. In particular, a wide-ranging G20 initiative aimed at broad policy cooperation through constructive cross-country surveillance, called the Mutual Assessment Process (MAP), was launched by the United States at the 2009 G20 leaders' summit in Pittsburg.[4] With the global economy mired in a new mediocre level of growth, the idea was that countries would make policy commitments that would be enforced through common oversight. In reality, however, G20 policymakers generally proposed policies that were already planned and then adopted a non-aggression pact in which country A would not criticize country B for not delivering on its commitments for fear of the reverse occurring. A later attempt by the Australian presidency in 2014 to revive the MAP as a more narrowly focused initiative aimed at boosting output by 2 percent over the next five years through structural reforms also failed to gain traction. These experiences are consistent with earlier patterns whereby international policy cooperation erodes after the immediate crisis fades. A good example of this is the contrast between the success of the Plaza Accord in 1985, agreed at a time when the overvalued dollar was a clear concern, and the failure of the 1987 Louvre Accord after the dollar had depreciated to more normal levels. The same loss of coherence has happened in the wake of the North Atlantic crisis as fears of a new global depression faded.

What is needed is a more integrated approach to *domestic* policies of the type that has been articulated in Japan. It is difficult to see how the *international* policy cooperation advocated by the G20 can work in the absence of effective *domestic* cooperation that uses a combination of monetary, fiscal, financial, and structural policies to generate inclusive and robust growth and bring inflation back to target. Such an approach will involve much greater cooperation between the central bank and the finance ministry, as well as with the other parts of the government responsible for structural reforms and financial stability, than has been typical since the generalized move to independent central banks in the 1980s. But how can this be arranged without forsaking the advantages of an independent central bank that is not under the sway of politicians?

* * *

Strengthening Domestic Policy Cooperation

It is striking and surprising that the attempts at reviving international policy cooperation has not led to a broader discussion on how to improve domestic policy integration. If it is appropriate to advocate a combination of monetary, fiscal, and structural policies to revive global growth, then surely it makes equal sense to push for the domestic equivalent. The complication here is the lingering distrust of policy integration as a result of the inflation of the 1970s and the focus on central bank independence that this engendered.

In particular, central banks have jealously guarded an extreme definition of independence. They have been reluctant to suggest appropriate fiscal and structural policies for fear that governments will respond by openly questioning monetary policy decisions. This careful approach may have made sense in the 1980s and 1990s when central banks were involved in the economically painful and politically unpopular business of wringing excess inflation out of the economy. Faced with such a difficult environment, it was understandable that central banks, who were often newly independent, would react by emphasizing the importance of ensuring that their decisions were technical and independent from the government.

However, low inflation was achieved in most advanced economies by the end of the 1990s and its economic benefits are by now widely accepted, so that there is little risk of undermining this consensus. In addition, rather than the narrow monetary issue of lowering excess inflation that confronted central banks in the 1980s and 1990s, the current policy challenges involve low underlying growth, lackluster inflation, and high debts that are unlikely to be solved using monetary policy alone. Meanwhile, the potential for a long period of low inflation and growth is real. Mild deflation was the pressing problem of the late nineteenth century as a lack of gold caused a gradual fall in prices after 1870; this period is now generally referred to as the Long Depression but at the time was labeled the Great Depression. Indeed, it was in response to persistent deflation that the US presidential candidate William Jennings-Bryan in 1896 made his famous pledge allow silver to be part of the US money supply so as not to be "crucified on a cross of gold".[5]

Central bank independence does not necessarily imply that the banks cannot cooperate with finance ministers or engage in a debate over the appropriate mix of monetary, fiscal, financial, and structural policies. Indeed, in the 1960s and 1970s the independent US Federal Reserve and German Bundesbank accepted the prevailing orthodoxy that monetary and fiscal policy should be cooperative. This suggests that the fundamental issue is less about whether the central bank is independent and more about the receptiveness of central banks to the inevitable to-and-fro on the appropriate monetary stance that a more cooperative approach to policies implies.

The need to revive growth through multiple policy channels suggests the importance of an organized process in which the options for different macroeconomic mixes are discussed.[6] Such an arrangement would replace the current compartmentalized approach to policies in which each institution focuses on its own assigned policy goal. It would encompass not simply monetary and fiscal policies but also financial and structural ones. This is a sensible response to the current "new mediocre" in global growth. Over time, however, policy integration is likely to become the new orthodoxy as the limitations of the compartmentalized approach is more fully recognized.

Such integration can be organized through regular meetings of the main domestic macroeconomic decision makers. These should include the head of the central bank, the finance ministry, the financial regulator, and those responsible for structural reforms (an added bonus from such as approach could be centralizing responsibility for structural reforms under one minister). The exact membership would likely vary by country depending on the institutional arrangements and (possibly) the economic challenges. The existence and timing of the meetings of these "economic all-stars" would be made public. Attendees and other experts such as outside commentators, institutions, and ex-policymakers would be encouraged to submit analysis on the appropriate mix of policies. All contributors would be asked to analyze the entire range of policies, rather than focusing on their own specific areas of expertise, so as to ensure that there was an informed debate about the appropriate joint settings for monetary, fiscal, structural, and financial policies.

The discussion between the top policymakers would be behind closed doors, to allow an appropriate level of frankness, but minutes would be made public as is currently the norm for central bank committees. This would include a summary of any agreements and disagreements about the appropriate mix of policies. While there would need to be a chairperson to ensure an orderly discussion, the outcome would not be binding on participants. In particular, although attendance at the all-star meeting would be mandatory so as to encourage a wider policy discussion, independent central banks would be allowed to make their own monetary policy decisions. The arrangements would thus respect institutional responsibilities and expertise. Policy integration would come organically out of the existence of a well-defined platform in which differing views on policies and their impact on the economy would be debated in an organized manner and the pros and cons of different policies analyzed. In terms of timing, the meetings would need to be sufficiently seldom that macroeconomic conditions would be likely to have altered but often enough to respond to new challenges. At least in current circumstances, in which macroeconomic instability is high, meetings might occur once every six months with the option for additional emergency meetings if circumstances warranted. For example, the unexpected vote for the United Kingdom to exit the European Union would likely have justified an emergency meeting.

One objection to such an arrangement is that key policymakers already meet regularly on an informal basis and that the policy mix is part of such tête-a-têtes. This objection, however, is unconvincing. First, it is difficult to believe that such discussions involve the detailed analysis of macroeconomic outcomes envisaged in the meetings of the "economic all stars". In addition, such meetings are generally between two institutions rather than a broader group. Perhaps the most compelling argument, however, is that such meetings do not involve or incorporate the insights from outside commentators, institutions, and ex-policymakers who have informed opinions on the appropriate policy mix. A wider and more formal discussion of the correct combination of policies has a much better chance of producing a carefully considered outcome.

Another objection is that monetary policy is the most flexible of policies and hence that intransigence by (say) fiscal policymakers could force the central bank into policies it would rather not follow. In terms of game theory, fiscal policymakers could end up using their inability to change plans quickly to force monetary policymakers to respond to facts on the ground. However, this is already the case in that fiscal policy is set less often than monetary policy, and hence monetary policy generally has to respond given a fiscal stance that has already been announced. It is difficult to see why organized policy discussion, in which the central bank could voice concerns about any problems created by fiscal and other policies, would not improve matters. Indeed, the logic of the all-stars meetings is to put pressure on institutions not to compete with each other, but rather to discover a mutually agreeable approach.

This line of reasoning also ignores the fact that the greater flexibility in changing monetary versus fiscal policy has to be put against the fact that fiscal policy feeds through into the economy faster. Budgets need prior planning and are generally implemented once a year (although emergency budgets can be organized more quickly), while most monetary policy committees meet every six weeks or so. But this faster implementation of monetary policy has to be set against the fact that changes in taxes or government spending boost output almost immediately while interest rate changes are generally believed to take around nine months to feed through to activity. It is thus far from clear that monetary policy delivers support for the economy faster than fiscal policy, a point that central banks could make in an organized discussion.

A final argument for insulating the independent central bank from wider discussion is that monetary policy is technical and that central bankers understand the macroeconomy better than others. Over the 1990s and 2000s there was an increasing belief in the science of central banking. The logic of this scientific approach was that monetary policy was best left to the august technicians housed in central banks who had the expertise to examine the tea-leaves of the economy and made far-sighted decisions that ensured macroeconomic stability. While there is no doubt that central banks have a lot of expertise, the North Atlantic crisis demonstrates that independent central banks are sufficiently fallible that they can allow major economic strains to fester and lead to economic collapse. The crisis exploded the myth of the omnipotent central bank should be left to make its own decisions rather than a more fluid and cooperative approach to macroeconomic policies in which the pros and cons of different policies are given a wider discussion.

The strongest case for considering this change in macroeconomic arrangements to allow more policy integration is the failure of current policies to deliver an acceptable outcome. When each institution focuses narrowly on its own narrow mandate the overall picture gets lost, strains go unresolved, and the economy becomes more brittle. Despite the best efforts of central banks, the North Atlantic crisis happened and the post-crisis period has seen low growth, low inflation, and chronic macroeconomic and political instability. Faced with the failure of the current myopic approach, it is essential to move to a more inclusive and cooperative one. A similarly eclectic approach is needed for macroeconomic theory.

* * *

A More Inclusive Approach to Macroeconomic Theory

The more market-orientated approach to macroeconomic policies, developed in response to the inflation of the 1970s, put an emphasis on economic theory. The failure of central banks to control inflation in the 1970s was ascribed to a mistaken belief that you could push unemployment ever lower without sparking an acceleration in inflation. In reality, however, attempts to drive unemployment down led to a destructive inflation spiral. In order to avoid future policy mistakes based on (apparently stable) empirical links that subsequently turned out to be malleable, macroeconomics increasingly moved to models based on microeconomic theory in which individuals maximized pleasure and firms maximize profits. This is exemplified by the increased use of dynamic stochastic general equilibrium (DSGE) models, in which the macroeconomy is seen as an amalgam of microeconomic theories for households and firms with policy rules defining the responses of central banks and fiscal policymakers.

The backbone of the microeconomic theories is "homo economicus". Homo economicus is an individual ("agent" is the preferred term) who maximizes pleasure ("utility") given his or her income and who ensures that the firms that (s)he owns maximize profits. Maximization is crucial, as it allows the full weight of the associated mathematics to be used. The assumption of maximizing behavior plus a natural unit to account for such behavior (money and prices) has allowed economics to become the most developed of the social sciences. At its most basic level, economics involves the law of supply and demand. When a price rises, firms have an incentive to produce more while consumers will demand less. This is the basis for Adam Smith's insight that the hidden hand of the market, in the form of price signals, produces a self-organizing and stable economic system.

Clearly, all sorts of imperfections that deviate from Adam Smith's ideal can distort the economy. Firms can exploit their economic power to raise prices above the socially optimal, generating "excess" profits that harm individual consumers. More generally, laws and regulations can be used to favor some groups over others. Inventiveness can be harmed by the ability of others to copy an original idea (hence the existence of copyright laws), but the efficiency of the economy can also be harmed if firms are allowed to hold onto a copyright for too long and avoid legitimate competition that would lower prices. All of these issues have been extensively analyzed in microeconomics, which focuses on behavior in particular markets. When such analysis is elevated from specific markets to the behavior of the macroeconomy, the need to link many sectors together leads to simplification. In particular, it is generally assumed that all firms and households behave in the same way. Hence, while in reality firms find themselves in a myriad of situations, from highly competitive markets to monopolies, in macroeconomic models it is generally assumed that all firms face the same level of competition. Similarly, households are assumed to work and spend in a highly stylized manner.

Even more importantly, macroeconomic models require assumptions about the future. To ensure that the resulting behavior is consistent with the underlying model, it is generally assumed that individuals and firms hold accurate views about its future path because they fully understand the workings of the economy and how central banks and other policymakers will react in any given set of circumstances. Such an approach, dubbed rational expectations, ensures that expectations about the future path of major macroeconomic variables such as prices, output, interest rates, budget deficits, and equity prices correspond to what the model says will occur (or, at least, what would occur if there were no further unexpected shocks). In this hyper-rational world people are assumed to fully understand the future.

The combination of microeconomic fundamentals and rational expectations is an impressive intellectual achievement that has generated powerful predictions about the macroeconomy. At the same time, such an approach finds it difficult to explain destabilizing behavior, including with respect to financial markets. Most prominently, theorists have found it essentially impossible to model "rational" financial bubbles. The basic issue is that far-sighted and well-informed investors will project the dynamics of the market and realize that the future path of assets prices is unstable and will at some point collapse. As a result, they will never start down the path towards a bubble as they understand that it is inherently unstable. This inability to model "rational" asset bubbles helped fuel the popularity of the efficient markets hypothesis—in which asset prices reflected the wisdom of crowds and were thus always accurate—that helped to lull policymakers into underestimating the risks emanating from growing financial imbalances in the United States and European economies.

More generally, the hyper-rational and far-seeing "homo economicus" has been elevated from a useful tool to something closer to a litmus test for economic modeling. Any macroeconomic analysis is seen as questionable unless the underlying behavior can be shown to derive from first principles. This approach has led to a focus on microeconomic incentives as a result of (say) lower marginal tax rates that largely ignores wider societal values such as inequality and economic fairness. It is the same desiccated approach that gave rise to the draconian English Poor Law of 1934.

While the experience of inflation in the 1970s underlines the importance of being careful about the use of *ad hoc* assumptions, the difficulty of theorists in producing a model of rational financial bubbles suggests that the pure theoretical approach also has its own limitations and should not be seen as an all-encompassing view of the world. In the end, economics is a practical science that should reflect underlying realities, akin to engineering or biology in which shortcuts are taken in order to explain real phenomena, rather than theoretical physics with its search for immutable principles. Indeed, even theoretical physics has accepted for around a century the existence of general relativity and quantum mechanics, two apparently incompatible approaches.

There is also a major issue as to whether a coherent view of the long-run path for the economy can be constructed. On a practical level, it assumes that individuals acting through the wisdom of crowds understand an awful lot about the economy. On a theoretical level, as discussed in an earlier chapter, the existence of "unknown unknowns" may make it impossible to calculate a well-defined future. In this case, *ad hoc* rules of thumb may be the best available option. The long-run may truly be a quantum process in which unexpected events cause shifts from one view of the world to another. Like physicists, economists may have to accept that that is an element of randomness at the core of the subject—that god does indeed play dice.

Another limitation with economic theory is that homo economicus, for all of his or her strengths, is not someone you would want as a neighbor. This is because (s)he is a loner who is completely self-focused. By contrast, one of the most striking features of real-life homo sapiens is that they are astonishingly social animals. Many of them live perfectly happily in big cities in which they interact regularly and closely with their own kind. They are extremely sensitive to each other's moods and social cues. Subtle social interactions are also evident in mass gatherings. A concert or a football game is much more fun if you are part of a large audience who are also appreciating the spectacle. Maybe most relevant to financial bubbles, speeders on the highway embolden others to speed. Risky behavior encourages other risky behavior—a response that homo economicus would not recognize.

Along with social interactions comes a set of views about fairness that homo economicus would also find bemusing. People give up their seats on buses for the elderly and disabled, they give special consideration to those who are pregnant, and they accept that kids behave differently from adults. These are obvious adaptions to allow complex societies to function smoothly despite personal diversity. While such conventions are not always followed, they are surprisingly pervasive even in extreme situations. The survival rate of male first-class passengers on the Titanic, while much higher than their third-class fellow passengers because of better access to the deck, was surprisingly low as a result of the principle of women and children first. The importance of social norms and harmony can also help to explain some recent evidence suggesting that economic inequality lowers growth. Such a macroeconomic perspective is not linked to the types of incentives—marginal tax rates, generosity of unemployment benefits, and access to financial markets—that drive the homo economicus and hence the microeconomic theory embraced by modern macroeconomic models.

More generally, people naturally want to impress others, to be attractive to others, and to be seen as nice by others. Such drives create a huge range of assessments that are alien to homo economicus. The desire for social acceptance that makes people want to fit in with the views of others provides an obvious conduit through which views about the long-run can form. The innate desire not to be seen as disruptive discourages individuals from questioning the perceived wisdom of other investors, as underlined, for example, in the account of how a few outliers did resist such pressure in the book about the financial crisis, Michael Lewis's The Big Short. More generally, Professor Robert Shiller of Yale, one of the few prominent economists who recognized that the US housing market was in a massive bubble before the crisis, has been one of several financial economists to suggest that financial market bubbles can be modeled as social waves in which ideas catch fire and become self-reinforcing before eventually deflating.[7] Such social eruptions can be modeled using similar tools to those used to examine epidemics, involving the probability of passing on an infection from one person to the other and a rate at which people stop being infectious, which define the height and longevity of the craze. Examples of crazes include hit records, Rubik's Cubes, and smart phone apps. This approach provides a way of thinking about asset price bubbles and the madness of crowds in a structured manner.

The increasing interest in behavioral economics provides another platform for considering how individuals deviate from pure rationality.[8] Behavioral economics, which examines how individuals actually behave in various economic situations rather than how they are supposed to behave, provides many insights but remains a specialized field. It has had only a limited effect on economic theory, in part because it is often difficult to generalize the results. A similar comment can be made about game theory, used in economics to model how individuals interact. Important insights have been generated by game theory, the most striking of which is the "prisoners' dilemma" in which two inmates who committed a crime are faced with the choice to confess or not confess. Unless they can communicate, each has an incentive to confess so as to minimize their sentence even though if they both deny the charge they will be set free. However, this is a simple and fairly stylized problem, and it rapidly becomes difficult to generalize how individuals will react in more complex situations.

Recognizing that homo economicus is only an approximation to the actual behavior of real-life homo sapiens does not imply rejecting the many insights that (s)he has generated. While people may on certain occasions deviate from self-centered maximization, it is clear that the pursuit of happiness is a pretty good description of most behavior. It is also clear that such models have provided extremely powerful insights into short-term activities in the real world, from explaining why asset prices are essentially unpredictable from day-to-day to the importance of maintaining a certain degree of policy predictability in maintaining macroeconomic stability. Rather, it implies accepting that there are more phenomena under heaven and earth than are dreamt of in homo economicus' philosophy: that asset prices are not always fairly valued and that predictable policies can create incentives to take excessive risks.

Economists should be wary of deviating from maximizing theory, but open to doing so if there is strong evidence that such behavior occurs. This is surely true of asset price bubbles. Financial market trading involves outguessing other traders and hence the underlying strategies are in constant flux. This suggests that the smooth adjustment typical in macroeconomic models should be combined with a more general approach that allows for fads and their collapse. While most fads are too localized to have macroeconomic consequences (think of the rise and fall in the popularity of the hula hoop, pet rocks, and cabbage patch dolls), financial market fads have the capability to create major disruptions. As the North Atlantic financial crisis amply demonstrates, unsustainable asset price bubbles fed by fads can create irrational rises and falls in asset prices that are extremely costly even if they are outside of the ken of homo economicus.

* * *

Toward a More Encompassing View of Macroeconomics

If the lesson from the inflation of the 1970s was to be wary about assuming that governments are omnipotent, the North Atlantic crisis repeated this insight for the private sector. This lesson has been absorbed with regard to financial markets, which are now more closely regulated and where the need for government intervention in the form of macroprudential policies to limit systemic imbalances has been widely recognized. But a more wide-ranging reevaluation of macroeconomics is in order, embodying a more inclusive view of the role of fiscal, financial, and structural policies, of the advantages of policy cooperation, and of the manner in which macroeconomic behavior is approached.

The pre-crisis macroeconomic orthodoxy essentially saw macroeconomic policies as providing a platform for the private sector to thrive. An independent central bank guided by an inflation target was primarily responsible for keeping inflation low and unemployment on an even keel by varying financial conditions. Such policies would allow private individuals to plan ahead with relative certainty about the future path of prices, employment, and wages. In a similar manner, the focus of fiscal policy was on keeping taxes and spending within reasonable limits and the government deficit and debt low and sustainable. Regulators were tasked with maintaining financial stability of individual firms, while those in charge of structural policies ensured robust growth by improving private incentives.

Despite the widespread problems of low growth and disappointing inflation in the post-crisis period, this remains to a large extent the current paradigm. To be sure, financial stability has been given more prominence as a macroeconomic issue as opposed to a microeconomic one. In addition, calls are regularly made for greater fiscal stimulus and structural reforms to move growth out of the doldrums. In reality, however, central banks have continued to be the main instruments for reviving growth and inflation, fiscal policy has focused on long-term objectives such as lowering debt or cutting taxes, and many macroeconomists remain wary of major structural reforms because of their potentially adverse short-term impact on growth. One exception to this general rule is Japan, which has tried to integrate monetary, fiscal, and structural policies to overcome the long-term problem of deflation and disappointing growth. The wider approach to macroeconomic policies taken in Japan should be repeated elsewhere, particularly given that the problems of low growth and inflation currently besetting some regions such as the Euro area bear a striking similarity to the longer-term experience of Japan.

Along with this broader approach to macroeconomic challenges and policy cooperation, macroeconomic analysis should also become more integrated. In particular, it should be recognized that there are some economic phenomena that cannot be modeled using rational and forward-looking individuals. This is particularly true of financial markets, where in the presence of "unknown unknowns" asset prices may have more to do with the gut instincts and the inclination of homo sapiens to agree with each other than with precise calculations of the future. Such a perspective can help to explain the origins of asset price bubbles. In addition, innate beliefs in fairness may help explain other deviations from narrow self-interest, such as recent evidence that higher inequality may be detrimental to growth over and above the narrow incentives involved in microeconomic theory. This more fluid approach to economic analysis would allow macroeconomics to come closer to the real world and make the economy more robust to shocks.

Chapter 9

WHITHER EMU?

Flaws in the design of the European Monetary Union (EMU) helped generate the North Atlantic crisis as well as amplify and elongate its costs. For almost a decade after the introduction of the Euro in January, 1999, a prolonged expansion eased the task of the European Central Bank (ECB). Indeed, the new currency union was viewed as a success that was promoting growing prosperity and a convergence in income between the less wealthy peripheral countries and the more prosperous core. In reality, these trends largely reflected unsustainable financial booms in the periphery, much of it financed by loans from undercapitalized mega-banks in the Euro area core. These growing imbalances were missed because policymakers overestimated the level of integration of the Euro area and hence its ability to cope with shocks to members. The financial chaos after the Lehman Brothers bankruptcy created deep problems for the undercapitalized core mega-banks system that were subsequently exacerbated by fiscal crises in the periphery, where Greece, Ireland, and Portugal were forced into economic recovery programs, Spain suffered a house price collapse that required major support from the government, and the sustainability of high Italian government debt was called into question.

The currency union so carefully negotiated in the Maastricht Treaty provided an inadequate response. The independent central bank lowered interest rates but its charter hampered it from providing more direct support to crisis-hit banks or governments. Rather, bank support was the province of national governments, putting pressure on public finances particularly in Greece, Ireland, Portugal, and Spain, the countries most affected by asset price collapses. Fiscal support for these crisis countries from the rest of the currency union was minimal given rules that explicitly excluded direct support from other governments or from the small federal budget.

The result was a Euro area depression. This was particularly evident in the periphery, as doubts about the viability of major banks and the sustainability of government finances fed on each other to drive an upward spiral in borrowing costs. Growth in the core also suffered a prolonged slowdown as weak banks pulled back from lending and recessions in the periphery crimped demand for exports. The downturn in output was made worse by the importance given to a rapid return to fiscal probity in the absence of a fiscal backstop as well as hints that weaker members might have to leave the union.[1] These largely self-inflicted wounds came to a head in 2012 as an upward spiral in borrowing costs in the periphery, most notably in Greece, put the viability of the currency union into question. In the end, the decision to move to a banking union provided cover for the president of the ECB to vow to do "whatever it takes" to preserve the Euro area, an announcement that rapidly calmed markets.

As discussed in Chapter 4, the deficiencies in the design of the Euro area reflected underlying tensions between the German and French concepts of the role of the currency union in economic integration. The German vision was that the currency union would come about only after successful economic and political integration, implying that the union would require minimal macroeconomic support beyond that provided by existing arrangements. By contrast, the French advocated an early currency union in order to promote economic convergence, combined with monetary and fiscal macroeconomic support to help members faced with recessions. The eventual unhappy compromise involved a "French" early move to a single money with a "German" independent central bank and minimal provisions for support for weaker members.

A crucial issue is whether the changes to Euro area design as a result of the crisis will allow it to respond better to future macroeconomic shocks or if more institutional surgery is needed. In other words, is the Euro area moving toward the smoothly functioning currency union that the French assumed would occur? Or is it likely to remain brittle and subject to major shocks and economic strife that will harm the future prospects of members? To answer these questions, it is first necessary to assess how much the architecture of the Euro area has improved.

* * *

The Institutional Response to the Euro Area Crisis

In the wake of the crisis, the Euro area has been made more responsive to large economic shocks by adding to the already extensive alphabet soup of European institutions. Rules about how to support countries facing a crisis have been expanded and codified through the creation of the European Stability Mechanism (ESM) and the ECB's Outright Monetary Transaction program (OMT). In addition, financial supervision has been centralized at the European Central Bank (ECB). At the same time, the fiscal rules in the Stability and Growth Pact (SGP) have been tightened in an attempt to avoid a repeat of the lax fiscal policies in Greece that helped to precipitate the crisis.

The European Stability Mechanism, activated in September 2012, is a permanent Euro-area-wide facility that can lend to members facing an economic or financial crisis. The ESM merged two temporary funds used to provide money for the crisis programs with Greece, Ireland, and Portugal—the European Financial Stability Facility and the European Financial Stabilisation Mechanism. The ESM's lending procedures are closely modeled on those of the International Monetary Fund. It can only provide a Euro area member with loans or precautionary funds (i.e., an overdraft facility in which money is only borrowed if it is needed) if the loans are accompanied by a Memorandum of Understanding outlining a program to restore financial health that has been vetted by the IMF, the European Commission, and the ECB (the European troika that organized the bailouts of Greece, Ireland, and Portugal over the crisis). The ESM has so far been used to support bank recapitalization by the Spanish government and a crisis program for Cyprus. In addition, although it has not done so, the ESM has some funds to directly recapitalize banks and take over their operations. The implications of this option will be discussed later in the context of the move to a single bank supervisor.

European Central Bank support to Euro area members in crisis has also been expanded and codified through its Outright Monetary Transactions program (OMT). The OMT program was announced in September 2012 on the heels of the speech by President Mario Draghi to do "whatever it takes" to preserve the Euro. It allows the ECB to purchase unlimited amounts of government bonds of a member that has an ESM program, bond yields at stressed levels, and full access to market financing, thereby providing a monetary backstop for members facing a crisis. Together, the ESM and OMT facilities provide an emergency safety net for members that is separate from the international one provided by the IMF (while still utilizing the IMF's expertise) and is more effective since it includes unlimited central bank support.

Another far-reaching institutional improvement brought about by the crisis was to switch the supervision of banks from national regulators to the ECB. Moving supervision of banks from competing national regulators to the ECB provides the potential for a true banking union in the Euro area. So far, however, the process is only half complete. While Euro area financial supervision has been centralized, the costs associated with bank support remain largely national. This is clearly true for retail deposit insurance, which remains the responsibility of member governments. The situation with regard to recapitalizing a troubled bank is more complex. A Euro-area-wide resolution fund to support insolvent banks has been agreed and is being gradually built using charges on banks. However, even when it is complete the fund will only comprise €55 billion (less than ½ percent of future Euro area output). This is too small a sum to provide meaningful guarantees for an industry dominated by mega-banks, even taking account of new rules to lower the cost of government rescues by requiring that uninsured lenders such as bond holders contribute to any recapitalization (called "bail-in" rules because private creditors participate in the rescue rather than being "bailed-out"). Once the Euro-area-wide fund is exhausted, the backstop remains individual Euro area members. There is also an option to provide centralized ESM funds to directly recapitalize banks, but the funds available to cope with such a crisis are again quite limited. The result is a half-formed banking union in which supervision is centralized but the costs of deposit insurance and of bank recapitalization basically remain with national governments.

Turning to fiscal arrangements, the Stability and Growth Pact was designed to prevent a crisis triggered by individual members using the credibility of the Euro area to borrow excessively. Despite the pact, however, the Greek government succeeded in doing exactly that in the run-up to the crisis. The October 2009 revelation that the Greek fiscal deficit was actually 12.5 percent of output (later revised up to 15.8 percent) rather than the official target of 3.7 percent triggered an abrupt rise in sovereign borrowing costs in the periphery. This was exacerbated by statements from the German government that high Greek debt put the Euro at risk and that Greece might have to leave the single currency. This drove interest rates even higher in Greece and other crisis countries as investors sought compensation for the risk that Greece and other crisis countries might leave the Euro area and repay their debts using a highly depreciated new currency (so-called denomination risk).[2] The rise in government borrowing costs fed through to bank funding, which had already spiked after the Lehman Brothers bankruptcy in September 2008 had raised the costs of intra-bank lending on concerns that European banks could meet a similar fate. This created an upward spiral in the sovereign-bank interest rates that almost tore the currency union apart, before President Draghi announced that the ECB was prepared to do whatever it took to preserve the currency union.

In response to the Greek debacle, new and stronger rules have been brought in to bolster the fiscal rules embodied in the Stability and Growth Pact. On the preventative side, governments are now under stricter surveillance rules including (for example) a requirement to follow better fiscal procedures, create independent national monitoring agencies and economic forecasts, and provide early submission of budget plans to the Commission and the European finance ministers. Rules on excessive deficits have also been tightened by making it more difficult for ministers to overrule any decision by the European Commission on sanctions for a country that is running an excessive deficit. In addition, the rate at which debt above 60 percent of output should be reduced has been codified. However no fiscal sanctions have ever actually been applied, suggesting that enforcement of fiscal rules continues to be problematic.

The key issue looking forward is whether the new SGP rules will be sufficiently tough to prevent a future fiscal crisis. This is because once a crisis has occurred, rules that require a return to fiscal stability are generally counterproductive. For example, after the Greek revelations in 2009, the SGP excess deficits procedures led to a rapid tightening of fiscal policy that worsened the Euro area recession. Between 2010 and 2013, the cyclically adjusted fiscal deficit was reduced by over 5 percentage points of output in Greece, Ireland, Portugal and Spain, and by 3 percent in France and Italy. To put this in context, the 3¼ percent consolidation for the entire Euro area over this three-year period was larger than the tightening required in the four years before Euro area entry in 1999, when governments were scrambling to achieve the Maastricht criteria. It was also tougher. Fiscal belt tightening in the run-up to the creation of the Euro was aided by accounting tricks and lower nominal interest rates. By contrast, over the Euro area crisis budgets were closely monitored while the increase in interest costs made it more difficult to lower the deficit.

The changes in design have made the Euro area better at combating future crises. In particular, access to centralized fiscal support through the ESM and to central bank funds through the OMT provide a convincing financial backstop. However, with the important exception of centralized banking supervision, little has been done to strengthen buffers to members that are not in crisis. Fiscal policy remains decentralized, and loans to support countries in difficulties are limited to members who are prepared to accept a program with the troika. The existence of this safety net provides some benefits even to governments that are not prepared to enter into a program, since it reduces the risk of members in crisis being forced to leave the Euro area involuntarily. In addition, the tougher approach to SGP surveillance makes it less likely that the Greek fiscal shenanigans in the run-up to the crisis will be repeated. However, it is also true that differences in government borrowing rates are higher than their (unsustainably) low level before the crisis and that fiscal flexibility in response to economic disturbances remains constrained. Similarly, in banking the glass is only half full since centralized supervision has not been supported by effective centralized support for failing banks.

The likelihood of further major changes to the underlying design of the Euro area is fading along with the immediate risks to the region. The history of the European Union is that major alterations occur at times of distress. As Jean Monnet, one of the architects of the European Union, said: "People only accept change when they are faced with necessity, and only recognize necessity when a crisis is upon them." It is extremely difficult to tinker with the design of the currency union in normal times, particularly since many of the rules are embodied in the Maastricht Treaty. Indeed, it is notable that none of the recent changes to the structure of EMU have involved major amendments to the Maastricht Treaty, which would involve reopening long-running Franco-German disagreements about the purpose of the single currency.

The difficulty in changing the rules also reflects the European Union's focus on consensus across countries.[3] The key driver of the European project is the 1957 Treaty of Rome pledge to work towards "an ever closer union of the European peoples". The "ever closer union" part commits members of the European Union to move towards a federated state with a single money, an arrangement that is usually backed by a political structure based on one-person-one-vote and majority rule so as to be able to adapt to changing circumstances. The mention of the "European peoples", on the other hand, committed the Union to widening its membership. A wide union involving diverse countries typically requires a confederated structure, where individual countries are protected against unwelcome changes by rules emphasizing one-state-one-vote and consensus. In practice, the power center of European Union—the Commission—has a confederated structure, which makes significant changes to Euro area arrangements difficult to achieve.

This suggests that the current design of EMU is likely to remain in place for some time, although as the book went to press the election of President Macron in France may yield further major changes. In any case, the key issue for the future of EMU is the validity of the key assumption in the French/Monetarist view of monetary union, namely that a single currency can create the economic integration needed for a smoothly functioning currency area. If this is correct, then the North Atlantic crisis was simply a major hiccup along the road to ever closer union. If this assumption is incorrect and the German/Economist view that a single currency will not generate rapid integration and hence that the currency union should have been delayed until after the union had become more economically and politically integrated, then the North Atlantic crisis may be a harbinger of future economic doldrums. Answering this question requires assessing the properties of an integrated and smoothly functioning currency union.

* * *

What Makes a Good Currency Union?

The theory of optimum currency areas is the branch of economics that examines the suitability of a region for a single currency. Adopting a single money has both benefits and costs. The obvious benefit is that it makes it easier and cheaper to transact with others within the union. A person in Chicago may find it easier and simpler to buy a widget from a firm in distant Los Angeles rather than one in closer Toronto because the former also uses the US dollar while the latter purchase involves the uncertainty and expense of paying in Canadian dollars. In short, a single currency promotes closer economic ties. This is the essence of the French/Monetarist argument that the Euro will create an integrated economy.

The cost of a single currency is that it limits monetary flexibility in response to shocks. A single money requires a single monetary policy. If Toronto is booming and Chicago is in an economic slump, then the Bank of Canada can tighten its policy in order to cool the situation in Toronto while the Federal Reserve can loosen policy to give support to Chicago. By contrast, if Los Angeles is booming and Chicago is in a slump then the Federal Reserve faces a dilemma. Should it tighten policies to cool the LA economy or loosen them to support Chicago? In practice, it would presumably split the difference and leave policies unchanged. This means that buffers other than monetary policy are needed to cushion shocks that create divergent economic conditions across a currency union.

This implies three approaches to assessing the suitability of a region for a single money. The first is the degree to which the members face similar economic shocks. If Los Angeles and Chicago tend to be hit by similar shocks, so that when LA is booming Chicago is likely also booming, then tighter Fed policies will suit both places. It is only when the shocks diverge significantly than a single currency creates issues.[4] The first criterion for a smooth functioning monetary union is therefore that economic disturbances across the members are similar—that they are coherent rather than incoherent.

A second criterion is the degree to which divergent shocks can be absorbed by other economic buffers that obviate the need for monetary support. The initial work on optimum currency areas by Robert Mundell in the 1960s focused on the importance of labor mobility in cushioning differing shocks.[5] If labor can move easily between Chicago and Los Angeles, then differences in underlying shocks would be solved by workers moving out of slumping Chicago and into booming LA. This is also linked with the ease of firms to move and hire and fire, since labor mobility only works if firms are sufficiently flexible to create new jobs.

In addition, fiscal policy can help to cushion the shock. Indeed, a federal fiscal system automatically provides more demand to regions in a downswing and withdraws it from regions in an upswing since federal tax revenues fall and spending rises in a slump while the opposite occurs in a boom. This is a regional equivalent to national automatic stabilizers. But there is a crucial difference, namely that the federal deficit remains unchanged because the higher deficit in Chicago is cancelled out by the lower one in LA. In essence, the federal tax system transfers money from Los Angeles to Chicago as their economic conditions diverge. Since the level of federal debt is unchanged, there is no reason for taxpayers in (say) Chicago to partially offset the boost to demand coming from the federal government in anticipation of higher taxes in the future. This provides a more effective stimulus than if Chicago tries to use its local taxes and spending to boost the economy, since the stimulus will be muted as taxpayers save part of the tax cut in anticipation of higher taxes down the road. However, a federal tax system also implies long-term transfers from rich to poor regions, which requires a high level of political cohesion that the Euro area has never achieved, which is why fiscal policy remains a national responsibility.

An integrated banking system can also play a role in offsetting divergent economic shocks, although this mechanism has been given little attention in the literature. If banking is regional, then the downturn in Chicago will put stress on local banks even as the boom in Los Angeles leaves its banks flush with cash. This will tend to loosen financial conditions in booming Los Angeles while tightening them in Chicago, exacerbating the initial divergent shock. While in theory LA banks could lend money to people in Chicago, in practice it is difficult for an LA bank to assess the risk of a loan to a person or firm in unfamiliar Chicago. Similarly, uncertainty about the financial health of Chicago banks may make their LA cousins reluctant to loan them funds through the interbank market. National supervision can help reduce these uncertainties, as it makes it easier for LA banks to assess the creditworthiness of individual Chicago banks, allowing them to channel their funds to sound institutions. National banks with operations in both cities can also provide support as such banks have the expertise to assess risks in both markets. However, national banks are a double-edged sword. If loans in Chicago are relatively profitable because the economy is slumping but the value of collateral such as houses remain strong, then a national bank will push resources into Chicago. If, however, the main problem is a slump in the value of collateral then a national bank may pull loans out of slumping Chicago and toward Los Angeles.[6]

A third criterion for assessing whether the Euro area is a natural currency union is the speed with which the union is becoming more economically integrated over time. Nobody believed in the early 1990s that the European economy was sufficiently integrated to comprise a natural currency union. Rather, the French assumption was that the single money would create the closer economic bonds needed to make a union work smoothly and generate the convergence that would justify its existence. Assessing the validity of this assumption requires a dynamic assessment of the rate at which the Euro has led to greater integration of the participants.

* * *

How Fast Is EMU Integrating?

How does the current Euro area stack up against these various criteria for a functioning currency union able to smoothly absorb regional shocks? The earlier discussion suggests three ways of assessing this issue. How far did the EMU increase economic integration across the participants, how much did it promote more similar economic shocks, and how far did it enhance the banking, fiscal, labor market, and corporate shock absorbers? In answering these question, I focus on the initial eleven members who joined the union in 1999 plus Greece, which adopted the Euro in 2001, the same countries that are examined in the first section of this book on the long-term origins of the crisis.[7]

How Far Did the Euro Boost Economic Integration?

How far did the creation of the Euro promote economic integration across the initial participants? A natural measure is the impact of the introduction of the Euro on international trade. There are several reasons for using trade as a measure of economic integration. It tracks a basic economic link across countries, namely the degree to which goods produced in a country cross international borders rather than staying within them. In addition, trade has the advantage of being well tracked by statistical agencies and of having a successful empirical literature explaining the level of trade including, as discussed below, the impact of a shared currency. On the other hand, it is difficult to do a comparison of intra-Euro area trade with intra-US trade, although the limited information available suggests that US trade is much higher. Researchers have also found that price movements across US regions are much more similar than across Euro area countries, suggesting that the United States is a more integrated union.[8]

Figure 53 shows trade of the initial Euro area members with each other, with other major advanced economies, with eastern Europe, with China, and with the rest of the world since 1980, all measured as a ratio of the output of the initial Euro members. Both the initial Euro area members and the other advanced economies were slow growing economies that were already highly integrated into the global trading system by 1980. By contrast, eastern Europe and China were much more dynamic economies that grew much faster by opening to the rest of the world and using low wage costs to develop manufacturing (the rest of the world largely comprises commodity exporters).

Trade across the early EMU members (the light gray dotted area) has risen gradually since 1980, from slightly under 20 percent of output in 1980 to its current level of just under 30 percent of output. Most of this expansion occurred between the agreement to move to a single currency in the early 1990s and the North Atlantic crisis of 2008 (with a notable fillip in 2000 with the advent of EMU) followed by stasis since the crisis. This basic pattern is repeated as trade with other advanced countries (such as the United States, United Kingdom, and Switzerland) also grew slowly. By contrast, the much smaller level of trade between the initial Euro members and eastern Europe and China expanded much faster in every time period. This spectacular rate of increase was boosted by rapid growth and pro-trade policies—the eastern European countries first left the Soviet sphere in the late 1980s and applied for EU membership in the 1990s while China entered the World Trade Organization in 2001.[9] Indeed, one of the surprises

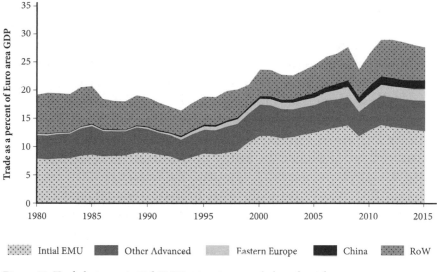

Figure 53: Trade between initial EMU entrants expanded moderately.
Source: IMF Direction of Trade Statistics and IFS.

about the European monetary union is that the German supply chain did
not move south to the periphery of the (then) Euro area but rather to lower
wage economies in eastern Europe. Trade with eastern Europe (as a ratio to
the initial Euro area entrants output) rose almost ten-fold between the early
1990s, as did trade with China. The fact that trade expanded much faster
with eastern Europe and China than across other early members of the
currency union implies that monetary union supported trade but was not a
game changer.

Comparing trade across the initial members of EMU and other advanced
countries reinforces the view that the single currency provided only a
modest boost to economic integration. The rise in the ratio of intra-EMU
trade to output is around 50 percent, somewhat faster than the 30 percent
seen for other advanced economies, with most of this divergence occurring
in the decade from the adoption of the single currency in 1999 to the North
Atlantic financial crisis of 2008. Within the initial Euro area members, the
boost to trade seems to have been largest in the more export-orientated
hard currency countries (Germany, the Netherlands, Belgium, Austria, and
Finland) than in the soft currency remainder, suggesting that the benefits
of the single currency were largest for those countries that were already
closely integrated into the global trading system.

These results are consistent with more formal analysis looking at the
impact of currency unions on trade. These studies use the empirically

successful gravity model of trade in which exports and imports between pairs of countries are linked with the size of the two economies and the distance between them (the name comes from the similarity with Newton's law in which gravitational force depends on the mass of the two objects and the distance between them). The results find that a single currency provides a moderate boost to trade that ranges from insignificant to 50 percent.[10] Comparing the increase in trade within early Euro adopters (50 percent) with the increase to other advanced economies (30 percent) suggests an impact somewhere around the middle of this range. As to timing, a study using the gravity framework to examine the impact of EMU over time confirms that most of the trade boost happened around adoption, with only limited evidence for continuing long-term benefits. Consistent with the fact that the European supply chain anchored around Germany expanded into the east rather than the south, the boost to trade from joining EMU seems to be larger for the newer eastern European members.[11] All of this suggests that the boost to trade integration from the introduction of the Euro has been modest. But did EMU make shocks more similar?

Did the Euro Make Shocks More Similar?

In the early 1990s, when a European currency union was in the offing, Professor Barry Eichengreen and I reported a simple approach to assessing the suitability of European countries for a single currency based on the similarity of their macroeconomic shocks.[12] The first part of our procedure identified macroeconomic shocks hitting different countries from the 1960s to the late 1980s. Next, we calculated the correlation between the shocks of potential EMU members and Germany, the anchor of any future monetary union. Finally, the results across European countries were compared with correlations between US regions and the Mideast, the anchor region of US monetary union that includes the financial hub of New York and the political capital, Washington DC. This approach remains widely accepted in the literature.[13]

The results indicated that the European countries were less well suited for a currency union than the United States. Both regions had a core with relatively similar underlying shocks and a periphery with less similar ones, but in both cases the European shocks were less coherent that those in the United States. The European core comprised the countries clustered around Germany and hence with closer economic ties—France, the Netherlands, and Belgium—coincidentally the members of the Euro area core identified in the first section of this book. Similarly, the currency union periphery we identified largely comprises the countries labeled earlier in this book as part of the Euro area periphery, including Italy, Spain, Greece, Ireland, and Portugal. In the United States, the core comprised a cluster around the Mideast—the Great Lakes, the Southeast, and New England—plus the Far West, dominated by the diversified economy of the California. The periphery comprised of the Rocky Mountains and the Southwest regions that specialized in mining and oil production, respectively.

Updating these results since the 1990s allows an assessment of whether the Euro area is now a better candidate for a currency union. In particular, by comparing the changes in correlations across the Euro area with those for US regions, the role of the introduction of the Euro can be assessed. Slightly ironically, the most important complication in this analysis is the North Atlantic financial crisis. This generates exceptionally large negative shocks across virtually all countries in 2009, including those in the Euro area. When included, the increase in the correlations of the shocks makes the Euro area appear to be a better candidate for a currency union even though the crisis almost destroyed it. Since 2009 involved a large global shock that has little to do with the suitability of the Euro area for a currency union, it is excluded from the analysis. For the US regions (where the exclusion of 2009 makes less of a difference) the recent correlations are similar to the 1960–88 results, a sensible baseline given that the US currency union has remained relatively stable over time.

Comparing the Euro area and US results for the recent period suggests that the Euro area remains less well suited for a currency union than the United States (Figure 54 shows correlations of aggregate supply shocks on the vertical axis and aggregate demand ones on the horizontal axis). The US continues to divide into a core with relatively high correlations of shocks with the anchor and a periphery with less similar shocks. Furthermore, the two groups have similar memberships to the earlier analysis.

The Euro area results are less easy to interpret. The shocks remain less coherent than in the United States, insofar as they are further away from the top right-hand corner. In addition, the dots are further from the lead diagonal, implying that some regions have significantly higher correlations in one shock than the other, a pattern also seen in the earlier time period. The most surprising result, however, is that the countries closest to the "good" upper right-hand corner comprise Italy, Portugal, Spain, Ireland, and (possibly) Greece—in other worlds the crisis countries. Their limited integration with Germany makes them implausible candidates for a Euro area "core", suggesting that the outcomes reflect distortions in the Euro area.

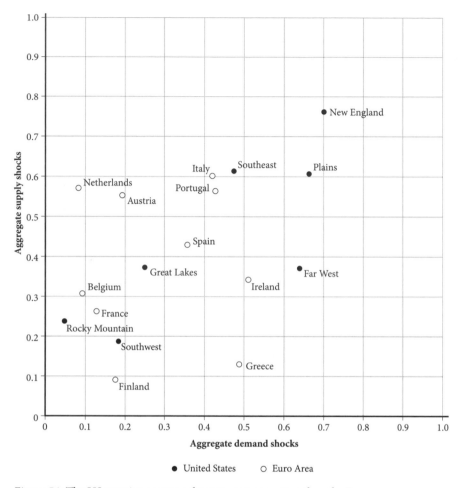

Figure 54: The US remains a more coherent currency union than the Euro area. Correlations with anchor region (Mideast in US, Germany in EMU). *Source:* Bayoumi and Eichengreen (2017).

Consistent with the discussion in the first part of this book, our analysis interprets the results as reflecting a Euro area banking super-cycle, as lax supervision of internal risk models drove a massive pre-crisis boom and a post-crisis slump in the periphery, linked to the fortunes of the export-led German economy.[14] These results suggest that rather than creating similar economic shocks to which a single monetary policy could respond, the creation of the Euro was accompanied by centrifugal financial forces that pulled regions apart, and were ill-suited to a single monetary policy. This implies that optimum currency theorists should have focused much more on the role of financial integration for a smoothly functioning currency union. In particular, it also underlines the potential for stronger and more centralized Euro area financial regulation to support the currency union. This brings us to the issue of the extent that non-monetary buffers can compensate for the loss of monetary autonomy as a result of a monetary union.

Is the Euro Promoting Better Shock Absorbers?

How far can non-monetary buffers to shocks make up for loss in national monetary policy? An obvious place to start is banking. While flawed financial integration helped to drive the 2008–2012 banking cum fiscal crises, the recent switch to ECB supervision of banks is a major change to the Euro area structure. Centralized bank regulation could impact a currency union in two ways. The first is by encouraging the creation of region-wide banks. European banking remained relatively splintered after the introduction of the Euro because supervision stayed in the hands of national regulators who showed more interest in promoting their own banks than in creating a truly integrated financial system.[15] Centralized supervision of the major banks by the ECB is likely to erode this resistance. In addition, centralizing the costs of bank rescues would eliminate the feedback from banking problems onto national debt that generated the sovereign-bank spiral featuring so prominently in the European half of the North Atlantic crisis.

The history of the US monetary union provides a way of examining the effects of the creation of national banks. Through the late 1970s, US banks were constrained to operate in one state and sometimes only in one branch within that state. This situation changed as earlier restrictions were lifted, and by the late 1990s national banks had appeared. Indeed, this transformed the geographic range of US banks more dramatically than any change as a result of centralized ECB supervision, since EU banks were not banned from cross-border mergers in the way regulated US banks were confined to operate in a single state, they were merely discouraged by local regulators.

The literature does indeed suggest that the spread of interstate banking made US regional business cycles smaller and more correlated, even if the similarity of pre- and post-1990 correlations of shocks suggests the impact was limited.[16] The theoretical impact on output volatility is ambiguous, as the benefits from having access to out-of-state loans over a credit crunch has to be set against the loss of local loans when there is a fall in collateral values. Empirical results, however, find that fluctuations in output in US states became smaller and more coherent as US bank integration increased.[17] Strikingly, this improvement occurred even as supervision of the regulated

banks was being tightened as a result of the introduction of prompt corrective action in the early 1990s. This suggests that part of the benefits came
from the fact that banks were constrained from excessive speculation.
Consistent with this interpretation, when the same framework is applied
across countries rather than US states there are few benefits and even
possibly some increase in volatility from bank integration, a more negative
pattern that is consistent with the fact the international debt flows are more
prone to speculation and contagion.

A strong case can also be made that centralized support for banks would
improve the ability of the Euro area to respond to shocks. The United States
has had federal bank support since the Great Depression, when the 1933
Banking Act created federal deposit insurance and the Federal Deposit
Insurance Corporation (FDIC). The FDIC oversees insured depositors but
also has a much broader mandate to resolve failing banks, for example by
arranging the sale of a failing bank to a competitor (US bank rescues often
involve a healthy bank buying the insolvent one for a low price).[18] The
FDIC is funded by levies on the banking industry, but also has a line of
credit with the federal government so that in practice bank deposits are
guaranteed by the full faith and credit of the US government.

Federal insurance greatly limited the feedback from earlier regional
banking problems on the local and national economy. For example, the US
experienced three significant housing busts from the late 1980s through the
mid-1990s. Real house prices fell by one-third in New England between
1988 and 1997, with similar outcomes in California (1989–97) and Texas
(1987–97).[19] Hence, from the late 1980s through the mid-1990s about a
quarter of the US economy was experiencing major falls in real housing
prices. While the economies of the three regions suffered (their growth rates
dipped some 1½ percent below their long-term average) the rest of the US
economy continued to grow at its long-term rate. And while these regional
slowdowns were accompanied by financial disruption, most notably in New
England, the housing slumps did not generate the kind of negative fiscal-
banking feedback loops that happened in the Euro area from 2009 to 2012
for the simple reason that the costs of cleaning-up banking were borne by
the federal government. The advantages of federal funding of bank rescues
was also be seen over the North Atlantic financial crisis, when the United
States was able to organize a coherent response to the banking crisis involving
federal support along with credible stress tests that forced banks to recapitalize. In the Euro area, the response was much less effective in large
part because member governments had to worry much more about the
potential costs to their own budgets.

The policy lesson is that the Euro area banking system needs two further reforms to switch from the amplifier of shocks seen over the crisis to an effective shock absorber. The first it to reign in the internal risk models that encouraged the creation of thinly capitalized mega-banks that were prone to speculation. The second is to switch to Euro-area-wide bank support by centralizing the funding of deposit insurance and bank rescues. This would allow the creation of an FDIC-like organization to oversee bank rescues across the Euro area to complement the centralized ECB role in bank supervision.

A similar underlying story about the importance of central funding applies to fiscal policy, although for slightly different reasons. Centralized banking support avoids the amplification of cycles coming from the need for individual countries to foot the bill for banking rescues. By contrast, fiscal policy can directly offset a shock to demand in a country through higher spending and lower taxes. As discussed earlier, in the case of the United States and virtually every other country in the world, the federal budget provides automatic support in response to divergent shocks within the currency union. Research suggests that in the US this amounts to a 20 cent offset for every dollar of shock. Hence, individual US states get a significant fiscal support in a slump even though almost all have balanced budget amendments that constrain their ability to respond through their own budgets.[20]

The Euro area has much less effective fiscal buffers because of the need for countries to fund their own fiscal response. Any fiscal boost to cushion a downturn involves a rise in national debt that will have to be offset by tighter future policies. Anticipation of these future costs blunts the impact of national fiscal support compared to the equivalent support from a federal system. While the size of this "Ricardian offset" to the fiscal stimulus coming from the anticipation of tighter future policies is difficult to measure, most estimates suggest it approximately halves the support provided by any increase in the fiscal deficit.[21] Hence, in order to provide the same support as the 20–cent fiscal boost coming from the US federal system, a Euro area member would have to provide a stimulus of 40 cents since the support to activity is only half as large, implying a need to deliberately augment automatic stabilizers. However, the European Stability and Growth Pact generally limits active policies in response to shocks.[22] The pact is designed to minimize the risks from excess borrowing using the credibility of the Euro area by limiting any build-up of debt rather than to respond to shocks. Fiscal deficits are supposed to be capped at 3 percent of output and by a "debt break" that requires members with government debt of over the

60 percent of output ceiling to reduce their debt ratio at a specific rate. If deficits exceed either cap, an excessive deficit procedure defines the rate at which countries should rectify the situation. While this calculation adjusts for the impact of the cycle on the deficit, so as to avoid excessively tight policies in the face of a downturn, there is no provision for active policies to support the economy. If history is any guide, Euro area members will run deficits close to the 3 percent limit in good times, constraining the ability to provide active government fiscal support in slumps.

Another buffer that can reduce the costs of diverse regional shocks is to improve the flexibility of an economy. Rather than reduce the impact of shocks, as with centralized banking and fiscal policy, a more flexible economy reduces the costs of coping with the consequences of shocks as labor and/or firms move from the region in a slump to the region that is booming. The United States, a large continent-wide currency union encompassing many different regions and economic realities, has relatively flexible labor and product markets. Such markets have helped the economy to adapt to unexpected changes such as the rise in oil prices in the 1970s (which supported the oil-producing Southwest region while hurting the manufacturing core of the Great Lakes economy), through the slump in oil prices later in the 1980s, the rise in the information technology sector in the 1990s, and the more recent oil shale boom. While these shocks have all involved regional winners and losers, the costs have been reduced by the ability of the US economy to adapt.

An important expectation for European monetary union was that the constraints of a single currency would inspire deregulation of labor and product markets.[23] This would increase the rate of growth of the region and make it more flexible and hence a better currency union. These incentives were expected to be particularly powerful on the more sclerotic southern members of the currency union that generally had the least flexible economies as a result of government rules and regulations. This process, which was supported by inter-governmental initiatives such as the Lisbon strategy launched in 2000 just after the introduction of the Euro, would accelerate overall growth and the convergence of incomes across the monetary union, making it more homogeneous in terms of underlying prosperity and flexibility.

There is indeed evidence that European labor markets are becoming more flexible over time. Recent analysis of European countries has found that the short-term role of migration in responding to labor market shocks has increased significantly between a pre-EMU sample (1977–99) and a largely post-EMU one (1990–2013).[24] In the pre-EMU period, migration absorbed about 20 percent of labor market shocks in the first two years after an employment shock. In the more recent period this has risen to more like 30 percent. There has been a similar increase in the (larger) role played by migration in absorbing labor shocks within EU countries, from 40 to 50 percent. The gap between the role of migration in intra- and inter-country mobility suggests that impediments such as language and culture continue to limit labor market adjustment between initial Euro area members. Consistent with this, analysis suggests that EU enlargement in 2004 and 2007 that added lower-wage eastern European countries to the single market aided the speed of labor market adjustment as these workers proved more willing to migrate.[25] Sadly, this has come at the cost of a political backlash against such migrants, as exemplified by Brexit and rising support for anti-immigrant parties elsewhere.

Despite these improvements, labor market flexibility across Euro area members remains significantly lower than within the United States even though the gap has narrowed. This reflects both the increase in labor mobility in the Euro area and a decrease in the United States. The US reduction may reflect a gradual lowering of regional divergences in labor market conditions across regions as the industrial structure has become more similar over time, which has reduced the incentives to migrate.[26] This is much less true in the Euro area. Differences in regional unemployment have always been larger in Europe than in the United States and, although the gap started closing after the introduction of the Euro, it has widened again since the crisis, suggesting that much of the earlier progress reflected unsustainable booms in the periphery. All in all, a sensible overall conclusion is that labor market adjustment to shocks across Euro area countries continues to be only about half the size of the United States.

Product market flexibility has also shown some convergence between EMU and the United States, as well as convergence within the Euro area. The Organisation for Economic Cooperation and Development (OECD) produces an index of product market regulation that combines assessments of the role of the state, barriers to entrepreneurship, and barriers to trade and investment for 1998, 2003, 2008 and 2013, conveniently spanning the decade from the creation of EMU until the eve of the crisis (1998–2008) and the early response to the crisis itself (2008–13). The numbers suggest that in 1998 the initial members of EMU had significantly more regulated product markets compared to other advanced economies and a much larger gap with the United States and the United Kingdom, the traditional leaders in this area. The gap between Euro area countries and other advanced economies reversed by 2013, when a typical Euro area country had less regulated product markets than other advanced economies, although it remained some way from the United States and the United Kingdom. There were particularly large improvements after 2008 in the crisis countries, especially Greece, Italy, and Portugal. The major uncertainty is whether the post-crisis impetus for faster reforms will take on a momentum of its own, or fade with memories of the crisis and the end of economic programs backed by the European Commission, the ECB, and the IMF.

Overall, the results suggest that EMU did help to create a more flexible Euro area economy both in absolute terms and compared to other advanced economies. However, not entirely surprisingly, the region remains well behind the United States. This helps to explain why business cycles across Euro area members remain less coherent than across US regions, and hence that Euro area members are more susceptible to regional shocks that a single monetary policy cannot solve.[27]

* * *

The Future of EMU

EMU occurred in spite of long-standing disagreement over its role in the European integration process. Since at least the Werner Report in the early 1970s, the French and like-minded countries held that an early currency union was needed to create the integrated economy that would produce a smooth-functioning currency union, while the Germans and their supporters felt that EMU should occur only after such integration had already been achieved. While this disagreement went into relative abeyance in the decade after the Euro was launched, when rapid convergence appeared to be occurring, it has resurfaced since the crisis, recast as a discussion about whether to loosen existing policy constraints in order to provide support for countries in crisis or maintain the rules so as to avoid further moral hazard in the future. Tension over this issue is unlikely to be resolved soon given that it has been simmering for almost half a century.

Since the crisis, progress has been made in providing better responses to diverse shocks with the Euro area. Banking supervision has been centralized, providing the potential for a truly integrated banking system of the type taken for granted in most currency unions, including the United States. The issue here is whether internal risk models will be curbed and deposit insurance and other forms of banking support will also be centralized. Such moves have the potential to greatly improve the workings of the monetary union while failure to follow through will leave an unstable, half-formed banking union that will be a significantly less effective shock absorber. In addition, tighter fiscal rules might convince Euro area members to run smaller deficits, allowing more leeway to provide stimulus in the face of negative shocks. Finally, significant progress has been made recently on structural reforms, most notably in the periphery whose economies were the least flexible at the outset of the single currency. As with banking union, the main uncertainty is whether this progress will be maintained as memories of the existential crisis fade and weariness with economic reforms grow.

If the crisis generates a true banking union, lower government deficits and debt, and further progress on structural reforms, the Euro area would to look more and more like the United States, another massive continent-wide economy. EMU would then be moving into the type of smooth currency union that the French/Monetarists predicted that a common currency would create. Such a currency union would find it much easier to cope with unexpected shocks. In particular, banking problems could be approached in a more organized and effective manner, while more fiscal leeway and more economic flexibility would blunt the inevitable trauma for those whose economies are hit with negative shocks. It might also create momentum for further fiscal and political integration.

There is, however, a much less optimistic future if progress stalls on banking reform, government deficits and debt remain high, and structural reforms slow. Under this scenario, the Euro area would continue as an unsatisfactory currency union with limited economic integration. Such a union would remain susceptible to divergent shocks that leave individual members in the economic doldrums for long periods. Such centrifugal economic forces would gradually erode the support for the single money. In this context, it is worth remembering the demise of the nineteenth-century Latin currency union, formed in the 1860s and eventually dissolved by mutual agreement in the 1920s, rather than in the white heat of a crisis. The circumstances are in many ways quite different. The Latin union existed under the classical gold standard that invoked relatively permanent fixed exchange rates and limited monetary autonomy. That said, however, it is very possible that, just like old soldiers, badly designed currency unions do not die but just gradually fade away.

FINAL THOUGHTS

This book explains the path that made the North Atlantic economy became so brittle that the failure of a medium-sized US investment bank precipitated a crisis, and the ensuing policy lessons. While enormous amounts have been written about the crisis, the focus has been either on what happened during the crisis and the lessons from that immediate experience or broader discussions of the failure of capitalism, rather than examining the historical context that led to this particular event. Symptomatic of this approach is that the US and Euro area legs of the North Atlantic crisis have often been treated as separate events, whereas the approach taken here underlines that there was a single crisis in which both sides of the North Atlantic were parasitically intertwined. A massive expansion in lending by banks in the Euro area core helped fuel financial booms in the Euro area periphery and the US housing market. When the resulting bubbles burst, they generated deep recessions on both sides of the North Atlantic that leeched into the rest of the world.

These financial excesses emanated from misguided financial reforms in Europe and in the United States driven by US deregulatory zeal and fractured Euro area policy processes. Both regions embarked upon radical financial reforms starting in the 1980s. In Europe the objective was to create a unified banking system. A key moment for the Euro area banking system 1996 decision by the Basel Committee on Bank Supervision to allow larger banks to use their internal risk models to calculate capital buffers for investment banking. This decision largely reflected the belief of the US Federal Reserve that market discipline worked better than government regulation, and that internal models represented a powerful method for banks to assess risk. In reality, the core Euro area mega-banks manipulated their internal models to reduce their capital buffers and redeploy the unused capital to back new loans. The resulting rapid expansion in lending went largely into investment banking in the United States and commercial loans in the periphery of Europe, regions that were seen as major growth opportunities. National regulators missed the erosion of capital buffers as they were focused on promoting their own national champions.

While lax regulation was allowing the European banks to expand, in the United States the distortions came from differences in rules between regulated and shadow banks. The regulated banks were saved from the excesses in Europe as they were required to hold large (and expensive) capital buffers against loans. However, this stricter system also gave them strong incentives to sell mortgages (and similarly standardized loans) to US investment and European universal banks whose capital buffers were thinner and business models less sound. A key moment for the US banking system was the 2003 decision by the Securities and Exchange Commission (SEC) to widen the collateral allowed in repurchase agreements. Repos were a way of obtaining dollar cash by temporarily loaning out safe assets with an agreement to repurchase them later at a fixed price. By the early 2000s, however, the market was being constrained by a dwindling supply of collateral. The SEC decision had the intended effect of expanding the repo market and making it more liquid. However, it also helped fund and internationalize the US housing bubble. By allowing mortgage-backed securities to be used as collateral for repos, it increased the demand for high-yielding mortgages, a demand that was satisfied by creating inadequately supervised subprime loans. By allowing foreign currency bonds to be used as collateral, the decision simultaneously increased the presence of European banks in US markets. The confluence led to a massive North Atlantic financial drift of European money into the US housing bubble.

The financial "yin" of more lending by banks with increasingly inadequate capital buffers was complemented by a macroeconomic "yang" as lower interest rates encouraged higher spending and borrowing by firms and households. The introduction of the Euro in 1999 and a surge in loans from the Euro area core led to a rapid fall in borrowing costs in the Euro periphery. In countries such as Italy, Spain, Greece, and Portugal that had always had high interest rates, lenders started charging similar rates to Germany and France. This result was a debt-financed boom in southern Europe that the northern mega-banks were happy to underwrite.[1] The macroeconomic "yang" explains why Euro area lending was concentrated in the periphery, even though the increased bank lending power was mainly in the core.

The US housing boom had an equally important macroeconomic "yang", as a steady fall in borrowing costs and inadequate supervision of mortgage terms allowed individuals to take on unwise loans. Major foreign financial inflows helped to drive down borrowing costs that fueled the housing bubble. A significant part of these inflows came from China and other emerging markets that built up reserves to protect themselves from financial instability and to support undervalued exchange rates.[2] An equally potent force, however, was financial inflows from European banks as they expanded into US markets. The Federal Reserve allowed easy financing conditions to continue because policymakers focused on inflation, which remained quiescent, even as house prices and the trade deficit soared. Again, the financial "yin" and the macroeconomic "yang" fed off each other.

One lesson is that financial regulation needs to be both tighter and more consistent across institutions. In response, regulations were tightened in both the Euro area and the United States. Higher capital buffers have been complemented by new requirements on liquidity.[3] Addition capital buffers have been added on "too big to fail" banks, repos, and securitizations, and US regulation has been extended to investment banks, the institutions at the heart of the shadow banking system. What has been less emphasized, however, is the remaining gap in the strength of regulation of major banks between Euro area and the United States. While both regions are under the same basic capital rules (Basel 3), the Europeans chose a stripped down version while US policymakers voluntarily added additional safeguards. In the Euro area, capital buffers of the mega-banks continue to be calculated using internal risk models which amplify financial booms and busts, allow banks to skimp on capital buffers, and afford the mega-banks a competitive advantage over their small competitors. And while there are plans to introduce more stringent rules in 2018 the devil will be in the details. By contrast, for the large US banks the results from internal risk models are constrained since they also need to comply with simpler and more transparent calculations of capital adequacy. Further reform of the Euro area banking supervision is urgently needed to lower risks of future lending booms, reduce the role of the mega-banks, and to avoid the potential for trans-Atlantic financial flows to restart exploiting regulatory differences. In the United States, the priority is to avoid rolling back tougher regulation of large banks, including investment banking.

The unsustainable macrofinancial booms on both sides of the North Atlantic were missed as a result of a series of intellectual blinkers associated with the pro-market ethos of the period. The flawed design of the Euro area failed to provide sufficient support for countries in crisis, turning a recession into a depression. More generally, three intellectual undercurrents were particularly important in creating a compartmentalized approach to policy-making that diverted the eyes of the policy community from the increasing risks. The efficient markets hypothesis eroded belief in the importance of financial regulation which allowed policymakers to sign off on internal risk models; analysis of the great moderation in output volatility led central banks to overestimate the effectiveness of monetary policy; and benign neglect led to a downgrade of international economic policy cooperation. These blinkers added to the size and costs of the crisis by causing policy-makers to miss the risks from trans-Atlantic financial capital flows and from the fractured design of the Euro area. The system that appeared to be so elegant and efficient turned out not to be robust as an intellectual bubble blinded policymakers to the growing macrofinancial bubbles. These ortho-doxies were embodied in state-of-the-art dynamic stochastic general equilibrium models that remain in wide use. The difficulty in adapting them to include more realistic features means that there is a risk that policymakers will continue to embrace the intellectual errors of the past.

A more comprehensive reboot of macroeconomics and policy regimes is needed. This will involve a wider canvas than the pre-crisis emphasis on inflation, business cycles, and monetary policy; more integration between those responsible for monetary policy, fiscal policy, financial stability, and structural reforms; and a more inclusive approach to macroeconomic analysis that can move beyond the self-centered, hyper-rational homo economicus and accepts that crowds can exhibit madness as well as wisdom. Turning to policies, one specific area where more government scrutiny is needed is on international debt flows, where rapid inflows followed by even faster outflows have driven a regular cycle of ever larger international crises, starting with the break-up of the Bretton Woods fixed exchange rate system in the early 1970s and culminating in the North Atlantic crisis almost forty years later. Finally, while some of the flaws in the design of the Euro area have been repaired, more needs to be done to ensure that the area can respond more smoothly to shocks in members, including completing the banking union.

An important legacy of the North Atlantic crisis has been an erosion in confidence in experts in general and economic experts in particular. This has been seen in the strength of populist parties at the ballot box. The failure to anticipate and avoid the crisis undermined the credibility of policy makers, including central banks. It is striking that no central bank has publicly apologized for the North Atlantic debacle despite that fact the preservation of financial stability is one of their basic responsibilities. It is simply not good enough to explain that inflation did not send the right signals and move on. Or to hide behind mathematical formulae that contain crucial simplifications. The crisis was a systemic failure of macroeconomics that requires a systemic revamp beyond tougher bank regulation.

The most important lesson from the North Atlantic crisis, however, may be the inability of financial policies on their own, including the introduction of the Euro, to create prosperity. A striking feature of the time between 1985 and 2008 was that financial deregulation was not accompanied by aggressive programs to improve the workings of the real economy of the type pursued in the 1980s by President Reagan in the United States and Prime Minister Thatcher in the United Kingdom. In the absence of structural reforms that provided new investment opportunities, financial deregulation simply pushed more money into the same places. Rather than being used to create more productive capacity, the additional lending was largely frittered away, mainly on higher land and house prices. Similarly, the massive expansion in mortgage-backed securities was driven by differences in regulation and had few social benefits, in contrast to earlier developments such as the emergence of junk bonds in the 1980s which, for all of the accompanying excesses, allowed small firms to access the bond market. Because it was filling a genuine economic need, the junk bond market continues to be vibrant to this day, in stark contrast to the moribund private securitization market.

There is a need to see economic progress in a more balanced manner, in which the financial sector provides an essential support to underlying changes in the real economy. This view that financial sector should be a support for real activity contrasts with the growing belief over the crisis that the financial sector was, in and of itself, a route to greater prosperity. The belief in financial alchemy, in which clever financial transactions can on their own create wealth without the tedious need to create new businesses or ideas, is a characteristic of most financial bubbles. The main difference in the case of the North Atlantic crisis was not the degree of self-deception but rather the sheer size of the economies that were involved. The enormous associated costs, however, underline the need to ensure that this experienced is not repeated. Hence the need for a more wide-ranging policy reboot from financial regulators, macroeconomic policymakers, and European leaders.

A final message from this narrative is the importance of being appropriately skeptical about financial improvements that create greater market opportunities for banks. Many of the crucial regulatory missteps involved reforms that allowed banks more latitude. Private banks pushed for the

1996 decision to allow capital buffers for market risks to be calculated using internal risk models and the 2003 decision that widened the eligible collateral for repo agreements. These changes made perfect sense from a certain perspective. Internal models were theoretically a better way of calculating risk, just as the US repo market was genuinely being limited by existing collateral rules. However, these narrow benefits turned out to be miniscule when set against the wider costs coming from excessively small capital buffers that internal models produced and the incentives to mass-produce high-yielding mortgages that the change in repo rules generated. Just as the epitaph to the Trojan war was to "beware of Greeks bearing gifts", the epitaph to the North Atlantic crisis should be "beware of bankers proffering improvements".

NOTES

Introduction: The Needle (and the Damage Done)

1. "National reputation hangs on IKB rescue", *Financial Times*, August 2, 2007.
2. Measured using the FTSEurofirst 300 index.
3. The exceptions are Greece and Ireland, where the IMF estimates provide implausibly small losses in output. For Greece, I simply assume the cost of the crisis was 30 percent of output, slightly larger than the equivalent figure for Portugal, and in Ireland I assume 5 percent of GDP rather than the positive number implied by IMF estimates.
4. For a discussion of the spillovers from the United States see IMF (2011).
5. For example, they are close to the "low" scenario reported in Cline (2017), Chapter 2.
6. For a useful discussion and comparison see Cline (2017), Chapter 2.
7. It has often ben remarked that no major bankers were prosecuted after the crisis, but just as striking is that no financial experts lost their jobs. One possible exception is Shelia Blair of the US Federal Deposit Insurance Corporation, who resigned at the end of her term in 2011. She, of course, was a fierce critic of Wall Street and a woman to boot.
8. In the United Kingdom, two major banks (Royal Bank of Scotland and Lloyds) had to be rescued and Barclays came under major stress; in Switzerland, the largest bank, UBS, also required government support. Both countries have interesting, if somewhat different, stories. The problems of UBS came from their major presence in the US markets, and hence is a case of US financial spillovers onto an otherwise sound banking system. The UK case is in many ways the opposite, a homegrown crisis with only limited dalliance in US markets except for Barclays bank.
9. Examples for the US include Wessel (2010), Paulson (2013), Geithner (2014), and Bernanke (2015), and for the Euro area crisis Pisani-Ferry (2014), Sandbu (2015), Brunnermeier, James, and Landau (2016), and Stiglitz (2016).
10. For example, Wolf (2014) and King (2016)
11. Clark (2012) and MacMillan (2013).
12. A similar view on the United Kingdom is provided by Haldane (2009).
13. Stiglitz (2016) and Brunnermeier, James, and Landau (2016).

1 European Banks Unfettered

1. Laeven and Valencia (2012), Table 1. The crises were assessed as systemic, except in the cases of France, Italy, and Portugal.

2. Price Waterhouse (1988), Murphy (1999), and Dermine (2002).
3. Merler and Véron (2015) report that banking made up 88 percent of financing in Europe, versus 30 percent in the United States.
4. The nationalizations were partially reversed by the incoming right-wing government of Jacques Chirac, although the banking system was not fully privatized until 2002 (Plessis, 2003).
5. Holton (1986); see also Sachs and Wyplosz (1986).
6. Price Waterhouse (1988), p. 8.
7. European Council Directive 88/361/EEC. Ireland, Portugal and Spain were allowed to maintain temporary restrictions, mainly on short-term movements, until 31 December 1992, and for Greece the deadline was 30 June 1994. As a safeguard, the directive included a clause enabling member states to take protective measures if short-term capital movements of exceptional size seriously disrupted the conduct of monetary policy, but the transition went smoothly and no country used the option. As a result, capital controls and the associated barriers to European-wide banking became a thing of the past in the European Union by the early 1990s.
8. Matthews (1992).
9. Focarelli and Pozzolo (2001).
10. European Central Bank (2000) has a detailed discussion.
11. While there was a modest increase in the fiscal responsibilities of the European Union, fiscal policy remained overwhelmingly at the national level.
12. James (2012), pp. 313–17.
13. It presumably also reflected lobbying by the national regulators who, like most institutions and people, preferred to retain their jobs.
14. In the final text, Article 105.5 of the Treaty stated that "The ESCB shall *contribute* to the smooth conduct of policies *pursued by the competent authorities* relating to the prudential supervision of credit institutions and the stability of the financial system" (emphasis added).
15. Véron (2013).
16. Basel Committee on Banking Supervision (2007). See also Goodhart (2011) who provides a detailed history of the Committee's actions from 1974 to 1997.
17. Tarullo (2008), Chapter 3.
18. Ibid., p. 45.
19. Goodhart (2011), Chapter 6, provides a detailed discussion of this process.
20. Basel Committee on Banking Supervision (1988), p. 1.
21. Ibid., paragraph 3.
22. Off-balance-sheet items were first given a "conversion factor" which translated then into the equivalent on-balance-sheet risk and then were assigned to the on-balance-sheet risk buckets.
23. Basel Committee on Banking Supervision (1993).
24. Goodhart (2011), pp. 247–9.
25. This issue was further confounded by the inability to reach agreement on uniform capital rules for market risk with the International Organization of Securities Commissions (IOSCO), which covered the US investment banking houses. The European universal banks were thus under a different regime for safety and soundness than the US investment banks, providing ample opportunities for requests to lower standards so as to provide a more level playing field.
26. Goodhart (2011), Chapter 7, Appendix J. The exact quote is that "roughly 7 to 10 of 15 banks produced estimates of risk within a range of plus or minus 25 percent of the median estimate".
27. Basel Committee on Banking Supervision (1996).
28. Greenspan (2008), pp. 372–3.
29. Financial Services Authority (2005).
30. Dermine (2002), Table 13.
31. Branches were a more popular method of entry in the southern countries than in the northern core.

32. An additional underlying factor was the information technology revolution, which tended to favor large banks with widespread operations over small banks with local knowledge.
33. The vertical axis shows the ratio of the book value of equity to total assets, the horizontal axis the ratio of Tier 1 capital to risk-weighted assets.
34. Vestergaard and Retana (2012). See also Blundell-Wignall and Roulet (2012).

2 US Shadow Banks Unleashed

1. For example Johnson and Kwak (2011). My analysis is based on longer historical over-views of US financial deregulation, such as Kroszner and Strahan (2014) and (for a more jaundiced view) Sherman (2009).
2. Colton (2002) and Federal Housing Finance Agency Office of Inspector General (2011).
3. The Emergency Home Finance Act allowed Freddie and Fannie to buy and sell mort-gages not insured or guaranteed by the federal government.
4. Over time, the caps on lending rates were gradually eliminated by a combination of favorable legal decisions, regulatory competition across states, and lower inflation. The major legal step was the 1978 Supreme Court ruling that the National Banking Act allowed a bank to charge up to the maximum rate allowed by its home state regardless of the location of the borrower. This created incentives for states to raise or eliminate the caps on interest rates so as to make their banks more competitive, particularly in the much less geographically constrained credit card business. Delaware and South Dakota were the first to eliminate their usury laws altogether, leading to a rapid expansion in their banks' credit card business. By 1988 a further 18 states had removed all restrictions. Elsewhere, the reduction in inflation in the 1990s made usury laws much less important except as regards extremely high-risk loans. By this time, however, the transfer of loans to the shadow banking system as a result of the simple leverage ratio was well underway.
5. Haltom (2013) provides more detail.
6. Federal Deposit and Insurance Corporation (1997a) contains for a detailed description.
7. Federal Deposit Insurance Corporation (1998) contains for more detail.
8. In addition, the act reduced the incentives for insured banks to take risks by introducing risk-based deposit insurance charges and the incentives to widen bailout to include non-insured creditors by directing the Federal Deposit Insurance Corporation to resolve a bank in the least costly way to the insurance fund.
9. In an important legal ruling, automatic teller machines were ruled to not constitute bank branches, allowing them to be set up without regard to rules on the location of bank offices.
10. Kroszner and Strahan (2014).
11. Calomaris (2000).
12. For example, Johnson and Kwak (2011).
13. Murphy (2013).
14. Kennedy (1999).
15. There are also separate regulators for credit unions and, before 2010, thrifts.
16. Greenspan (1996).
17. Moseby (2016).
18. Greenspan (1996).
19. Their origins lay in financing physical trade. Merchants would accept money from investors in return for providing a portion of the profits from the voyage assuming the ship and its cargo arrived safely. Investment banks would accept such paper at a discount that reflected the uncertainties involved in the voyage. From the start, they were heavily involved in making markets work.
20. For discussions and definitions of the shadow banking system see Pozsar and others (2013), Adrian and Shin (2009), and Adrian and Ashcraft (2012).
21. A famous early exposition is Lewis (1989).
22. See Edwards (1999) for more on hedge funds.
23. Ibid.

24. Of the three main rating agencies (S&P, Moody's, and Fitch), one looked only at the likelihood of default and not at the amount of money that could be recovered should the security default, another took both default and losses into consideration, while the last focused on loss given default. These methodologies are easily available on their web sites.

25. The repo data include federal funds transactions, but since these were lent at a penalty rate it can be assumed the vast majority of the funds are private repos.

3 Boom and Bust

1. In addition, the core northern European banks expanded into other regions and businesses, such as Eastern Europe and trade credit. This development helped spread the impact of the subsequent North Atlantic financial bust to the rest of the world.

2. Securities and Exchange Commission (2003b). As preparation for this in March 2003 the SEC had issued a Final Rule that delegated the authority to "expand the categories of permissible collateral" for such repos to the Director of the Division of Market Regulation (Securities and Exchange Commission, 2003a, Section IIIA).

3. Securities and Exchange Commission (2003b).

4. It also extended safe haven status to other collateralized loans such as swaps, in which banks "swapped" interest payments on loans linked to interest rates of different maturities (e.g., 3-month and 1-year rates) or in different currencies.

5. Basel Committee on Banking Supervision (2005a and 2005b). Regulations on covered bonds were also modernized. Covered bonds, mainly used by European banks, were bonds that were backed by specific loans on a bank's balance sheet, which meant that they would pay out even if the bank went bankrupt as long as the borrowers of the loans continued to pay.

6. Basel Committee on Banking Supervision (2005a), paragraph 3.

7. Kiff and Mills (2007) discuss mortgage originations and Justiniano, Primiceri, and Tambalotti (2016) discuss the dynamics of mortgage-backed asset spread.

8. Mayer, Pence and Sherlund (2009) and Amromin and Paulson (2010) discuss the deterioration in subprime loans over time.

9. Tarullo (2008), p. 89.

10. Mortgage loans attracted a risk weight of 50 percent while mortgage-backed securities had a weight of only 20 percent.

11. McDonough laid out three rationales for such a review. In the face of more intense competition, arbitrage strategies were undermining the value of Basel 1; that capital adequacy rules should be supplemented by supervision and market discipline; and the need to attend to operational risk from unlikely but major shocks. Tarullo (2008), pp. 91–2.

12. While the preamble to the proposal advocated a three-pillar approach, comprising capital rules, supervision, and market discipline, the Committee's work was and would continue to be focused on capital rules.

13. The biggest rise in capital occurred when using the foundation internal risk-based model, implying little or no incentive for banks using the standard approach to adopt this model. On the other hand, the advanced approach produced the smallest increase in overall capital charges, with a fall in capital for credit risk more than offsetting additional charges for operational risk.

14. Tarullo (2008), p. 113.

15. In addition, the Committee started coming under pressure from politicians, including, for example, German concerns over the risk weights for small- and medium-sized enterprises.

16. Tarullo (2008), p. 114.

17. On the way to the final rule a third consultative paper was released but it did not contain any fundamental changes in course.

18. Tarullo (2008), p. 160.

19. The Office of the Comptroller of the Currency, the Board of Governors of the Federal Reserve System, the Federal Deposit Insurance Corporation, and the Office of Thrift Supervision (2006).
20. The 15 percent figure involved weighting banks by their capital, which put more weight on banks with large capital buffers.
21. Summary section of the report.
22. Basel Committee on Banking Supervision (2006).
23. The Basel study aggregated results for QIS-4 and QIS-5, and adjusted the results for QIS-4 by the new 1.06 scaling factor for internal-ratings-based capital requirements (this scaling factor was not included in the US agencies' report).
24. Financial Services Agency (2005).
25. Quoted in Alford (2010).
26. In the words of Alan Greenspan, testifying to the US Congress in October 2008: "I made a mistake in presuming that the self-interest of organizations specifically banks and others were such that they were best capable of protecting their own shareholders."
27. Tarullo (2008) and Herring (2007) contains trenchant contemporary assessments of the US process, and Getter (2014) for a more recent discussion.
28. Jickling and Murphy (2010).
29. All Euro area banking systems increased their assets by 40 to 150 percent of output between 2002 and 2009 except Ireland (where it rose by an astonishing 660 percent). Luxemburg is excluded as it is essentially an off-shore center.
30. While equivalent data are not available, it seems likely that the UK banks also expanded into investment banking. This was certainly true of the Irish banks—which were also under "light-touch" regulation—whose ratio of commercial loans to assets had sunk to one quarter by 2008, the lowest in the Euro area.
31. The inclusion of Austria and Finland in the periphery group is for convenience and makes little difference to the calculations as their economies are small.
32. Pagano and others (2014) discuss this trend in more detail.
33. Fender and McGuire (2010).
34. The assets reported for the investment banking groups are considerably larger than the assets of the broker-dealer sector reported earlier, underlining that broker-dealers only represented the core institutions within these wider investment banking groups.
35. Lane (2013) contains an analysis.
36. Bernanke (2008).
37. Shin (2012).
38. The impact of private sector safe assets on interest rates and the macroeconomy are discussed in Gorton and Ordoñez (2013) and Caballero, Farhi, and Gourinchas (2016).
39. This is calculated by summing data on holdings of US debt by foreign official institutions and holdings of GSE securities by the five most important emerging markets. The latter adjustment reflects the use of GSE bonds as reserves by some countries, most notably China.
40. This calculation assumes that all of the asset purchases went into US securities, which seems reasonably given the rapid reduction in such assets after the crisis.
41. Bergsten and Gagnon (2017).

4 A Flawed Monetary Union

1. Brunnermeier, James, and Landau (2016).
2. Simms (2013).
3. Marsh (2011), pp. 45–6.
4. Brunnermeier, James, and Landau (2016) contains a much more detailed treatment.
5. Marsh (2011), Chapter 1.
6. Eichengreen (2008), pp. 15–16.
7. James (2012), pp. 74–85.
8. Werner (1970).
9. Quoted in Marsh (2011), p. 62.

10. Ibid., p. 63.
11. Enormous amounts of energy were extended on the details of this proposal, essentially deciding whether to reduce the stringency of monetary constrains by widening the bands around the dollar while leaving European bands unchanged or to tighten monetary cooperation by leaving dollar bands unchanged and tightening European ones. In the end they chose the latter, with US exchange-rate bands left unchanged at 0.75 percent and European bands narrowed from 1.5 percent to 1.2 percent.
12. James (2012), p. 107.
13. Ibid., Chapter 4.
14. Ibid., p. 152.
15. Ibid., p. 154.
16. Samuel Brittan of the *Financial Times*, quoted ibid., p. 181.
17. Short (2014) provides an entertaining biography of Mitterrand.
18. Moravcsik (1991), p. 30.
19. Marsh (2011), pp. 66–8.
20. Ibid., p. 122.
21. Ibid., p. 124.
22. The deliberations were taped, so we have a good record of what was said, as discussed in James (2012).
23. Ibid., p. 238.
24. Ibid., p. 237.
25. Marsh (2011), p. 129.
26. James (2012), p. 247.
27. Ibid., p. 249.
28. Ibid., p. 251.
29. Ironically, it was governor de Larosière who supported an effective supervisory mechanism in Stage 2 and beyond.
30. James (2012), p. 253.
31. Marsh (2011), p. 129.
32. James (2012), p. 211.
33. Marsh (2011), p. 143.
34. Ibid., p. 144.
35. Ibid., p. 153.
36. Ibid., p. 202.
37. Ibid., p. 110.

5 Intellectual Blinkers and Unexpected Spillovers

1. Honorable exceptions include Bill White at the Bank of International Settlements and the academics Nouriel Roubini and Robert Shiller.
2. Fox (2009).
3. King (2016).
4. Greenspan (2008), p. 489.
5. Bank of England website.
6. Lane (2013) and Fagan and Gaspar (2008).
7. Blanchard and Simon (2001) and Stock and Watson (2003)
8. The weight on high volatility sectors, such as durable goods and construction, that contributed disproportionately to the volatility of output remained largely unchanged over time. Similarly, while greater access to loans would smooth consumption of goods that provided immediate satisfaction (such as meals) this would not necessarily occur for goods that provided their services gradually over time, such as cars. Yet volatility had also fallen in the latter sectors.
9. Stock and Watson (2003) and Ahmed, Levin, and Wilson (2002).
10. Bernanke (2004).
11. Barro and Gordon (1983).
12. Arce, Hurtado, and Thomas (2016).

13. Kohn (2006).
14. Ibid.
15. Bergsten and Green (2016) contains an extensive discussion of the Plaza Agreement.
16. The University of Toronto has an excellent website with all of the main G7 documents, including the communiqués.
17. For more detailed critiques of DSGE models see Romer (2016) and Bayoumi (2016b).
18. Romer (2016) observes that in the models built by academics, monetary policy often had implausibly limited effects, while Bayoumi (2016b) argues the monetary effects are too large in models built by policymakers.
19. See, for example, Benes and Green (2016).
20. Greene (2004) provides an excellent intuitive explanation of the problems involved.

6 A History of the International Monetary System in Five Crises

1. On the benefits of international trade see International Monetary Fund, World Bank, and World Trade Organization (2017) and Krugman, Obstfeld, and Melitz (2015).
2. International Monetary Fund (2012b), p. 13, paragraph 16. The references contained in the original have been taken out for the sake of readability. See also the main paper, IMF (2012a).
3. The US crisis had some elements of a domestic sudden stop as some of the speculative money was transferred to treasuries, which may explain the lower costs to the United States (although all crises had significant involvement of domestic speculators). The Euro area crisis did not have this characteristic as there were few centralized funds to support crisis countries.
4. Recent changes to balance of payments statistics allow a finer breakdown between debt and equity purchases than the one used here, in particular as regards foreign direct investment. The overall result, however, is similar and since the data does not go back reliably over time I use the simpler definition of debt and equity flows.
5. There is a similar, if less direct, increase in risk for investors who lend in dollars, as a depreciation in the value of the pound increases the cost of dollar repayments for all foreign investors, thereby making all of the loans riskier.
6. Jeanne and Zettelmeyer (2005) provide a survey. See Krugman (1992) on the first generation models and Obstfeld (1996) on the second generation.
7. This is closely related to earlier models of bank runs, in which a run is always a risk unless government insurance gives depositors the assurance that their money is safe. Diamond and Dybvig (1983).
8. Bergsten and Green (2016).
9. IMF (2012b) paragraph 18 and references therein.
10. Garber (1993) contains a more detailed description of the collapse of the Bretton Woods system.
11. Eichengreen (1992).
12. Eichengreen (2008) contains a description of the evolution of capital market regulation over time.
13. Skidelsky (2001).
14. The Bretton Woods system came to maturity in 1960 after the termination of the European Payments Union (EPU), an arrangement that curtailed even current account transactions because of the severe shortages of dollars after the war.
15. Federal Deposit Insurance Corporation (1997b), Cline (1984 and 1995), Cohen (1992) and Dooley (1994) contain descriptions.
16. Quoted in Federal Deposit Insurance Corporation (1997b), pp. 197–8.
17. Ibid., p. 204.
18. Seidman (2000), pp. 127–8.
19. L. William Seidman, quoted in Federal Deposit Insurance Corporation (1997b), p. 207.
20. James (2012), Chapter 4, provides a blow-by-blow account of the snake.
21. Marsh (2011) contains a lively description.
22. James (2012), pp. 174–7.

23. For descriptions see Corsetti and others (1998) and Goldstein (1998).
24. Goldstein (1998), p. 13.
25. Bayoumi and Gagnon (2016).
26. Dooley (1994) is the only description of the crisis that argues that banks lent on the expectations of a bail-out.
27. A partial exception may be the break-up of Bretton Woods, since its likely demise was in the words of one commentator "one of the most accurately and generally predicted of major economic events", Garber (1993). However, fuzzy acceptance of the limitations of the system did not prevent participants from trying to shore it up, suggesting that there was less uniformity on its terminal state that this quote suggests.
28. There are many approximations in these calculations. For example, growth is measured in real terms while the trade balance in nominal terms. However, the misery index still provides an intuitive measure of the size of a crisis.
29. The United States for the break-up of Bretton Woods, Mexico and Brazil for the Latin American crisis, the United Kingdom, Italy, and France for the ERM, Thailand, Malaysia, Indonesia, and South Korea in the Asian crisis, and the United States, Italy, Spain, Ireland, Portugal, and Greece for the North Atlantic experience.
30. Washington Leaders' Summit Communiqué, from the University of Toronto "G20 Information Center" website.
31. An alternative is to have permanent capital controls, but this runs the risk of reducing the benefits from access to international debt markets in normal times.

7 Will Revamped Financial Regulations Work?

1. Basel Committee on Banking Supervision (2011).
2. Howarth and Quaglia (2015).
3. Getter (2014) describes the US approach.
4. Davis Polk (2014) provides details.
5. Goldstein (2017), Cline (2017) and Dagher and others (2016).
6. European Banking Authority (2016).
7. Schoenmaker and Véron (2016) contains a fuller description.
8. Posen and Véron (2014).
9. For a useful summary of Dodd–Frank see Morrison and Foerster (2010).
10. Goldstein (2017) and Aikman and others (2014).
11. On holdings of government debt see Véron (2016). Within these broad aggregates there are interesting country variations. In the periphery, assets as a ratio to output shrank most in crisis countries with easily identified bubbles and/or financial programs. Within the core countries, the adjustments have been larger in Germany and Belgium than in France and the Netherlands.
12. the IMF's April 2017 Global Financial Stability Report.
13. The investment banks are proxied by assuming their assets are double those of the broker-dealers, as discussed in Chapter 3.

8 Making Macroeconomics More Relevant

1. http://www.imf.org/external/np/tr/2008/tr081115.htm.
2. International Monetary Fund (2015) and Svensson (2016).
3. Quoted from the communiqué, available on the University of Toronto website on the G20.
4. Faruqee and Srinivasan (2012) discuss the Mutual Assessment Process in detail.
5. A series of gold discoveries in the late nineteenth century, most notably in Australia, ended the Long Depression.
6. Bayoumi (2016a).
7. Shiller (2017).
8. For a survey see Hirshleifer and Teoh (2009).

9 Whither EMU?

1. Saccomanni (2016).
2. Ibid.
3. Bayoumi (2016c).
4. This ignores the zero lower bound, which has created problems for the monetary response to the region-wide shock caused by the North American crisis.
5. Mundell (1961).
6. A formal model is contained in Morgan, Rime, and Strahan (2004).
7. Germany, France, Italy, Spain, the Netherlands, Belgium/Luxembourg, Greece, Austria, Ireland, Portugal, and Finland.
8. Beck, Hubrich, and Marcellino (2009).
9. Finally, trade with the rest of the world seems to be less stable, reflecting the inclusion of a lot of major commodity exporters whose trade is affected by commodity prices.
10. Glick and Rose (2016) provide a succinct review of the literature.
11. Many thanks to Professor Andrew Rose of Berkeley for running these custom regressions for me.
12. Bayoumi and Eichengreen (1993).
13. For example, Gagnon (2012) and Campos and Macchiarelli (2016).
14. Bayoumi and Eichengreen (2017).
15. Posen and Véron (2014).
16. Morgan, Rime, and Strahan (2004) and Morgan and Strahan (2004).
17. Dao, Furceri, and Loungani (2014).
18. In the case of the bankruptcy of Continental Illinois Bank in 1982, the FDIC used its powers to guarantee other creditors and noninsured depositors so as to avoid further financial spillovers.
19. There was also a more localized fall in house prices in Michigan over 1979–84.
20. Bayoumi and Eichengreen (1995).
21. Bayoumi and Masson (1998) contains a discussion and estimation of the differences in automatic stabilizers. Röhn (2010) contains more recent evidence on the Ricardian offset.
22. European Commission (2013).
23. European Commission (1989).
24. Beyer and Smets (2015).
25 Jauer and others (2014).
26. Dao, Furceri, and Loungani (2014).
27. For example, Beyer and Smets (2015) find that "the greater homogeneity of the US economy is reflected in the fact that the US factors plays a more important role in accounting for both employment growth and employment rate [i.e. unemployment] fluctuations".

Final Thoughts

1. The exception was Ireland, where the lending boom and subsequent crisis was driven much more by banking competition than by a sudden reduction in borrowing costs.
2. Bergsten and Gagnon (2017).
3. The literature on whether these charges are still too low is summarized in Cline (2017).

REFERENCES

Adrian and Ashcraft (2012): Tobias Adrian and Adam Ashcraft, "Shadow Banking: A Review of the Literature", Federal Bank of New York Staff Report No. 580, 2012.

Adrian and Shin (2008): Tobias Adrian and Hyun Song Shin, "Liquidity and Financial Cycles", BIS Working Paper No. 256, from the Bank of International Settlements, 2008.

Adrian and Shin (2009): Tobias Adrian and Hyun Song Shin, "The Shadow Banking System: Implications for Financial Regulation", *Banque de France Financial Stability Review*, No. 13 (September 2009), pp. 1–10.

Ahmed, Levin, and Wilson (2002): Shaghil Ahmed, Andrew Levin, and Beth Anne Wilson, "Recent U.S. Macroeconomic Stability: Good Policies, Good Practices, Or Good Luck?", International Finance Discussion Paper, Board of Governors of the Federal Reserve System, International Finance Division No. 730, July 2002.

Aikman and others (2014): David Aikman, Mirta Galesic, Gerd Gigerenzer, Sujit Kapadia, Konstantinos Katsikopoulus, Amit Kothiyal, Emma Murphy, and Tobias Neumann, "Taking Uncertainty Seriously: Simplicity Versus Complexity in Financial Regulation", Bank of England Financial Stability Paper No. 28, 2014.

Alford (2010): Roger Alford, "Some Help in Understanding Britain's Banking Crisis, 2007–09", LSE Financial Markets Group Special Paper No. 193.

Amromin and Paulson (2010): Gene Amromin and Anna L. Paulson, "Default Rates on Prime and Subprime Mortgages: Differences and Similarities", *Profitwise: News and Views* (published by the Federal Reserve Bank of Chicago), September 2010.

Arce, Hurtado, and Thomas (2016): Óscar Arce, Samuel Hurtado, and Carlos Thomas, "Policy Spillovers and Synergies in a Monetary Union", *International Journal of Central Banking*, Vol. 12, No. 3 (September 2016), pp. 219–77.

Ayadi and Pujals (2005): Rym Ayadi and Georges Pujals, "Banking Mergers and Acquisitions in the EU: Overview, Assessment, and Prospects", SUERF Study 2005/3, June 2005.

Ball and others (2016): Laurence Ball, Joseph Gagnon, Patrick Honohan, and Signe Krogstrup, *What Else Can Central Banks Do?*, Geneva Reports on the World Economy, No. 18, 2016.

Barro and Gordon (1983): Robert Barro and James Gordon, "Rules, Discretion, and Reputation in a Model of Monetary policy", *Journal of Monetary Economics*, Vol. 12, pp. 101–21.

Basel Committee on Banking Supervision (1988): "International Convergence of Capital Measurement and Capital Standards", July 1988.

Basel Committee on Banking Supervision (1993): "*Measurement of Banks' Exposure to Interest Rate Risk*, consultative proposal by the Committee", April 1993.

Basel Committee on Banking Supervision (1995): "Proposal to Issue a Supplement to the Basel Capital Accord to Cover Market Risks", April 1995.

Basel Committee on Banking Supervision (1996): "Amendment to the Capital Accord to Incorporate Market Risks", January 1996.

Basel Committee on Banking Supervision (2005a): "The Application of Basel II to Trading Activities and the Treatment of Double Default Effects", July 2005.

Basel Committee on Banking Supervision (2005b): "Amendment to the Capital Accord to Incorporate Market Risks", November 2005.

Basel Committee on Banking Supervision (2006): "Results of the Fifth Quantitative Impact Study (QIS 5)", June 2006.

Basel Committee on Banking Supervision (2011): "Basel III: A Global Regulatory Framework for More Resilient Banks and Banking Systems", December 2010, revised June 2011.

Bayoumi (2016a): Tamim Bayoumi, "The Dog That Didn't Bark: The Strange Case of Domestic Policy Cooperation in the 'New Normal'", in Tamim Bayoumi, Stephen Pickford, and Paola Subacchi (eds), *Managing Complexity: Economic Policy Cooperation After the Crisis*, Brookings Institution Press, Washington DC, 2016.

Bayoumi (2016b): Tamim Bayoumi, "Dynamic Stochastic General Equilibrium Models and Their Discontents", *International Journal of Central Banking*, Vol. 12, No. 3 (September 2016), pp. 403–11.

Bayoumi (2016c): Tamim Bayoumi, "Will the Real European Union Please Stand Up?" Real Time Economic Issues Watch, Peterson Institute for International Economics, June 29, 2016.

Bayoumi and Eichengreen (1993): Tamim Bayoumi and Barry Eichengreen, "Shocking Aspects of European Monetary Union", in Fransisco Torres and Francesco Giavazzi (eds), *Adjustment and Growth in the European Monetary Union*, Cambridge University Press, Cambridge, 1993.

Bayoumi and Eichengreen (1995): Tamim Bayoumi and Barry Eichengreen, "Restraining Yourself: The Implications of Fiscal Rules for Economic Stabilization", *International Monetary Fund Staff Papers*, Vol. 42, No. 1 (March 1995), pp. 32–48.

Bayoumi and Eichengreen (2017): Tamim Bayoumi and Barry Eichengreen, "Aftershocks of Monetary Unification: Hysteresis with a Financial Twist", *International Monetary Fund working paper* WP 17/55 (March 2017).

Bayoumi and Gagnon (2016): Tamim Bayoumi and Joseph E. Gagnon, "Unconventional Monetary Policy in the Asian Financial Crisis", *Pacific Economic Review*, forthcoming.

Bayoumi and Masson (1998): Tamim Bayoumi and Paul R. Masson, "Liability-creating Versus Non-liability-creating Fiscal Stabilisation Policies: Ricardian Equivalence, Fiscal Stabilisation, and EMU", *The Economic Journal*, Vol. 108, Issue 449 (July 1998), pp. 1026–45.

Beck, Hubrich, and Marcellino (2009): Guenter W. Beck, Kirstin Hubrich and Massimiliano Marcellino, "Regional Inflation Dynamics within and across Euro Area Countries and a Comparison with the United States", *Economic Policy*, Vol. 24, Issue 57 (January 2009), pp. 141–84.

Bergsten and Gagnon (2017): C. Fred Bergsten and Joseph E. Gagnon, *Currency Conflict and Trade Policy: A New Strategy for the United States*, Peterson Institute for International Economics, Washington, DC, 2017.

Bergsten and Green (2016): C. Fred Bergsten and Russell A. Green (eds), *International Monetary Cooperation: Lessons from the Plaza Accord after Thirty Years*, Peterson Institute for International Economics, Washington DC, 2016.

Bernanke (2004): Ben S. Bernanke, "The Great Moderation", speech given at the meetings of the Eastern Economic Association, Washington DC, February 20, 2004.

Bernanke (2005): Ben S. Bernanke, "The Global Saving Glut and the U.S. Current Account Deficit", speech given at the Homer Jones Lecture, St. Louis, Missouri, on April 14, 2005.

Bernanke (2015): Ben S. Bernanke, *The Courage to Act*, W. W. Norton Press, New York and London, 2015.

Beyer and Smets (2015): Robert C. M. Beyer and Frank Smets, "Labour Market Adjustments in Europe and the US: How Different?", *European Central Bank Working Paper* No. 1767, March 2015.

Blanchard and Simon (2001): Olivier Blanchard and John Simon, "The Long and Large Decline in U.S. Output Volatility", *Brookings Papers on Economic Activity*, No. 1, 2001, pp. 135–64.

Blundell-Wignall and Roulet (2012): Adrian Blundell-Wignall and Caroline Roulet, "Business models of banks, leverage and the distance-to-default", *OECD Journal: Financial Market Trends*, Vol. 2012/2., 2012.

Brunnermeier, James, and Landau (2016): Markus K. Brunnermeier, Harold James, and Jean-Pierre Landau, *The Euro and the Battle of Ideas*, Princeton University Press, 2016.

Caballero, Farhi, and Gourinchas (2016): Ricardo J. Caballero, Emmanuel Farhi, and Pierre-Olivier Gourinchas, "Safe Assets Scarcity and Aggregate Demand", *NBER Working Paper* No. 22044 (February 2016).

Calomaris (2000): Charles W. Calomaris, "Universal Banking 'American Style'", in Charles W. Calomaris, *U.S. Bank Deregulation in Historical Perspective*, Cambridge University Press, Cambridge, 2000.

Campos and Macchiarelli (2016): Nauro Campos and Corrado Macchiarelli, "Core and Periphery in the European Monetary Union: Bayoumi and Eichengreen 25 Years Later", *Economics Letters*, Vol. 147, Issue 3 (2016).

Clark (2012): Christopher Clark, *The Sleepwalkers: How Europe Went to War in 1914*, Penguin Books, London and New York, 2012.

Cline (1984): William R. Cline, *International Debt: Systemic Risk and Policy Response*, Institute for International Economics, Washington DC, 1984.

Cline (1995): William R. Cline, *International Debt Reexamined*, Peterson Institute for International Economics, Washington DC, 1995.

Cline (2017): William R. Cline, *The Right Balance for Banks: Theory and Evidence on Optimal Capital Requirements*, Peterson Institute for International Economics, Washington DC, 2017.

Cohen (1992): Daniel Cohen, "The Debt Crisis: A Post Mortem", in *NBER Macroeconomics Annual 1992*, Vol. 7, Olivier Jean Blanchard and Stanley Fischer (eds), MIT Press, Cambridge, MA, 1992.

Colton (2002): Kent W. Colton, "Housing Finance in the United States: The Transformation of the U.S. Housing Finance System", Joint Center for Housing Studies Harvard University, July 2002.

Committee for the Study of Economic and Monetary Union (1989): "Report on Economic and Monetary Union in the European Economic Community", (Delors Report), April 1989.

Corsetti and others (1998): Giancarlo Corsetti, Paolo Pesenti, and Nouriel Roubini, "What Caused the Asian Currency and Financial Crisis? Part 1: A Macroeconomic Overview", NBER Working Paper No. 6833, December 1998.

Dagher and others (2016): Jihad Dagher, Giovanni Dell'Ariccia, Luc Laeven, Lev Ratnovski, and Hui Tong, "Benefits and Costs of Bank Capital", IMF Staff Discussion Note SDN/16/04, March 2016.

Dao, Furceri, and Loungani (2014): Mai Dao, Davide Furceri, and Prakash Loungani, "Regional Labor Market Adjustment in the United States and Europe", *IMF Working Paper* WP/14/26, February 2014.

Davis Polk (2013): "U.S. Basel III Final Rule: Visual Memorandum", available at davispolk.com.

Davis Polk (2014): "Supplementary Leverage Ratio (SLR): Visual Memorandum", available at davispolk.com.

Davis Polk (2015): "Federal Reserve's Proposed Rule on Total Loss-Absorbing Capacity and Eligible Long-Term Debt", available at davispolk.com.

Dermine (2002): Jean Dermine, "European Banking: Past, Present, and Future", paper given at *The Transformation of the European Financial System*, Second ECB Central Banking Conference, Frankfurt am Main, October 24–25, 2002.

Diamond and Dybvig (1983): Douglas W. Diamond and Philip H. Dybvig, "Bank Runs, Deposit Insurance, and Liquidity", *Journal of Political Economy*, Vol. 91, No. 3 (June 1983), pp. 401–19.

Dooley (1994): Michael P. Dooley, "A Retrospective on the Debt Crisis", *NBER Working Paper* No. 4963, December 1994.

Edwards (1999): Franklin R. Edwards, "Hedge Funds and the Collapse of Long-Term Capital Management", *Journal of Economic Perspectives*, Vol. 13, No. 2 (Spring 1999), pp. 189–210.

Eichengreen (1992): Barry Eichengreen, *Golden Fetters: The Gold Standard and the Great Depression 1919–1939*, Oxford University Press, Oxford, 1992.

Eichengreen (2008): Barry Eichengreen, *Globalizing Capital: A History of the International Monetary System*, 2nd edn, Princeton University Press, 2008.

El-Erian (2016): Mohamed A. El-Erian, *The Only Game in Town: Central Banks, Instability, and Avoiding the Next Collapse*, Random House, New York, 2016.

European Banking Authority (2016): *EBA Report on the Leverage Requirements Under Article 511 of the CRR*, EBA-Op-2016–13, August 2016.

European Central Bank (2000): *Mergers and Acquisitions Involving the EU Banking Industry*, European Central Bank, 2000.

European Commission (1990): "One Market, One Money: An Evaluation of the Potential Benefits and Costs of Forming an Economic and Monetary Union", *European Economy*, No. 44, October 1990.

European Commission (2013): "Vade mecum on the Stability and Growth Pact", Occasional Papers, No. 151, May 2013.

Fagan and Gaspar (2008): Gabriel Fagan and Vitor Gaspar, "Macroeconomic Adjustment to a Monetary Union", *European Central Bank Working Paper* No. 946, October 2008.

Faruqee and Srinivasan (2012): Hamid Faruqee and Krishna Srinivasan, "The G-20 Mutual Assessment Process—A Perspective from IMF Staff", *Oxford Review of Economic Policy*, Vol. 28, No. 3, pp. 493–511.

Federal Deposit Insurance Corporation (1997a): "The Savings and Loan Crisis and Its Relationship to Banking", Chapter 4 in *A History of the Eighties – Lessons for the Future*, Vol. 1: *An Examination of the Banking Crises of the 1980s and Early 1990s*, December 1997.

Federal Deposit Insurance Corporation (1997b): "The LDC Debt Crisis", Chapter 5 in *A History of the Eighties – Lessons for the Future*, Vol. 1: *An Examination of the Banking Crises of the 1980s and Early 1990s*, December 1997.

Federal Deposit Insurance Corporation (1998): "Open Bank Assistance", Chapter 5 in *Managing the Crisis*, 1998.

Federal Housing Finance Agency Office of Inspector General (2011): *A Brief History of the Housing Government-Sponsored Enterprises*, 2011.

Fender and McGuire (2010): Ingo Fender and Patrick McGuire, "European banks' US dollar funding pressures", *BIS Quarterly Review* (June 2010), pp. 57–64.

Financial Services Authority (2005): "Better Regulation Action Plan", Financial Services Authority, December 2005.

Fiordelisi (2009): Franco Fiordelisi, *Mergers and Acquisitions in European Banking*, Palgrave Macmillan Studies in Banking and Financial Institutions, Palgrave Macmillan, London and New York, 2009.

Focarelli and Pozzolo (2001): Dario Focarelli and Alberto Pozzolo, "The Patterns of Cross-Border Bank Mergers and Shareholdings in OECD Countries", *Journal of Banking and Finance*, Vol. 25, No. 12 (December 2001), pp. 2305–37.

Fox (2009): Justin Fox, *The Myth of the Rational Market*, Harper Business, New York, 2009.

Friedman (2006): Benjamin M. Friedman, *The Moral Consequences of Economic Growth*, Alfred Knopf, New York, 2006.

Gagnon (2012): Joseph Gagnon, "European Monetary Unification: Precocious or Premature?", Chapter 10 in Jacob Funk Kirkegaard, Nicolas Véron, and Guntram B. Wolff (eds), *Transatlantic Economic Challenges in an Era of Growing Multipolarity*, Peterson Institute for International Economics, Washington DC, 2012.

Garber (1993): Peter Garber, "The Collapse of the Bretton Woods Fixed Exchange Rate System", in Michael D. Bordo and Barry Eichengreen (eds), *A Retrospective on the Bretton Woods System: Lessons for International Monetary Reform*, Chicago University Press, Chicago, 1993.

Geithner (2014): Timothy F. Geithner, *Stress Test: Reflections on Financial Crisis*, Crown Publishers, New York, 2014.

Getter (2014): Darryl E. Getter, "U.S. Implementation of the Basel Capital Regulatory Framework", Congressional Research Service, Washington DC, April 2014.

Glick and Rose (2016): Reuven Glick and Andrew K. Rose, "Currency Unions and Trade: A Post-EMU Reassessment", *European Economic Review*, Vol. 87, Issue C (2016), pp. 78–91.

Goldstein (1998): Morris Goldstein, *The Asian Financial Crisis: Causes, Cures, and Systemic Implications*, Peterson Institute for International Economics, Washington DC, 1998.

Goldstein (2017): Morris Goldstein, *Banking's Final Exam*: Stress Testing and Bank-Capital Reform, Peterson Institute for International Economics, Washington DC.

Goodhart (2011): Charles Goodhart, *The Basel Committee on Banking Supervision: A History of the Early Years 1974–1997*, Cambridge University Press, Cambridge, 2011.

Gorton and Ordoñez (2013): Gary Gorton and Guillermo Ordoñez, "The Supply and Demand for Safe Assets", *NBER Working Paper* No. 18732, January 2013.

Greene (2005): Brian Greene, *The Fabric of the Cosmos: Space, Time, and the Texture of Reality*, Vintage Books, New York, 2005.

Greenspan (1996): Alan Greenspan, "Bank Supervision in a World Economy", speech given at the International Conference of Banking Supervisors, Stockholm, June 13, 1996, available from the Federal Reserve website.

Greenspan (2008): Alan Greenspan, *The Age of Turbulence: Adventures in a New World*, Penguin Books, London, 2008.

Haldane (2009): Andrew Haldane, "Banking on the State", *BIS Economic Review* No. 139, 2009.

Haltom (2013): Renee Haltom, "Failure of Continental Illinois May 1984", Federal Reserve History, 2013, available at the Federal Reserve website.

Herring (2007): Randall J. Herring, "The Rocky Road to Implementation of Basel II in the United States", *Atlantic Economic Journal*, Vol. 35, No. 4 (February 2007), pp. 411–29.

Hirshleifer and Teoh (2009): David Hirshleifer and Siew Hong Teoh, "Thought and Behavior Contagion in Capital Markets", in Thorsten Hens and Klaus Reiner Schenk-Hoppé (eds), *Handbook of Financial Economics: Dynamics and Evolution*, North Holland, Amsterdam, 2009.

Holton (1986): Richard Holton, "Industrial Politics in France: Nationalisation under Mitterrand", *West European Politics*, Vol. 9, Issue 1, 1986.

Horton, Kumar, and Mauro (2009): Mark Horton, Manmohan Kumar, and Paolo Mauro, "The State of Public Finances: A Cross-Country Fiscal Monitor", IMF Staff Position Note SPN/09/21, July 2009.

Howarth and Quaglia (2015): David Howarth and Lucia Quaglia, "The Comparative Political Economy of Basel III in Europe", University of Edinburgh School of Law, Research Paper Series 2015/19 and Europa Working Paper 2015/03, 2015.

Independent Evaluation Office of the International Monetary Fund (2005): *The IMF's Approach to Capital Account Liberalization*, International Monetary Fund, 2005.

Independent Evaluation Office of the International Monetary Fund (2015): *The IMF's Approach to Capital Account Liberalization: Revisiting the 2005 IEO Evaluation*, International Monetary Fund, March 2015.

International Monetary Fund (2009): "The State of Public Finances: Outlook and Medium-Term Policies After the 2008 Crisis", International Monetary Fund Policy Paper, March 2009.

International Monetary Fund (2011): "The United States: Spillover Report", *IMF Country Report* No. 11/203, July 2011.

International Monetary Fund (2012a): "Liberalizing Capital Flows and Managing Outflows", International Monetary Fund Policy Paper, March 2012.

International Monetary Fund (2012b): "The Liberalization and Management of Capital Flows: An Institutional View", International Monetary Fund, November 2012.

International Monetary Fund (2015): "Monetary Policy and Financial Stability", International Monetary Fund, August 2015.

International Monetary Fund, World Bank, and World Trade Organization (2017): "Making Trade an Engine of Growth for All: The Case for Trade and for Policies to Facilitate Adjustment", prepared for discussion at a meeting of G20 Sherpas, March 23–24, 2017.

James (2012): Harold James, *Making the European Monetary Union*, Harvard University Press, Cambridge, MA, 2012.

Jauer and others (2014): Julia Jauer, Thomas Liebig, John P. Martin, and Patrick A. Puhani, "Migration as an Adjustment Mechanism in a Crisis? A Comparison of Europe and the United States", *OECD Social, Employment, and Migration Working Papers*, No. 155, January 2014.

Jeanne and Zettelmeyer (2005): Olivier Jeanne and Jeromin Zettelmeyer, "Original Sin, Balance-Sheet Crises, and the Roles of International Lending", in Barry Eichengreen and Ricardo Hausmann (eds), *Other People's Money: Debt Denomination and Financial Instability in Emerging Market Economies*, University of Chicago Press, Chicago, 2005.

Jickling and Murphy (2010): Mark Jickling and Edward V. Murphy, "Who Regulates Whom? An Overview of U.S. Financial Supervision", Congressional Research Service, Washington DC, December 2010.

Johnson and Kwak (2011): Simon Johnson and James Kwak, *13 Bankers: The Wall Street Takeover and the Next Financial Meltdown*, Vintage Books, New York, 2011.

Justiniano, Primiceri, and Tambalotti (2016): Alejandro Justiniano, Giorgio E. Primiceri, and Andrea Tambalotti, "A Simple Model of Subprime Borrowers and Credit Growth", *Federal Reserve Bank of New York Staff Report* 766, February 2016.

Kennedy (1999): David M. Kennedy, *Freedom from Fear: The American People in Depression and War, 1929–1945*, Oxford University Press, Oxford, 1999.

Kiff and Mills (2007): John Kiff and Paul Mills, "Money for Nothing and Checks for Free: Recent Developments in U.S. Subprime Mortgage Markets", *IMF Working Paper* WP/07/188, July 2007.

King (2016): Mervyn King, *The End of Alchemy: Money, Banking, and the Future of the Global Economy*, W. W. Norton, London and New York, 2016.

Kohn (2006): Donald L. Kohn, "Monetary Policy and Asset Prices", speech given at *Monetary Policy: A Journey from Theory to Practice*, a European Central Bank Colloquium held in honor of Otmar Issing, Frankfurt am Main, March 2006.

Kroszner and Strahan (2014): Randall S. Kroszner and Philip E. Strahan, "Regulation and Deregulation of the U.S. Banking Industry: Causes, Consequences and Implications for the Future", in Nancy L. Rose (ed), *Economic Regulation and Its Reform: What Have We Learned?*, University of Chicago Press, Chicago, 2014.

Krugman (1992): Paul Krugman, *Currencies and Crises*, MIT Press, Cambridge, MA, 1992.

Krugman, Obstfeld, and Melitz (2015): Paul R. Krugman, Maurice Obstfeld, Marc Melitz, *International Trade: Theory and Policy*, Pearson, Cambridge, MA, 2015.

Laeven and Valencia (2012): Luc Laeven and Fabián Valencia, "Systemic Banking Crises Database: An Update", *IMF Working Paper* WP/12/163, June 2012.

Lane (2013): Philip R. Lane, "Capital Flows in the Euro Area", *European Commission Economic Paper* No. 497, April 2013.

Lewis (1989): Michael Lewis, *Liar's Poker*, Norton Books, New York, 1989.

MacMillan (2013): Margaret MacMillan, *The War That Ended Peace: The Road to 1914*, Profile Books, London, 2013.

Mallaby (2016): Sebastian Mallaby, *The Man Who Knew: The Life and Times of Alan Greenspan*, Penguin Press, New York, 2016.

Marsh (2011): David Marsh, *The Euro: The Battle for the New Global Currency*, Yale University Press, New Haven and London, 2011.

Matthews (1992): Barbara C. Matthews, "The Second Banking Directive: Conflicts, Choices, and Long-Term Goals", *Duke Journal of Comparative & International Law*, Vol. 2 (1992), pp. 89–128.

Mayer, Pence and Sherlund (2009): Christopher J. Mayer, Karen M. Pence, and Shane M. Sherlund, "The Rise in Mortgage Defaults", *Journal of Economic Perspectives*, Vol. 23, No. 1, pp. 27–50.

Merler and Véron (2015): Silvia Merler and Nicolas Véron, "Moving Away from Banks: Comparing Challenges in China and the European Union", in *China's Economic Transformation: Lessons, Impact, and the Path Forward*, Peterson Institute for International Economics Briefing 15–3, Washington DC, September 2015.

Moravcsik (1991): Andrew Moravcsik, "Negotiating the Single European Act", *International Organization*, Vol. 45, No. 1 (Winter 1991), pp. 19–56.

Morgan, Rime, and Strahan (2004): Donald P. Morgan, Bertrand Rime, and Philip E. Strahan, "Bank Integration and State Business Cycles", *Quarterly Journal of Economics*, Vol. 119, No. 4 (November 2004), pp. 1555–84.

Morgan and Strahan (2003): Donald P. Morgan and Philip E. Strahan, "Foreign Bank Entry and Business Volatility: Evidence from U.S. States and Other Countries", *Bank of Chile Working Papers* 229, October 2003.

Morrison and Foerster (2010): "The Dodd–Frank Act: A Cheat Sheet", available at media. mofo.com.

Morrison, Roe, and Sontchi (2014): Edward R. Morrison, Mark J. Roe, and Christopher S. Sontchi, "Rolling Back the Repo Safe Harbors", *Business Lawyer*, Vol. 69, No. 4 (August 2014).

Mundell (1961): Robert A. Mundell, "A Theory of Optimum Currency Areas", *American Economic Review*, Volume 54, No. 4, pp. 657–665 (September 1961).

Murphy (2013): Edward V. Murphy (2013), "Who Regulated Whom and How? An Overview of U.S. Financial Regulatory Policy for Banking and Securities Markets", Congressional Research Service Report for Congress, Washington DC, 2013.

Murphy (2000): Neil B. Murphy, "European Union Financial Developments: The Single Market, the Single Currency, and Banking", *FDIC Banking Review*, Vol. 13, No. 1, pp. 1–18.

Obstfeld (1996): Maurice Obstfeld, "The Logic of Currency Crises with Self-Fulfilling Features", *European Economic Review*, Vol. 40, pp. 1037–47.

Office of the Comptroller of the Currency, Board of Governors of the Federal Reserve System, Federal Deposit Insurance Corporation, and Office of Thrift Supervision (2006): "Summary Findings of the Fourth Quantitative Impact Study", Washington DC, February 2006.

Pagano and others (2014): Marco Pagano, Sam Langfield, Viral Acharya, Arnoud Boot, Markus Brunnermeier, Claudia Buch, Martin Hellwig, André Sapir and Leke van den Burg, "Is Europe Overbanked?", *Report of the European Systemic Risk Board*, No. 4, June 2014.

Paulson, (2013): Henry M. Paulson, *On the Brink: Inside the Race to Stop the Collapse of the Global Financial System*, updated edition, Business Plus, New York, 2013.

Pisani-Ferry (2014): Jean Pisani-Ferry, *The Euro Crisis and Its Aftermath*, Oxford University Press, Oxford and New York, 2014.

Plessis (2003): Alain Plessis, "The History of Banks in France", manuscript available on the world wide web at http://www.fbf.fr/en/french-banking-sector/history-of-banks-in-france/the-history-of-banks-in-france, January 2003, translation October 2003

Posen and Véron (2014): Adam Posen and Nicolas Véron, "Europe's Half a Banking Union", Op-ed, *Europe's World*, June 15, 2014.

Pozsar and others (2013): Zoltan Pozsar, Tobias Adrian, Adam Ashcraft, and Hayley Boesky, "Shadow Banking", *Economic Policy Review* of the Federal Reserve Bank of New York, December 2013, pp. 1–16.

Price Waterhouse (1988): "The "Cost of Non-Europe" in Financial Services", *Research on the "Cost of Non-Europe", Basic Findings*, Vol. 9, Commission of the European Communities, 1988.

PricewaterhouseCoopers (2006): "European Banking Consolidation", Pricewaterhouse Coopers LLP, April 2006.

Röhn (2010): Olivier Röhn, "New Evidence on the Private Saving Offset and Ricardian Equivalence", *OECD Economics Department Working Paper*, No. 762, 2010.

Romer (2016): "The Trouble with Macroeconomics", speech delivered as Commons Memorial Lecture of the Omicron Delta Epsilon Society (forthcoming in *The American Economist*), January 5, 2016.

Saccomanni (2016): Fabrizio Saccomanni, "Policy Cooperation in the Euro area in Time of Crisis: A Case of Too Little, Too Late", in Tamim Bayoumi, Stephen Pickford, and Paola Subacchi (eds), *Managing Complexity: Economic Policy Cooperation After the Crisis*, Brookings Institution Press, Washington DC, 2016.

Sachs and Wyplosz (1986): Jeffrey Sachs and Charles Wyplosz, "The Economic Consequences of President Mitterrand", *Economic Policy*, April 1986, pp. 261–322.

Sandbu (2015): Martin Sandbu, *Europe's Orphan: The Future of the Euro and the Politics of Debt*, Princeton University Press, Princeton, 2015.

Schoenmaker and Véron (2016): Dirk Schoenmaker and Nicolas Véron (eds), *European Banking Supervision: The First Eighteen Months*, Blueprint Series Vol. 25, Breugel Institute, Brussels, 2016.

Securities and Exchange Commission (2003a): "Customer Protection—Reserves and Custody of Securities Delegation of Authority to the Director of the Division of Market Regulation", Release No. 34–47480, March 11, 2003, available at https://www.sec.gov/rules/final/34-47480.htm.

Securities and Exchange Commission (2003b): "Order Regarding the Collateral Broker-Dealers Must Pledge when Borrowing Customer Securities", Release No. 47683, April 16, 2003, available at http://www.sec.gov/rules/other/34-47683.htm.

Seidman (2000): L. William Seidman, *Full Faith and Credit: The Great S & L Debacle and Other Washington Sagas*, Beard Books, Washington DC, 2000.

Sherman (2009): Matthew Sherman, "A Short History of Financial Deregulation in the United States", Center for Economic and Policy Research, Washington DC, July 2009.

Shiller (2017): Robert J. Shiller, "Narrative Economics", presidential address delivered at the 129th annual meeting of the American Economic Association, January 7, 2017,

Shin (2012): Hyun Song Shin, "Global Banking Glut and Loan Risk Premium", *IMF Economic Review*, Vol. 60, Issue 2 (July 2012) pp. 155–92.

Short (2014): Philip Short, *A Taste for Intrigue: The Multiple Lives of François Mitterrand*, Henry Holt, New York, 2014.

Simms (2013): Brendan Simms, *Europe: The Struggle for Supremacy, from 1453 to the Present*, Basic Books, New York, 2013.

Skidelsky (2001): Robert Skidelsky, *John Maynard Keynes*, Vol. 3, *Fighting for Freedom, 1937–1946*, Penguin Group, London and New York, 2001.

Stiglitz (2016): Joseph E. Stiglitz: *The Euro: How a Common Currency Threatens the Future of Europe*, W. W. Norton, New York and London, 2016.

Stock and Watson (2003): James H. Stock and Mark W. Watson, "Has the Business Cycle Changed and Why?", in Mark Gertler and Kenneth Rogoff (eds), *NBER Macroeconomics Annual 2002*, Vol. 17, MIT Press, Cambridge, MA, 2003.

Svensson (2016): Lars E. Svensson, "A Simple Cost-Benefit Analysis of Using Monetary Policy for Financial Stability Purposes", in Olivier J. Blanchard, Raghuram G. Rajan, Kenneth S. Rogoff, and Lawrence H. Summers (eds), *Progress and Confusion: The State of Macroeconomic Policy*, MIT Press, Cambridge, MA, 2016.

Tarullo (2008): Daniel K. Tarullo, *Banking on Basel: The Future of International Financial Regulation*, Peterson Institute for International Economics, Washington DC, 2008.

Véron (2013): Nicolas Véron, "Banking Nationalism and the European Crisis", Blog Post, Bruegel Institute, Brussels, October 2013.

Véron (2016): Nicolas Véron, "Breaking the Vicious Cycle", *Financial World*, October–November 2016.

Vestergaard and Retana (2012): Jokob Vestergaard and María Retana, "Behind Smoke and Mirrors: On the Alleged Recapitalization of Europe's Banks", Danish Institute for International Studies 2013:10, 2013.

Werner (1970): Pierre Werner, "Report to the Council and the Commission on the Realisation by Stages of Economic and Monetary Union in the Community", (Werner Report), October 1970, available online at the Archive of European Integration.

Wessel (2009): David Wessel, *In FED We Trust: Ben Bernanke's War on the Great Panic*, Crown Business, New York, 2009.

Wolf (2014): Martin Wolf, *The Shifts and the Shocks: What We've Learned—and Have Still to Learn—from the Financial Crisis*, The Penguin Press, London, 2014.

INDEX